I have argued and fled from God.
I have made excuses,
Dwelt on nameless fears,
And let fanciful dreams
Cloud my ability to reason.
In the end, I do not write for glory or fame,
But for release.
For over a decade,
These words have grown in my heart,
And now, they spill forth,
In delicate ink upon the page.
And I am like a new parent,
Amazed at the smallest detail of what
I am giving to the world,
And how it struggles forth in great travail.

-The Author

A Faraway Ancient Country:

A Spiritual Journey into Roman Catholicism And Biblical Defense of the Faith

By Emissary

Nihil Obstat
    Pending

Imprimatur
    Pending

ISBN
    978-0-615-15801-3

Acknowledgments

I would like to extend my deepest appreciation and gratitude to Reverend John Putnam, Jr., B.S., S.T.B., M. Div., J.C.L., and his staff at Sacred Heart Catholic Church, Salisbury, NC. It was their support and assistance that helped to make it all possible.

A special thanks belongs to Father Stephan Heimann of Christ the King Anglican Church, in Salisbury, NC. Though our positions were theologically different at times, Father Heimann served as a general history resource, sounding board, and clearing editor, often catching errors that the others overlooked.

And to my husband, I say: "Thanks for believing in me when others did not."

Introduction

Do you have the courage and the open mind that it takes to read this book? It could change how you look at the world and the Christian faith, for it embraces a "terrible cause." The Revolutionary War, the Civil War, World War II, and the Civil Rights Demonstrations in American history are terrible causes. These conflicts define their participants, forcing choices that carry a heavy cost. One can lose friends, family, and even life in the struggle. But you fight for what you believe in because it is right. This book embraces a "terrible cause," and I am in labor. And in bringing forth this literary child, I have pleaded with God, saying, ***"Give this assignment to someone better qualified, who more fully emulates the Christian ideal."***

My child is a message to the Body of Christ. And I am just a messenger. As the Apostle Paul once said, ***"If I am a Christian, then I am the least of you."*** I see myself as a serving girl around the table of God, hopelessly flawed with an imperfect past and well-known weaknesses. I still lose my temper, say colorful phrases, speak out of turn, and will often be stubborn, proud, and ambitious. My words do not come from some lofty moral or theological position, but out of love, respect, and humility towards Christians everywhere.

This book covers my spiritual journey from Protestant Fundamentalism into Catholicism. Moreover, it shares Catholic doctrines and beliefs with Protestants while addressing many of the myths and misconceptions surrounding my faith. Because this is a true story, (with actual people, places, and events) names and certain details have been changed or omitted to protect the privacy of all concerned. My identity is not as important as the story that I must tell and the faith that I am driven to share.

Humanity has this tendency of "killing the truth" or at least putting it on life support. Once an idea has been repeated long enough and often enough, it becomes accepted as "fact." Whether the "fact" is really true becomes irrelevant. When I stop at Protestant bookstores, I continue to be shocked and dismayed at the harsh commentary aimed at Catholics. Some Protestant writers take a particular action or quote out of context without looking at Catholicism as a whole while others twist history to fit their own particular world-view. It's sad, but the frightening part is that many readers totally accept an author's words without question as if they were Holy Scripture. Christians should always be devoted to the truth, never allowing inflammatory rhetoric to affect reason and common sense.

Because I prize truth, reason and common sense, I would like Protestants to see and experience Catholicism through my eyes, hopefully giving a glimpse inside a world that few outsiders understand. When you finish this volume, you will have solid answers to many popular assumptions and conclusions made by Protestant authors.

The reaction to this work is mixed within my own parish. Most of my friends are fascinated and want a peek at the manuscript, but some seem withdrawn and resentful, saying something like: ***"Why do we have to explain ourselves to Protestants? If they can't accept our views, it's their problem."***

That mentality is unwise. Catholics and Protestants coexist with one another. They work together, play together, and even share households. Neither group lives in its own separate world. Like it or not, there is a twisted view of Catholicism that Protestants are accepting as truth. Any Catholic who does not fight to correct this image is, in some way, validating it. If we do not defend our faith, we, by our silence and indifference, lend opposing ideas credence.

In the American South, Catholics must show particular diligence in helping to change attitudes and mind-sets. "Catholic bashing" has become a sport. But when we address myth and fallacy with biblical truth, we can easily unravel the logic behind this anti-Catholic viewpoint. Communication (the first step in healing any rift) demands that we cross linguistic and cultural barriers.

For example, while American and British citizens speak essentially the same language, the meanings of various words change drastically in each country. The word "pants" in America means slacks or jeans. The English refer to their underwear with that word. America recognizes "chips" as a snack food while Britain views "chips" as another term for French fries. And although Americans and Brits share many concepts, they entertain different social, religious, and political views, each bred from its own respective culture.

In many ways, Catholics and Protestants speak the same language of devotion to God, discipleship to Christ, forgiveness of sins, salvation, and eternal life. But there are subtle and important differences in words and viewpoints. These discrepancies are rarely explained, and they desperately need to be so. Otherwise, we can look forward to more ignorance, misinformation, bigotry and malice. It's time to correct the image, to clarify doctrines and beliefs, and lay to rest the old myths.

Part I

In The Beginning, When God Thundered And Roared...

Let me quiet my soul and speak of this journey. It wanders not to exotic cities or fabled lands, but crosses the wide expanse called the human soul. If we could visualize the terrain, we might witness peaceful valleys and brooding glens, travel and explore wide oceans and turbulent rivers, and climb to magnificent summits.

My spiritual odyssey begins with my birth in the mid-1960s. The city in which I was born (and which I still call home) is a lovely place, one of the oldest towns on the Eastern seaboard. In its heart, stands a grand dame in her court of myrtle trees. Cast in bronze, her wings lift skyward as she cradles a fallen warrior. For close to a century, this famous lady has greeted visitors and welcomed back old friends to our tree-lined streets, antebellum houses and majestic churches.

While much of the American South suffered a fiery destruction at the hands of the Union Army, our city was spared. This is mostly due to the generosity and hospitality of one citizen and his family. His actions bought our collective safety and helped to preserve homes, businesses, and churches. Today, seasonal tours feature an intimate look at many of our larger, more distinguished homes. And our genealogy department at the city library has become important to local and regional historians.

If you walk down the streets of my hometown in the morning, you can smell the heady aroma of hickory and pecan fires. Various barbecue restaurants are already about the business of smoking pork, for which our region is quite famous. While many people believe barbecue must involve the use of heavy sauces, we smoke and lightly garnish our meat in spices, sweet red slaw, and hushpuppies. This taste is a favorite among barbecue aficionados, once they get used to the idea.

Home is steeped in small town "Americana." We have cozy shops specializing in crafts, furniture, antiques, fine linens and drapery as well as the usual fare of coffeehouses and restaurants. One of my favorite hangouts is the Ice Palace; a store offering New Orleans-styled shaved ice treats. Then, there's Darla's Ice Cream, whose specialties are homemade frozen treats, and a wondrous collection of salads, soups, and subs. If it's a hamburger or hot-dog you crave, you have only to pop over to Marty's Grill, which boasts the best in town. Although it has grown considerably over the years, there is still the feeling of a close-knit community and its traditions, established by over two and half centuries of English, Scottish, Irish, German and African families. Like many Americans, my heritage is a mosaic of these nationalities coupled with Native American roots.

Regarding religion, my roots are devoutly Christian and feature a mixture of denominations, primarily Methodist, Baptist, and German Quakers. Our family was once part of a sect of independent Wesleyans. The Wesleyan faith is branched from the Methodist church. Since we were independent Wesleyans, our church was an offshoot of an offshoot. The 60's and 70's encompassed an age of pilgrimages to the East for religious enlightenment. However, in our world, faith came as easy as breathing air. We purchased this spirituality by divesting ourselves of worldly things. In fact, the term "worldly" was synonymous with heresy and defined as any infraction of established rules of dress or conduct set down by our elders.

Women did not wear any makeup, jewelry (not even a wedding band), pants, shorts or other revealing clothing. Short hair was forbidden for women, but a directive for men, who were also expected to wear the most conservative form of dress. Community activities such as attending public school, sporting events, and movies were also frowned on. One did not drink, smoke, or attend dances under any circumstances. And while radios were tolerated, possessing a TV was unthinkable.

I love to joke that we were like a light version of the Amish. We had a lot of rules, but did manage to keep electric power and automobiles. Of course, there were some concessions to these stringent rules. Women could wear perfume, lotions, and body powders; watches were allowed for "utilitarian" purposes only; and occasionally, a man might let his hair grow to cover the nape of his neck. The latter offense was one for which my father received a moderate amount of teasing. Daddy had a marvelous mane of raven hair. Sometimes, he would find it longer than the ideal length because it was luxurious and grew so fast. But for all the restrictions, we lived a rich spiritual existence.

My mind still wanders back to witness the wonder of that time. There were long summer evenings when I would fall asleep on my father's lap. We sat on the front pew next to an open door that let the night breeze in. Sunset would fade into blue-green twilight with its occasional lightning bug twinkling in the distance. The preacher's voice would grow quieter as visions of the Bible crept into my head.

Then, there were other times when sleep was not an option- even for a child. I also remember the raw power of God sweeping through the sanctuary. Respected elders would run up and down the aisles- some shouting and praising God while others shook like dolls in a mighty wind. Witnessing that kind of display was an unnerving experience. I would sit welded to my seat, my body taut and unable to breathe, knowing that I was watching something both sacred and private. Spiritual intimacy has a bonding effect that is empowering for those involved and embarrassing for those who are not. Many people may dismiss ecstasy as mass hysteria, but it is very real. Generally speaking, we hardly knew when an event like that would take place, but when it did, the world stopped spinning and held its breath.

Even so, most of us had an idea that things would get wild during our yearly camp meeting. Camp meetings were like summer camp for Christians, and we had a large campground. Hundreds of people would come - some brought campers or rented cottages on the premises while others stayed in the large dormitory over the dining hall. The hall was a wonderful place with its delicious smells and social activity. Families and old friends held informal reunions, many traveling from different counties or states. But the centerpiece of this property was the large arbor or tabernacle.

For those unacquainted with such a structure, it was two-sided with a roof and electricity for the podium and sound system. The other "walls" were composed of well-spaced timber pillars that lent support. This permitted summer breezes to flow through the sanctuary like rudimentary air conditioning. Its "floor" always had a thick carpeting of pine shavings. Even now, the smell of freshly cut pine brings back old memories of that white temple nestled in its protective grove.

I can never forget attending services during thunderstorms. There's nothing like hearing a fire and brimstone service punctuated by thunderclaps. The sky would deepen to purplish-blue and flash with long fingers of lightening, and the wind would rustle through the congregation, bringing with it the green incense of the surrounding forest. Even the trees would bow under its force as if paying homage to the Creator. This was God in His most raw and elemental form, and my child's eyes witnessed the violent beauty of the universe as it was created so long ago.

Blending Divisive Elements

If I had a recipe to create someone like myself, the central ingredient would be my religious life. I believe it would be accurate to say that that portion of my existence was unusual, especially in the age of hippies and "free-love." We seemed insulated from the social and political unrest that permeated American society at the time. But that was not entirely true. There were radical elements in my life that seemed to add balance.

My father had a set of cousins who brought excitement and fun whenever they visited. They were a bohemian group of artists, the chief of which was Julian, a talented still-life painter. He, his wife, Margot, and their five kids infected us with a love and zest for life that lingers today. Even spending the night in their rambling old farmhouse was an adventure.

The house was a cross between Pipi Longstocking's home and Frankenstein's lab, boasting dogs, cats, chickens, and the occasional goat. But strangest of all were the peacocks. At one time, a complete flock with males, peahens, and chicks roamed the yard, leaving brightly colored feathers in their wake. When anyone drove up, they made an awful racket. The building itself was a treasure chest of fun: artwork everywhere, all kinds of toys, a pool table, oriental bird cages, antiques, and other unusual items, some of which defy description. Once, I remember seeing a real human skeleton crumpled into a pile of bones in the entrance hall, an acquisition from a local school lab.

I have wonderful memories of my cousins bustling about, hanging out with their friends or riding motorcycles. Julian would often return from his studio and find Margot cooking supper in her kitchen. And all the adults would spend the evening reminiscing and catching up with the family's latest exploits. I remember sleeping in the den with its large flagstone fireplace and hardwood floors. My cousins often served as the template of the all-American family, but they were not the key influence in my personal development. That honor belongs to my grandmother.

Olivia Fitzpatrick (whom I called, "Nana") was a wisecracking, no nonsense kind of matriarch who lived in a large white house in an adjacent suburb. Her home occupied much of a city block and boasted a profusion of flowers and plants. There were azaleas, roses, peonies, lilacs, hibiscus and magnificent September bushes that would burst with purple blossoms. A canopy of two-hundred-year-old oaks stood watch over the pink and white dogwoods and flowering mimosa in the front yard while weeping willows, cedar, and red bud trees shaded the sides and back. My favorite trees were the red buds, the heralds of spring. Tiny buds would sprout from their barren limbs, creating a deep pink cloud in the backyard sky.

I cannot think of Nana without thinking of flowers. My mother remembers when she and her family first moved there; the yard was nothing but red clay, broken bottles, and trash. People thought my grandmother silly to waste her time on such an eyesore, but when she was done, the land had been transformed into a lush playground complete with a formidable vegetable garden. This was accomplished by bringing whole truckloads of rich black soil to cover the clay and provide an optimum medium for plant growth. According to those who were around, the first crop of grass resembled more like plush carpeting than ground cover.

My grandmother's creativity was a testament to her indomitable will. Nana was what some call a "force of nature." Besides the domestic arts, in which she excelled, Olivia had a shrewd mind. Nana wrote for different newspapers, dabbled in politics and real estate, and ran a succession of businesses to keep her family clothed and fed. As a Methodist minister, my grandfather was lucky to receive food and shelter as compensation for his work. Olivia's income helped fill in so many gaps. Even in the Great Depression, a time when people begged for food and work, my grandmother ran a boarding house, and was a nanny and seamstress to rich families. Mother never wanted for the necessities of life in an age when other children (including my father) did without.

Olivia was also my first teacher. We began with the primary skills of sewing, crafts, and cookery. I could hold a needle by the age of six, knew my way around a kitchen by eight, and apprenticed in ceramic art at fourteen. Next came the lessons of the world. Nana whispered stories of political intrigue, scandals of every kind, and wrangling with "the powers that be." I still have the volumes of history, archeology, exploration, language, and folklore/mythology, which she purchased for birthdays or Christmas or "just because." They're old and crumbling now, having seen many late night readings. I still look at them and see old friends. Olivia taught me to seek knowledge and use it as a weapon against the world.

Books were precious things. Even their smell spoke of wisdom. While both of my older sisters were the socialites of our family, I was a wild child, lost in a realm of adventure. Books took my imagination around the world, roaming the myths and legends of ancient Greece, Rome, China, and the Middle East. I dreamt of being a great scholar and a world traveler. One day, I would explore the Egyptian pyramids, discover lost ruins in the jungles of Peru, or unlock the secrets of Atlantis.

Visiting my grandmother was also an exercise in the forbidden. Nana sold cosmetics, so she was never short on makeup, lipstick or eye shadow. I remember raiding her jewelry box and adorning my person in yards of costume pearls and gemstones. But the most exciting thing about Olivia's home was the TV in her living room. It introduced me to Hollywood's greatest actors, actresses, and plays. There were musicals, westerns, films noire, and crime dramas. We also saw our daily fill of Phil Donohue, game shows, and soap operas. Oddly enough, my grandmother never disallowed any show. If she saw it, then I could as well. But Nana was always quick to state her opinion if she considered something right or wrong. While my religious life could be restrictive, it was balanced with the freedom to explore, learn, and grow that my grandmother offered.

Olivia had a very egalitarian outlook. Though more likely to sneer at the term, my grandmother was a classical feminist. She saw the sexes as basically equal; though distinct and different from one another, both genders were important. Men and women had to work in concert with one another to have a happy family. Gentlemen were expected to go out, earn a living, provide for their families, protect them from harm, and be the strong arm to lean on when things went wrong. Ladies were the stewards of family treasure, the wise counselors for their husbands and children, the creative elements that made a home a pleasant, cheerful place, and the spiritual wells from which their families drew succor.

It was an honor and privilege to be female. While men conquered lands, women conquered hearts. If men were ships, then women were the masts that held the sails. This viewpoint was largely due to a Quaker background and the belief in one of the oldest principles known to man- that of balance. If one sex were allowed total power over the other, it would be corrupted by that power. So, the best marriages and families balanced authority with love.

It would be fair to say that I had a dichotomous life from the start, but public school made things unbalanced. Before second grade, my parents decided it would be best to enroll me in the local elementary school due mainly to the financial pressures of attending parochial school. Away from everything that was familiar and comforting, I experienced culture shock. Most adults find it nerve-wracking, so you can imagine how a seven-year-old felt. Crowded and chaotic, public school terrified me. Life in a strict religious sect made it hard to blend in, so I also became the perfect target to bully or pick on. At early ages, kids can be cruel. I remember how it felt to be punched, kicked, or snubbed by the social elite who would twist their cherubic faces into wicked sneers and say, *"Inferior. Unacceptable. Not one of us!"* I clung to my teachers like a drowning man clutches a life preserver and became immersed in books.

That was the beginning of a slow transition into pop culture. When I was nine years old, I received my first pair of jeans. I saw this simple item of clothing as the beginning of "normal" childhood and must have worn that one pair until they grew threadbare and fell apart. Fourth grade also saw me looking more like my peers with a new haircut. Thanks to Nana, I broke that strict rule, only to find that my hair grew faster and thicker because of it. The ends curled up so beautifully that everyone seemed to love my new look. But the damage was already done at school. I would remain the weird little girl who never seemed to fit in.

I am an extrovert today, but the outcome would have been very different had I continued on that earlier course. But, my mother determined that I should learn to swim and enrolled me at the local YMCA. For the first time, I found acceptance and friendship within my own age group and even among the older kids. Many scholastic officials love to point out the value of public school as a socializing agent. But my experiences in public school were more survival and less socialization. The Y was my passport into adulthood, instilling social skills, self-reliance, self-esteem and self-respect.

Because my parents worked and Nana tended to be a homebody in her latter years, I was left to function on my own in everyday activities. Summer mornings were spent in swim classes and at our downtown library followed by lunch at an old-fashioned soda fountain in the heart of town. It featured homemade orangeades made from freshly squeezed oranges, corn syrup and water (so good on a hot day.) I would spend my vacations playing at the pool, and return to school happier and better adjusted.

Then, there was Alex. Alexandra Marie Haskell and her brother Theodore (called Teddy) were Air Force brats who would occasionally spend time at their grandparents' home, which was next door to my own grandmother's house. Over the years, Alex and I have cultivated a kind of strange friendship. There were years when we would not see one another, and when we would finally meet again, time would melt away. (It still does; Alex once remarked that she couldn't remember a time when I wasn't there. Our friendship spans over a quarter of a century.)

My first and oldest friend, Alex acted as another window to the outside world. She was beautiful and street wise, with an easygoing nature and a winning smile that made her popular. Alexandra spent much of her childhood abroad in exotic places such as Panama and Japan, acquiring fascinating stories and an unusual pet, a large parrot named Carlos. Just being with her was a trip into the world of "cool." Yes, the Y helped greatly, but I was still quirky, socially inept, and a little withdrawn, my main problems being overweight coupled with the rejection for not following the crowd like the average kid. Alex never really seemed to mind. We were opposites, truly an "odd couple."

But we had marvelous fun. As children, we played "dress up" and cultivated the most fanciful stories with time travelers, feuding queens, renegades and outlaws- many so involved that one adventure might last a couple of days. We even had imaginary lovers, husbands, and children. In adolescence, we dabbled with makeup, fine-tuning our appearance. We practiced kissing on Alex's cousins and brother, Teddy. Alex taught me how to dance, play poker and gin rummy. On summer nights, we would steal away from our families and whisper ghost stories or read the latest romantic confession magazine. Memories of Alex are still vibrant after all this time, occupying a special place, which nothing else can fill. It's odd how we affected one another. Despite my family's occasional fears, Alex made me more socially aware, and I brought her down to earth with my religious training. I'm in my thirties, and still rambunctious while Alex went from being the mischievous military brat to a conservative Christian (the irony of it all.)

Music also acted as a balancing agent in my personal development. Yes, there was lots of Gospel music with The Cathedrals, The Imperials, and the Gaither Trio being my favorites. However, I also developed a taste for other genres such as jazz, swing, rock-n-roll, funk, and new wave. If it had a beat with a catchy melody, I was into it. I cut my teeth on everything from Elton John to beach music. Late teenage years saw a love affair with groups like U2 and The Miami Sound Machine as well as country groups like The Charlie Daniel's Band and Alabama. Music and books were a refuge when getting to the Y was not possible, and Alex wasn't around. The notes, words, and stanzas would wrap me in a protective cocoon when my world became too much to handle.

I think that all of these factors brought out my gregarious nature. The ugly episodes in public school were tempered with the growing ability to connect and make friends. (My husband loves to joke that aliens could abduct me, and I would meet someone I know in the next holding cell.) In my late to middle adolescence, I had friends from all over the world. There were Caucasians, African-Americans, Asians, Hispanics, Muslims, and Hindustanis; we learned, laughed, and played together.

And through all of this, I was becoming increasingly aware of the different Christian denominations in my hometown. And the most fascinating of these were the Catholics. This is probably because of the proximity of the local Catholic Church to the Y. It sat on the adjacent corner and was separated by only a small side street. Built in the Spanish mission style, the building was composed of pink granite stone with a tall bell tower and a lovely rosette window over its massive wooden doors. I wondered for years what it looked like on the inside until a Catholic playmate invited me in.

It was a hot afternoon, and we were a little bored with our usual activities, so we wandered across the street and into its cool and quiet walls. It was serenity itself when I walked through those doors. The carpet was a rich emerald green, and sunlight glinted through the brilliant stained glass, setting it afire with a kaleidoscope of bright colors. The altar was different from what I was used to, being polished and inlaid wood draped with a delicate lace cloth. Behind it stood the tabernacle in gleaming brass where the communion bread was stored. Of course, there were the saints staring down from each window, the Stations of the Cross on the walls, and the beautiful statues of Mary and Joseph holding a very young Jesus.

But the focal point to the room was the massive cross with Christ upon it. So lifelike was that form that those ribs might have expanded for one last breath of air or the head might have lifted and the eyes opened to look down at me. Strangely haunting, my first impression of that church spoke of ancient biblical times and what the earliest Christians must have been like.

Memory tucked those images away in a small corner of my heart. How could I have known that this experience was my first baby step into another realm and that I would confirm and become a child of Rome in this very place? My adventure could have been simply the product of childhood curiosity, or was it? We Catholics believe that Jesus calls us by name. Did I hear His voice, drifting in the still air of that darkened sanctuary?

Rites of Passage

Have you ever completed a large, cumbersome, jigsaw puzzle? Or analyzed a painting or mural? If you have, then it becomes apparent that seemingly non-relevant colors, shapes, and hues blend together to form one picture. This is what a human being is like, a complex creation with many colors, shapes, and hues.

It is a fact that events that occur in childhood and adolescence shape the human psyche and often make or break us. Though these incidents may be secular elements, they blend with spiritual aspects to form a kind of picture or tapestry of the total individual. One element or aspect may seem insignificant, but take it away, and the person changes. There were three crucial events in my adolescence that irrevocably changed who I was and how I viewed the world.

As hard as it is to admit this, one of these rites of passage was a fight. Membership at the YMCA cultivated my outgoing nature that, in turn, slowly encouraged more school participation. In addition to good grades in high school, I took up drama plays and entered oratorical contests. My junior year saw me replace my high school chorus with participation in DECA (The Distributive Education Clubs of America). This garnered both local and state trophies. But in spite of my nerdy achievements and close circle of friends, I was still occasionally bullied.

This aggravation came to an abrupt end at the beginning of my senior year when I finally snapped after eleven years of abuse. My long fuse, which had tolerated all sorts of mistreatment, simply blew. Some people have no idea what it's like to be excluded, picked at, humiliated, and physically threatened on a daily level. For example, I have needed glasses since the age of nine and am severely myopic. One abuser was cruel enough to flush a brand new pair of particularly beautiful (and expensive) frames down a commode.

I have always been a nonviolent person, often electing to talk my problems to death, but this was one time when I refused to be cornered anymore. All that I can say was that a hazy rage descended over me as I faced this last school bully. She was a "leather queen," with a nasty reputation, but I just didn't care anymore. The brawl that ensued was a good old-fashioned catfight, in which my opponent lost. If it had ended there, then both of us would have gone home, cleaned up and been back at school the next day- no problem.

But the incident happened on a school bus, which was school property. Angered that her image as a tough girl had been compromised, the "leather queen" (whom I'll call Georgina) wanted revenge, insisting that Mr. Sanders, our principal, discipline me. Imagine her surprise when the principal suspended both of us. Sanders said that both Georgina and I had been mutually guilty in the incident. I remember quietly smiling as my bully ranted and raved. We were each suspended for five days. Yes, my grades would suffer, but I knew that I would still have a B average, while Georgie was not that lucky.

I did worry a little about telling my parents; they had always held high standards as far as conduct was concerned. But Mom and Dad were kind and supportive, being aware of all the misery that I had endured in public school. I spent most of my time away as I usually did in the summer, bumming around town, swimming at the Y, and reading at the library.

When I came back, I found that some teachers were stunned at what happened. I was normally such a mild-mannered mouse that my homeroom teacher thought that my name on the list of those suspended was a "typo." Other instructors were sympathetic, offering me lots of extra credit to shore up my grades. The general consensus of the faculty members who knew both of us was that a bully had received some of what she deserved.

The second event was the death of my beloved Nana. Though she passed away when I was sixteen, I saw her as dead when she lost her mental capacity completely the year before. Alzheimer's disease is a horrible way to die; taking tiny pieces of the mind until nothing is left. And while the body may survive for a period of time, you end up hoping and praying for death to come as you witness your loved one suffering in a physical kind of purgatory, suspended between life and death.

Olivia Fitzpatrick was a brilliant woman; with an IQ some believed to be at or above genius level. I can't tell you how painful it was to watch her slowly disappear. When I was fourteen, our respective positions of charge and caregiver began to reverse. A year later, that transition was complete. When other teens were absorbed in academics, football, and dances, I dealt with the increasingly violent and confused shell that was my grandmother- until our family could no longer trust her on her own while I was at school. Olivia spent her final months in a vegetative state at a local nursing home.

Upon her death, all that I could feel was a joyous peace. I must have glowed at the wake. Dressed in an elegant black skirt and heels with a white moiré taffeta blouse, and glinting with the occasional flash of gold, I laughed, joked, and socialized with attending friends and family. To be anything less would have been dishonorable to Olivia's memory. I knew that her spirit was somewhere close by, and that she was pleased by this display. I felt anointed with Nana's presence, as if every good thing that she was had survived in me.

Nana's last lesson for me was about social justice. One of the saddest things about the American healthcare system is the fact that many of us cannot get the proper care that we need without liquidating everything that we own. Insurance companies often make insurance too expensive or impossible to get for those who need it the most. Pharmaceutical firms prey on the elderly and those who suffer from chronic or life-threatening conditions, constantly raising the price of drugs.

Witnessing the financial problems that a terminal illness brings has made me a firm advocate of a national healthcare plan, so that other Americans who've worked hard to have the small piece of Americana won't have to sacrifice everything that they have to receive adequate healthcare. What good is paying taxes, if it does not increase the quality of life for those who contribute? The wealthy have plenty of assets to absorb astronomical medical bills, and the poor have specific programs and funding, but the middle class, who contributes the most taxes, gets the least benefits. The injustice of it cries to heaven.

The first two incidents, though largely secular in nature, have left their mark on my personality. While I paid for my mistake, the fight gave me a newfound confidence and ease, instilling a feisty spirit that isn't afraid to assert itself. And I still retain little tolerance for any kind of bully, whether the physical kind or other brands which are infinitely more pernicious. Although I didn't know it at the time, the concept of social justice is deeply rooted in Roman Catholicism and comes from Christ Himself. Jesus instructed His Disciples to care for the least of humanity, those who are poor, imprisoned, sick and dying. It is our responsibility as Christians, and when we fulfill His command, we also minister to Jesus because He is present in these little ones. Preying upon the weakest members of society is against the very nature of Christianity and an affront to God. So, in a strange way, my Protestant grandmother had some share in my conversion to Catholicism, which brings us to the last and most fateful of these rites of passage into adulthood.

I grew up in a compartmentalized world. This continued even after my grandmother's death and my return to my parents' home. On weekends, I played the part of a strict devotee- a member of a Wesleyan fundamentalist sect that governed even the smallest aspects of everyday existence. Then, there was life during the week as average teen that wore jeans, jewelry, and short hair. The real me loved the movies and would frequently disappear into the pages of a favorite novel. Looking back at those years, I've wondered exactly when the division between my two opposing worlds was complete. Was it when I formally left my father's church or had my mind been set against it all from the start?

I used to feel occasionally guilty as if I were a hypocrite- unable to be the same thing all the time. But the freedom I had found away from church was intoxicating. I loved being a wild child, playing in Nana's overgrown gardens. Strangely enough, my devotion to God did not diminish. In the face of mainstreaming, my heart was still deeply religious, but I found it hard to reconcile both aspects of my young life.

The church that I grew up in had two problems. The first was politics. One of the biggest difficulties of independent churches is their leadership. There are too many "called preachers" who lack the spiritual discipline to go to seminary school. It is simply not enough that God has called someone to preach. They need to know biblical history and languages such as Latin and Greek, and be able to cultivate interpersonal skills, especially in the realm of counseling. Now, some might argue that the Disciples were simple men who did not attend modern colleges, but to be fair, most of the Apostles spent three years learning at the feet of God Incarnate- the ultimate seminary experience! Today, it is imperative for a minister to be a learned individual.

To further compound the problem of politics is the aspect of the continuing splits and fracturing within the body of Christ that goes with it. Most independent churches tend to break apart after a few years. When this happens, a flock will be divided between two or more groups in the wake of some big disagreement and will radically change in its membership. This is one of the most destructive practices that I know of. It is sad to realize that pride and arrogance will not allow even a small amount of unity within these churches, some of which number less than two hundred people. My childhood memory is littered with instances of missing different people due to their leaving, having followed someone to another sanctuary. While it is emotionally jarring to be moved from home to home and city-to-city, it can be devastating to leave a group of individuals with whom you worship. People, especially children, crave stability, and our religious environment was anything but stable.

But, politics aside, the worst problem was their dogmatic views on dress and conduct. This group of people could be extremely loving and generous, so much so that a person could almost forget their harsh, unbending rules. I said, ***"Almost."*** While it is a good thing to look modest, church elders could be legalistic, even cruel when enforcing their rules and opinions on how members attired and conducted themselves.

I remember hearing my mother tell about the time Mrs. Garby, one of our church's most devout matriarchs, attended a service in a lovely red dress. The minister got up and preached against the color red. Embarrassed, the poor lady sunk deeper in her seat as the sermon wore on. Mrs. Garby was not dressed in a sleazy fashion; she was a good and honorable lady who would never do such a thing. Her grave spiritual error was wearing the wrong color on the wrong day.

Another incident dealt with a Mr. Orbach, a minister whom the whole church was fond of. His wife, Martha, had exceptionally long, thick hair that reached around her ankles. It was usually piled upon her head in a heavy bun. Now, Martha had three children to keep up with, but she was constantly plagued with headaches so severe that she would take to her bed and be unable to look after her family. After the usual round of tests and examinations, the final cause of this pain was determined to be her hair. It weighed so heavily upon her head that it was placing a strain on her neck and shoulders. The physician advised Mrs. Orbach that she would need to cut her hair, if she wanted no more headaches. She did so, opting for a shoulder-length style. Nevertheless, this incident caused such a problem among the elders of the church that our beloved minister left his post. While it is true that a woman's glory is her hair, is it so glorious to stay sick from the length of it? There seemed to be a serious lack of common sense in this situation.

If it were just two incidents, then the eccentricities of the church could be overlooked. But these events are simply a taste of the extremism. I remember my parent's first TV set, a little black and white thirteen-inch model. We would hide it in the closet when church people came to visit. (My mom will flatly deny this; however, she was not usually the one who had to move it. I remember picking up that thirty-pound monster.) There were even reports of radical Wesleyans from up north who did not allow their flocks to wear sandals in the summer. Some elders forbade drinking carbonated soda. (In all fairness, both of those edicts didn't last long.) But to put it mildly, there were times when I found the whole affair a ridiculous waste of time.

Two types of children issued from the families within our church. Some teens dutifully did whatever was the proper thing while others not only broke the dress and conduct codes, but went a little nuts in doing anything that offended society as a whole. These kids did drugs, broke the law, and were sexually promiscuous behind their parent's backs. Authoritarian parents have a tendency of rearing either children who lack independence or rebels who reject everything their parents stand for.

Luckily, my family produced rebels who weren't that crazy. Church was balanced with a home that emphasized giving children some autonomy in small day-to-day affairs with adherence to a few basic guidelines. Christian virtues, good grades, and proper manners were the watchwords in my parents' home and at Nana's house. The rest was negotiable. My upbringing was authoritative, not authoritarian, which made all the difference.

Because I was mainstreamed into the outside world at an early age, I never fit in at church either, but being a social misfit gave me the distinct advantage of being able to be with less popular people without worrying about falling out of the "in" crowd. I had nothing to lose. Most churches have a "street" ministry geared toward bringing the "unchurched" to God. Our van would pick up kids from "the wrong side of the tracks" and take them to the sanctuary. They were a rough crowd who did not always dress and act the preferred way, but I would always make it a point to treat them the same as everyone else.

God gives us revelations in our lives, and my revelation that I did not truly belong with my church family came in the form of a young girl who had been riding in the van for a few Sundays. One morning, she took me aside and said, *"You are the only one here who's been good to us."*

She continued to confide that one of our teenage socialites had told her, *"I don't like the way that you dress. Leave my church."*

There was something extremely unchristian in those words. At that moment, I was so taken aback and ashamed that I came to the realization that I needed to go. Some careless comments from an immature teenager could have been excused. But beneath it all, there lay something more insidious. This statement reflected the views of the leaders of the church, in general, only amplified in teenage callousness. The socialite had simply acted the way she had been taught.

Leaving the church into which you were born and raised is akin to leaving the family home. After my graduation, this was my first big decision. My father took the news a little better than I thought he would. (I had been very apprehensive. My mother and sisters had left earlier, and I felt as though Dad might believe me to be deserting him. We had attended services together for years.) Our current minister heard that I was soon to go, and came over for a talk. I told him how I felt and why I had made my decision. He furnished a few excuses, but I remained unmoved. At the end of the interview, frustrated at losing the discussion, the minister told me, *"If you leave, your soul will be in danger!"*

I had respected our pastor- until that moment. His words confirmed that what I was doing was the right thing. Showing him to the door, I closed it and doing so, shut away the past.

Recently, I sat down and began to carefully look at my childhood church with new eyes. Our elders always seemed to be obsessed with the biblical books of Deuteronomy, Numbers, and Leviticus. For the unschooled, these books are simply from the Old Testament. But, biblical scholars know that they contain within them the Mosaic Code.

The Mosaic Code is more than the Decalogue (the Ten Commandments) and is extremely long and cumbersome. It controlled every aspect of life for the Jew before and at the time of Christ, and it continues to do so for many Orthodox Jews today. Its function was to separate the Jews from other people in the world and prepare the Jewish people for the coming of the Messiah.

When Christ came into the world, He fulfilled the law. Our Savior told us to love God with all of our being and to love our neighbor as ourselves. This was the law and the prophets; everything else was commentary. Jesus did not pick at people because they did not follow the letter of the law; instead, He always emphasized the spirit of the law. Christ was more interested in the heart and soul of a person, rather than outward appearances.

Now, some people enjoy bringing the Apostle Paul and his letters into the argument, especially the books of Corinthians. But they really do not understand to whom and why he is writing. Corinth had a large, very Orthodox, Jewish contingent, and the church at Corinth was trying to lead these people to Christ. Paul knew that unless Corinthian Christians looked and acted like their Jewish brothers and sisters, they would not be accepted within the community. So, it was imperative that they adopt certain Mosaic standards in order to do this; otherwise, the Jewish Corinthians would have simply ignored them. Yes, Paul does quote the law, but he also finishes with the statement: *"But if any man seem to be contentious, we have NO such custom, neither the churches of God." (I Corinthians 11:16, KJV)*

Paul tells the Corinthian Christians to respect Jewish customs to better lead Jews to Christ, without needless conflicts over dress and conduct. Once converted to Christianity, the Jews would learn that they were, in fact, freed from the law. Furthermore, Paul addresses the importance of being free from the Mosaic Code in his letter to the Galatians:

> *Knowing that a man is not justified by the works of the law, but by the faith of Jesus Christ, even we have believed in Jesus Christ, that we might be justified by*

> the faith of Christ, and not by the works of the law: for by the works of the law shall no flesh be justified.
>
> But if, while we seek to be justified by Christ, we ourselves also are found sinners, is therefore Christ the minister of sin? God forbid. For if I build again the thing which I destroyed, I make myself a transgressor. For I through the law am dead to the law, that I might live unto God.
>
> I am crucified with Christ: nevertheless I live; yet not I, but Christ liveth in me: and the life which I now live in the flesh I live by the faith of the Son of God, who loved me, and gave Himself for me. I do not frustrate the grace of God: for if righteousness come by the law, then Christ is dead in vain. (Galatians 2:16-21, KJV)

Just as with the Church in Galatia, some Christians are still enslaved in strict dress and conduct codes when they truly do not need to be so. James warns us that we should always strive to meet the spirit of the law, not the letter. Listen to his words when he says, *"For whosoever shall keep the whole law, and yet offend in one point, he is guilty of all. For he that said, 'Do not commit adultery,' said also, 'Do not kill.' Now if thou commit no adultery, yet if thou kill, thou art become a transgressor of the law."* (James 2:10-11, KJV)

Looking at this passage, it becomes clear that the exact letter of the law will judge those who deliberately ignore this warning and adopt the legalistic stance, and infringing on one point will make those individuals guilty of the ***entire*** Mosaic Code.

How many of us enjoy ham dishes, cheeseburgers, pizza, lasagna, shrimp, and lobster? Sorry, can't have it. It is forbidden to eat pork, mix milk and meat, or eat seafood with no scales. One cannot stir or turn anything on the Sabbath. You cannot cook or even start a car engine. And the Sabbath is from Friday evening to Saturday evening. This is just a small taste of the legalism involved in the law. There are hundreds of rules and regulations within the Mosaic Code. If a person decides to live by certain points in the law, that individual must adopt every standard, even the dietary ones, or be guilty of it all. One cannot pick and choose. It is all or nothing.

This is why my old church was wrong. They half-clung to the old standards and forgot about the downside to legalism. In the process, they hindered the faith of others and stunted new believers in their spiritual growth. Worse yet, they could not handle the freedom Christianity gives, electing to place themselves back under the law (at least partially) when Christ came to deliver us from its iron rule.

Could I have ever truly stayed and become obsessed with appearances and the approval of a select few? What kind of a life is that? I was born and bred to be free, instilled with voracious curiosity and a thirst for knowledge. It was inevitable that I would leave, looking for new spiritual vistas, and the challenges that accompany them.

Epiphany

By the time I had left my family's old church, I had a suitable replacement. During high school, I had formed a friendship with a Baptist minister's son. For at least a year, he did his best to get me to go to his church. I had a good mezzo-soprano voice, and they needed people in the choir. So, when the time came, my transition was relatively smooth. Daddy would drop me off in front of the sanctuary and continue on to his church, then retrieve me after everything was over.

I enjoyed being a member. For the first time in my life, I could dress like an average person. I have never liked having to change my appearance just to fit in. Now, I could enjoy wearing makeup, jewelry, and trendy outfits without the guilt. It felt good that my spiritual and secular lives were more blended, and I began to bloom in this friendly environment. One of my fondest memories is my baptism, which took place in their baptistery, a little room above the choir loft. I remember wearing a white gown and the warmth of the water.

Another good thing that happened due to my membership was the eventual enrollment of my mother and sister. For a long time, neither of them went to any services due to bitter memories at the Wesleyan Church. Mom and Gwyneth had gotten embroiled in a conflict with the other matriarchs, which ended badly. By the time I was nine, both of them had completely mainstreamed into American culture while leaving our old flock behind. It's sad how politics can turn someone off to religious life. But their exile ended when they found a home in my new church. (Incidentally, Mom and Gwyneth are still there.) I think it's funny when Baptist family friends refer to me as "Gwyneth's sister," forgetting that I was there first. But to be fair, most of these events happened over seventeen years ago. I doubt that my nephews can even remember me as a Baptist.

It was at this time that I had one of the most vivid religious experiences of my life. This epiphany happened on my first real job, which I landed shortly before my eighteenth birthday. I entered the workforce as an inventory clerk in a firm that contracted with Revco Drugs. We would do a store a day, some Revcos having inventory values of less than fifty thousand dollars while others were worth as much as half a million. I remember traveling all over the Carolinas, Tennessee, Virginia, West Virginia and Ohio. Trips to Myrtle Beach, South Carolina and Newport News, Virginia were a lot like working vacations. This environment was anything but conducive to religious experiences.

One morning, as I counted a section of cold medicines, my mind began to wander as I hit the keys. The music and words of a favorite hymn, *"He is so precious to me,"* came to mind. As a child, I had always seen the picture of Christ with His lambs standing at a closed door, His hand raised as if knocking. For some strange reason, the image became poignant at that moment. It conveyed a feeling of intense longing, though not on my part. It was as if I were experiencing Christ's desire to commune with His followers.

As all of these images and emotions engulfed me, I felt an unbelievable presence. It was staring through penetrating eyes from behind. And there was incredible pain and love beyond imagination. I froze, unable to turn around. I knew in my heart that He was there in all of His radiance, and if my head had even rotated a few degrees, I might see with my own eyes the person who died two thousand years ago for my sins. The pull was strong but I couldn't bring myself to look in those eyes. Instead, I began to sob, tears falling silently in an unbroken stream. I'm not sure how long this episode lasted, but the beautiful presence disappeared when someone came down the aisle towards me. The rest of the day seemed to echo with a sense of lost glory. I tried to return to that mindset in hopes of reliving that special moment, but my efforts were in vain.

I had always known and accepted the possibility of miracles and visions. This was an intrinsic part of my upbringing. So, you can imagine how unsettled I was when I told my Baptist minister about this incident and found his reaction less than enthusiastic. I expected him to express awe, wonder, or at least, sympathy and understanding, but the man didn't even acknowledge my words or want to discuss something so special. Instead, my pastor acted as if he had "stepped" in something. I guess some Christians believe that modern man cannot experience God the way the prophets and Disciples did. That's sad because it inhibits the ability of the Holy Spirit to bear witness in our lives.

The minister's response to my little epiphany made me feel out of place in my new church home and left a craving for the spirituality that I had known as a child, but in a less legalistic form. I realized that this church could only offer temporary shelter from the outside world; it would never satisfy the need to touch the supernatural world and transcend the senses. But my hunger to touch the divine would send me on a search down other avenues, some which were dark, shadowy, and very dangerous.

A Glorious Sunset

My parents gave me life, but Olivia was the one who truly affected me during my formative years. Nana spent the most time with me. I didn't just visit my grandmother, but lived with her during the week while seeing my parents on weekends. Mom and Dad worked outside the home (which I do not begrudge), and both of my sisters were married by my fourteenth birthday. So, it was easier and more economical to live with Olivia. Logically, it would stand to reason that I would grow to be more like my grandmother than anyone else is. In fact, it has been said on more than one occasion that I am very much like she was. But that has not always worked to my advantage.

For everything that she was, Olivia had her faults. She was anti-Catholic, socially ambitious, and often entertained racist views. (I patently object to these ideas.) My father is half-Native American, the son of an Eastern Band Qualla Cherokee woman and a humble sharecropper. Though once influential, Dad's family had lost its fortune during the Great Depression. So, Nana, who had wished for an affluent, Anglo-Saxon son-in-law was deeply frustrated when my mother fell in love with this young upstart from out of town who had a questionable heritage. It is a fact that my grandmother created a rift between herself and my parents due to her refusal to accept my Dad as one of the family.

Let me say that I love my father very much. He has always been a good, decent man who has worked tirelessly to provide for his family. And Dad gave me a strong religious foundation, for which I will be eternally grateful. But when a child develops a personality reminiscent of a parent's biggest familial adversary, it can become a stumbling block in the parent/child relationship. Being so much like Nana, the frustration once directed at her became subconsciously aimed at me.

After high school and a childhood of extremism and premature responsibility, I wanted to bum around a little, enjoy life, and go to college. At times, my father would gravitate between treating me as a ten-year-old and forcing my independence at a time when I had no training or skills. This ambivalence was more than a little vexing. School was also a quandary. All through high school, I had wanted to be an archeologist, having a total fascination with history's legends and lore. The local technical school didn't really offer much. So, I quickly lost interest in my first major, computer programming.

But, my social life was taking off. Mina, my surviving high school friend, introduced me to **Doctor Who**, a popular British Sci-Fi series. Together, she and I created our own fan club, a subsidiary group of a national club called **The Companions of Doctor Who**. And along with Mina came a host of new friends and acquaintances.

First there was Patrick, Mina's brother, who had a monster collection of all sorts of science fiction movies, episodes and film clips, some of which were rare British bloopers. His contacts from the United Kingdom were always sending some tape that other groups didn't dream of having. So, if entertainment was a problem, he was the man to see, especially if you wanted to impress someone.

Then, there was the unlikely duo of Sydney and TJ. Sydney, a lanky kid with wire-rimmed glasses, loved **Star Trek** and Bill Cosby. (What a combo!) TJ was a big military buff that "believed" that almost any problem could be solved with the suitable application of high-end explosives. Those two would get into animated discussions on everything from quantum physics to the latest fantasy novels.

Martin, a close friend of Patrick from high school, was a large black guy who preferred cowboy boots and a "ten gallon" hat to the favorite African American fashions of the day. This odd outfit once earned him the moniker, "Sheriff" from the British star, Jon Pertwee. Sentimental and old fashioned at times, Marty had a weakness for oriental women and long hair. He would often fuss whenever he saw me with a new haircut.

This colorful bunch was like a second family to me. We spent weekends together, traveling all over our state, meeting other fans and raising money for our local Public TV station during their Festival Campaigns. I also loved going to local conventions as well as those out of state in places such as New Orleans and Atlanta. I had the pleasure of meeting various American and British actors/actresses, writers, artists, and producers.

Science fiction fans have always been pictured as foolish and silly. But the subculture is like a smorgasbord for the mind. Pick a subject, and there will always be someone who has an opinion or has read the latest article. This is especially true when it comes to social issues. Beneath the strange costumes and carnival atmosphere, a good convention is a fertile place to explore religion, sexual issues, social problems, and politics. I might add that sports and entertainment have their own respective obsessive fans. I wonder how many of them have deep and meaningful conversations on the nature of the universe.

Contrary to popular opinion, Sci-Fi fantasy fans do have lives. Most of us have families, jobs and are part of various religious communities. And, while one might see a lot of teens and young adults at a convention, that person is just as likely to see a businessman in his custom suit buy a bunch of comics and tuck them into his briefcase. Fans come from every aspect of society and are not limited to the stereotype that most people imagine.

With my introduction into this offbeat culture, I, like many other kids in the eighties, took up running characters in role-playing games. It's sad how religious zealots have turned role-playing into a dirty word when my con buddies and I had so much fun. In addition to the infamous **Dungeons and Dragons** game, there were so many other types of games such as **Star Fleet Battles (Star Trek), Dr. Who, In Her Majesty's Secret Service** (spies and espionage), **Time Traveler,** and **Chill** (battling ghosts, vampires, werewolves, etc.) I have run characters and been around numerous gamers for seventeen years, and I have absolutely no recollection of anyone being hurt either physically, emotionally, or spiritually from playing those games.

There's been a lot of joking, laughter and munchies, but I can't remember us ever trying to sacrifice Cousin Fred on a Saturday night. It didn't happen, folks. Anyone who blames a game for aberrant behavior is ignoring the obvious fact that the person was unstable in some way long before he/she took up gaming. **Dungeons & Dragons** is largely based on the legends and lore of cultures worldwide as well as the literary creations of writers such as JRR Tolkien and HP Lovecraft. I was already familiar with much of this before I created my first character.

It's interesting to see how the public has received the **Lord of the Rings Trilogy**, understanding it to be one of the great literary classics brought to life, with stunning scenery, special effects, and superb acting. All three movies have thrilled viewers worldwide. Tolkien's world is the basis of the typical D&D adventure featuring: mischief at the local pub, exploring forbidden places, battling evil wizards and mythical creatures, and finding that magic item that's more trouble than it's worth. Sound familiar? This sort of adventure is a kind of fairytale for adults.

Now, you may wonder about how all of this fits into a spiritual journey. The answer is people are not two-dimensional figures, but complex individuals with varied interests. Science fiction/fantasy demands the open mind and heart of a child and truly finds it in the fandom subculture as opposed to the mundane world that cannot abide with that quality. This was the new social life that I had created for myself, and it served a strange purpose as it set the scene for one of the great defining moments in my life.

My personality, lack of collegiate enthusiasm, and thriving social life did place a strain on family life. But to be fair, I was still a good kid. Even as a young adult, I stayed away from drugs, promiscuity, and crime. I never kept my parents up with worry. If I was out and might return home later than originally agreed upon, I would always call to let them know. By most standards, I was trustworthy and responsible. My biggest problem was that I needed a little more focus.

I suppose that had nothing significant happened to change the situation, I would have probably saved up my pennies for college tuition in a four-year institution and moved out to some campus. But those plans were derailed when I was nineteen. I was at a Sci-Fi convention in Macon, Georgia called MOC I. It was late March, and people were milling to and from the con suite. A con suite is a place for the enjoyment of all the conventioneers, offering snacks, sodas, conversation, and films. I bumped into this guy on his way through the sliding glass doors to the pool outside.

Many fans collected buttons to wear at conventions and meetings, some of which were very funny. It was customary to stop someone and read/inspect their buttons. That's how I met Michael, only he had so many buttons that he wore them on the back of his shirt. (I thought this very unwise at the time, as there was a real possibility of getting stuck by the thick pins that held them on.) We talked for a little while, and then went our separate ways.

Mike turned up again on the following night. Conventions are largely done on weekends, so that attendees can get away from work. Friday is the first day, but Saturday is when things get into high gear. There's usually a lot of dressing up and talent shows. My costume for Saturday evening was one that I had designed and made of white chiffon over white gauze trimmed in silver, very Grecian in line and form. I bound my hair up in clear Austrian crystals, and a friend had lent me a long CZ earring in pastel colors. A large solitaire CZ in the other ear balanced this. In the eighties, the long/short earring paring was the rage. My eyelids were a mix of blue, purple, and pink, while my lips and cheeks were done in a rich wine color.

Sci-Fi fans enjoy freaking out the normal population in a city, so our group decided to raid a fast food restaurant in costume. The fascinated looks from surprised "mundanes" were vastly entertaining as fifteen to twenty of us entered the store that evening. Amid my friends and the accompanying stragglers, I saw Michael again.

From that moment on, we seemed inseparable. Our first date was one long talk session. Back in the lobby of the hotel, we discussed so many subjects that it felt like surfing from topic to topic, so easy and fluid. At times, he would stare at my eyes as if he were drowning. In the least, Michael seemed blown away by my getup, christening me "his vision in white." Around midnight, we went to his hotel room to meet up with more friends. My husband's greatest memory of that convention was our first kiss, but mine is somewhat different.

In the middle of a physical passion that was dangerous, I demonstrated resolution and gave him the test that I had given every person that I had ever dated. It was a pass or fail situation, in which the wrong answer would have proven him unsuitable to date. I looked him in eye, and calmly said, *"I am a virgin, and will remain so until I marry."*

Michael looked like a miner who had just struck a large vein of gold. Staring at me, as if seeing a mythic unicorn, he smiled broadly and answered. *"I respect virgins. I'm a Catholic."*

That was the beginning of an interstate courtship that featured little physical contact and hours on the phone. I think we drove both sets of parents buggy with the long distance bills. Mike spent nearly three hundred dollars alone in the first month. (My first bill was a demure hundred forty bucks.) We dated on the phone and visited one another every two to three months. When we did see one another, Michael was sure to bring me tons of stuffed animals and other pretties such as crystal sun catchers. We went to great restaurants and talked incessantly about every facet of living.

I was extremely impressed with his family when I first met them. Mike is the seventh child in a family of nine kids, and every one of these siblings seemed extremely well read and intelligent. I spent most of my life searching for interaction with people who were on the same intellectual level as I was. Now, I felt strangely outnumbered. I loved their dinners that were always punctuated with noisy, boisterous commentary, and delicious dishes from all over the world. Whether Hispanic, Greco-Roman or Chinese, the food was always freshly prepared and a pleasure to eat. The Gunns even made hand-stuffed sausage, which was so lean and thick that one had to boil it down in water, and then brown the outside.

The patriarch of this clan was John who worked for the State Board of Transportation for Florida. He was once a Notre Dame seminarian who had dreamed of the priesthood. But his heart was lost to Jean, his wife. Even today, they are extremely devoted to one another. My husband has fond memories of seeing his father nuzzle his mother's neck as she sat about creating some meal in the kitchen- a task that they shared, often commenting on the day's events.

One of the greatest secrets in finding a mate is to examine and note how members of one's gender are treated and the dynamic present in various relationships. Chances are that you will be treated in the same fashion once and if you become part of the family. John had a saying that my husband has adopted. *"A man is the head of the family, but the woman is its heart!"* Watching carefully, I noted the affection and respect women were given, and I liked it.

During this period of courtship, I rekindled my lost interest in Catholicism. I figured that if I was considering becoming part of the family, I needed to find out as much as possible about Michael's faith. One morning, I got the courage to dial up the very church that I had played in as a child. The answering voice had a rich New York accent. It was my first true contact with Catholicism, a man that I will call Father Leo.

Charming and charismatic, with the demeanor of a Roman general and the heart of a poet, Leo could disarm with a word and fascinate with a gesture. He was Italian with black hair that was thinning on top and eyes the shade of warm chocolate. Those deep-set eyes could peer into the soul, and this priest's kind affability made anyone want to trust him implicitly. We met weekly, over a six-month period, covering every aspect of the Catholic faith.

As my first Christmas with Mike approached, I wanted to give him something very special for Christmas. It has been said that I sing rather well, so during this time, I decided to assist the choir at the Catholic Church in their presentation of Midnight Mass in addition to my participation with the local Baptist choir in their seasonal cantata.

Midnight Mass became a pivotal experience in my life. After the concert, I sat transfixed as the celebrant priest, Monsignor Pierce, blessed the bread and wine. Wanting so much to be a part of it all, I wandered up with the rest of church for this sacred feast. I had no clue that I was not supposed to go until Father Leo gently put me off. But he didn't let me go away completely empty-handed. Leo laid his hands on my head and gave me a blessing. That night filled me with a deep longing to be a part of the priestly people that the world calls Catholics.

The Long Dark Night of My Soul

*I confess to Almighty God,
And to you, my brothers and sisters,
That I have greatly sinned,
In my thoughts and in my words,
In what I have done, and in what I have failed to do,
Through my fault, through my fault,
Through my most grievous fault;
Therefore I ask the Blessed Mary, ever-Virgin,
All the Angels and Saints,
And YOU, my brothers and sisters, to pray for me to the Lord, our God.*

-From the Mass Penitential Rite

Twilight's Fingers

Faith begins as a small stream. The struggles and conflicts that we encounter are the stones and boulders that fall in. Sometimes, a boulder can misdirect the water off its appointed course or even scatter it, but in many instances, a spiritual obstacle can deepen the water with its depression. Without the conflicts that life throws at us, faith stays a weak stream, never a strong river. The greatest of these spiritual boulders are dark nights. They can reveal to us our fears and failures, force critical choices between good and evil, and lay our souls bare before God, sometimes the world. If we survive the onslaught, we continue our journey, slowly growing with a new maturity and grace.

I wish that I could say that I've never committed a grievous offense against God, but that would not be true. Satan has something for everyone; he knows our weaknesses and enjoys exploiting them. There are those who are driven by consuming ambition. Some others can be sexually enslaved. And many lose themselves in the abyss called drug abuse- or it can be a recipe of these and other factors. Whatever these pitfalls are, they seek to pull an individual from the presence of God.

While I prize reason, intellect, and logic, these pursuits have always been balanced by a devout belief in the spiritual world. There is a disturbing thread that winds it way through my family tree, the ability to draw spirits. My grandmother had this strange gift, and to some extent, so do I. The only way to describe being around ghosts and malevolent beings, is the feeling that unseen eyes are watching you, and if you turn suddenly, you might get a glimpse of an unearthly face. Nana instructed me to always use the Trinity to turn dark spirits away. This is said aloud, over and over until the presence is gone.

*In the name of the Father, and the Son, and the Holy Spirit,
I banish you back from whence you came.
Let evil be separated from me as far as the North is from South,
And the East is from the West. Amen.*

The ability to draw spirits comes with a natural fascination with the occult. The American South is a haunted place filled with legends of native battles and massacres, civil war conflicts, lost lovers and their betrayers, pirates, and slaves. One of the little known secrets of my home state is its link with witchcraft. There is a rumor that we have one of the largest schools of Wicca on the East Coast situated in our mountains. Famed with majestic beauty, these misty blue giants hide centuries of folk magic and native spirituality.

When I was nineteen, I bought an exquisitely illustrated tarot deck, and began to diligently learn the meaning behind each card, right side up or inverted. A tarot deck is a psychic extension of an individual, much like a leg or arm. To make this possible, the reader must carry with them at all times, handle the cards as much as possible, even sleep with the deck under a pillow. As I became more adept at the cards, I found it easy to spiritually connect with those I cast readings for. Occasionally, individuals would be surprised at what I said.

The most positive reading I ever did was for my own future, shortly after I had met Michael. It spoke of all sorts of trials and hardships, but the final card was the Ace of Cups, right side up. Its illustration depicts a large chalice or cup, filled with water. Rays of light fall down upon it from the sky, as a dove circles above. These symbols are synonymous with the Trinity and a pure, self-sacrificing kind of love that theologians call *agape.* How prophetic! God has played a major role in our lives, and we seem to be bound in mystical relationship- far beyond the modern idea of romantic love or marriage. In many ways, our union is that of twin souls, separated by four years and three states, but brought together by Providence.

But another reading still gives me chills. I cast the cards for my con buddy, Martin, and in revealing the final card, I told him to expect a job promotion in the future. That was a laugh. We both knew that his chances of promotion were nonexistent, as the company he worked for was extremely small with a workforce that rarely changed, especially in the higher positions. A few weeks later, I was stunned to learn that one of the associates had suddenly died, and Martin had been chosen to fill the vacancy. His promotion had come courtesy of "dead man's boots." Marty's reading brought a new feeling that was more intoxicating than any drug- power. There's nothing like being able to reveal intimate details of a stranger's life or having a fleeting glimpse of the future. It probably was all coincidence, but that didn't lessen the incident's effect.

And the experience underscored something much deeper than mere fascination. Remember the craving I spoke of earlier. As a child, I had studied ancient cultures and religions and had even witnessed the kind of Christian mysticism that could make a person want to touch the divine. But, as a young adult, I had become a wanderer, increasingly hungry to experience what I had once known. No matter how kind or devout my Baptist church home was, it could not satisfy that need. I wanted more than they could give me. After my minister's lack of enthusiasm regarding my religious epiphany, I no longer talked about spirituality to fellow Christians at church. They simply did not understand. Instead, I secretly began to explore and look for something else.

While I wanted to believe that what I was doing was right, I felt every fiber in my being cringe from my activities. I was both terrified and intrigued, staring down a winding staircase that seemed to melt away into darkness. My parents were blissfully unaware that the wine satin bag in my bedroom contained an element of divination. It wasn't until a few years ago that I told my mother and father about my tarot deck and the misadventure that caused me to shrink from its use.

I had landed a job working as a waitress in a small diner. One day, I made the mistake of bringing my deck to work. People naturally ask, even beg for readings, especially if they're free. (I did not like the idea of charging for the service, though once I had charged a small fee for readings during a charity drive.) One girl at work was very insistent for my services. As I was doing her cards, I let it slip that I could draw spirits. It was a casual comment, but she became almost obsessed with the idea of a séance.

Recently the coworker, Leta, had lost a good friend in a traffic accident. Leta felt that the girl was still with them and wanted to help her go to her rest. Now, reading tarot was one thing, but conversing with the dead was entirely different. I was both thrilled and nervous at what might happen. I tried to say no, but just couldn't get the words out. Before I knew it, I was roped into the whole affair. The appointed time was two days before Thanksgiving, the night before the city's annual holiday parade.

That evening, I took my deck, but I also took a Bible, a Christian songbook, and my silver cross necklace. There was a small little voice that whispered that things could go horribly wrong. I was steadfastly against allowing something unseen to enter my mind and soul. I prayed for divine protection, and upon reaching the house, anointed each person there with prayer. Some of the kids wanted to play harsh rock music, but I felt that would be unwise.

It wasn't the Hollywood version of a séance; nothing much happened that evening. I believe now that my prayers kept whatever it was at bay. The air in that apartment bristled with frustration and anger. When I was delivered home, Leta and her friends wanted me to come back and try again the next day. I said no, having volunteered to ride in the church float in the parade. I also made them promise not to try without me, as someone could get hurt. (Actually, I had determined that this was my first, last, and only séance. Something about it left me feeling creepy.)

The day of the parade was very cold, and as we were loaded in the float, it began to slowly drizzle. I was wearing my mother's brown fur coat and holding an umbrella, but it was not enough. At the end of the parade route, I felt like a human ice cube. After eating a good, hot meal, it was early to bed. Imagine my surprise when I was awakened to frantic pounding on our front door early Thanksgiving morning. My dad called me, and I sleepily wandered out to see what was wrong. The kids from the séance were back. Screaming and crying hysterically, they were begging to see me. Sending my father back to bed, I shut the door, and stood with them on the porch.

Against my warning and advice, they had done another séance. This time, there was no protection. I was told that one of the girls had begun to act strangely, speaking in a masculine voice. They were desperately seeking my help. So, at 2 am, I ran back into the house, dressed hurriedly, and went with them. I spent the morning praying for those teenagers, especially the girl, Holly, whom I found passed out on a nearby bed. There were no masculine voices, just a group who grew surly because I refused to do another séance. It was around early Thanksgiving afternoon, when I decided that I was weak and tired of the whole business. I told them that I needed a ride home, which they refused to give me. So, I called my dad, and in fifteen minutes, he was there.

I was very quiet coming home, but Dad was brimming with questions. To be honest, I couldn't bring myself to tell him what had happened. It would have scared and hurt him to know about my excursions into that dark world. I know that Nana would've certainly disapproved. Séances looked adventurous on TV and in the movies, but that was all make believe. What I had been involved in was real.

If that had been the end of it, then there wouldn't really be a story to tell. But it was only the beginning. The next day, I checked back with Leta, to warn her and her friends not to do this again. I was too late. They had made contact with what seemed to be a dark spirit, not the spirit of their deceased friend. Dismissing me, they announced that they would seek the help of a real witch, and adding one last statement, *"It did not like you. We even think it could come after you."*

Now, I was frightened out of my wits. I couldn't go to my Baptist minister; he was too close to my family and not bound by strict confidence. So I turned to Father Leo. (I also understood that Catholic clergy had a reputation of successfully battling demonic forces, just in case things did turn ugly.) Leo was very kind. After a short but emphatic "you-shouldn't-have-done-that" lecture over the phone, we met at the rectory and discussed the incident at length. I was so afraid, not just for me, but for the possibility that whatever these kids set loose would find its way to my home and wreak havoc on my parents.

In answer to this, the priest took me into the kitchen, and opening the cabinet, procured a large empty coffee can. Leo filled it with water from the tap and seasoned it with salt. Then, he blessed it, marked my forehead, and said; *"Now you must bless your house. Mark all the windows and doors and sprinkle the perimeters inside and outside. You must draw the cross on each along with the alpha and omega symbols.* As you do this, pray and pray hard."

Upon reaching home, I took up the task. Taking special pains to keep mother from understanding what I was up to, I set about moving in a circle around the house with handfuls of water. Whenever she wasn't looking, I marked everything that I came to. Mom did comment and wonder why I was restlessly milling about the house, disinterested in relaxing in the living room, as was my habit late evening.

It was after dark when I encircled my home with blessed water while praying my banishment prayer. Afterthought suggests that I should've have started from outside and worked my way in, but at that time, my feverish mind wasn't very logical. Once all this was done, a kind of protective peace came over me. I felt safe and rejoiced that my family remained unharmed.

But everything comes with a price. My brief flirtation with occult resulted in the loss of my job. When Leta's mom found out about the incident, I was blamed for the whole thing. No one minded the fact that I had tried to dissuade those kids from doing the séance in the first place, and that they had ignored my warnings. A few days later, I received a phone call at work. As soon as I picked up the receiver, the woman, identifying herself as Leta's mother, began a verbal assault, cursing and calling me every unsavory name she could think of. Disquieted, I hung up and went about my duties. A week later, I called work for my schedule and was informed that my name had been taken off.

I went over to find out what was wrong. My manager refused to answer. She was tight-lipped, only saying that I was fired without giving much of a reason. I was pretty good at my job: coming in on time, trying to stay busy, and socializing with customers. There had been no warnings; it was all so sudden. To this day, I am thoroughly convinced that Leta's mom exacted her revenge without considering the mutual guilt of everyone involved. Parents often look for someone to blame when their children do wrong.

And I could not dismiss the idea that my tarot deck had indirectly cost me my job. Even the harsh words the woman spoke would not leave me. It became hard to even pick up the deck. After that time, I rarely took my cards out again. I finally ditched them in the trash two years later, saving only the title card. Today, it's sealed in one of my old photograph albums, a vivid reminder of a foolish and dangerous excursion into realm of spirits.

Nightfall

As I relive much of the memories of that time, I understand that my tryst with the occult was the only the beginning of an emotional and spiritual trial of fire that still wounds my spirit to this day. Another foreshadowing of future events was a costly betrayal of friends. There are few things that I prize more than loyalty. Unfortunately, some acquaintances have not always had the same standards. One of the hardest lessons that life gives you is the realization that people you trust can be opportunistic and betray you with casual flippancy, even campaign against you.

The first betrayal began innocently enough. I was to meet Michael at the Atlanta Fantasy Fair to celebrate both our birthdays, which are on the same day. And instead of tagging along with my usual con buddies, I decided to go with a friend of the group called Anna and her group of friends. Over the preceding year, I had gotten to know this teen and her mom, Gwendolyn, and felt at ease with them. It had been decided that the girls would stay in one room and the boys in another. We had all paid for a room with a bed to sleep in. The hotel beds were supposed to be full beds, so that two people could crash on each for the evening.

No one was thrilled when Anna and another girl announced that they intended to use one room for themselves and their boyfriends. The rest of us were consigned to sleeping the remaining room for the duration of the con. To worsen the situation, the beds were twin-sized, forcing most of us to sleep on the floor. One poor soul ended up curled up in the bathtub. (I had to tell him to move when I took my morning shower.) If you're thinking about a massive party with lots of sex and drugs, forget it. We were just people who were trying to navigate through those two nights without needless interpersonal friction, a hard thing to do in cramped accommodations.

But the worst part of the weekend came when I was left in the heart of Atlanta with only ten dollars to my name. It was my twentieth birthday and Michael's twenty-fourth, and despite the aggravation with the hotel rooms; we were handling the whole affair with a sense of humor. That afternoon, I had brought my things down and was ready to go. Since Gwendolyn had yet to arrive in her red truck to pick us up, I decided to go to the restroom in the lobby, so that I wouldn't have to stop on the road. I was gone less than five minutes. When I came back down to the garage, I found a dumbfounded Michael staring at the opening gate out into the street.

Apparently, Gwen had decided to leave me, refusing to wait for just a few minutes. When Mike tried to stop her, she nearly ran him down. While I may have cried a little, I only remember being speechless. This was a person whom I had completely trusted. I couldn't believe anyone could be that callous, cruel, and utterly selfish. Unbelievably, this person was a mother herself. All that I kept saying was, **"What if this had been Anna? How would Gwen have liked it if someone had left her daughter in Atlanta with very little money and no way home?"**

Luckily, Michael stepped in, took me to his home where he and two other siblings stayed and put me up until he could deliver me home to my parents, three states away. This event cemented our relationship. Michael's actions seem to communicate a deeper bond, possibly love. If he hadn't been such a stand up guy, we wouldn't be married today and more than likely, the book that you're reading would not exist.

However, our relationship was about to be put to an awful test. The fiasco in Atlanta was just a brief taste of treachery; the worst type of betrayal comes at the hands of those we hold closest to our hearts. It is slow, quiet and secretive, and does not fully reveal itself until the last possible moment, which renders a devastating effect.

By the time I turned twenty, my relationship with my parents had reached a fevered pitch. We fought over everything and could not be in the same room without exchanging harsh words. And to be honest, Michael was surely on their list of things that was wrong with my life (his main defect being the fact that he was a Catholic.) Dad also thought that Mike was not strong enough for me. But I wasn't interested in a bossy boyfriend as much as I wanted someone I could genuinely connect with on all sorts of levels, particularly intellectually. I had always wished for a man who was as smart as or smarter than I was. God has a sense of humor; he brought someone into my life that still amazes me with his intelligence. There was no way that I was going to give Michael up.

But my social and romantic lives as well as my natural sense of independence and strong will were causing a domestic turmoil, which had a volatile nature. It was becoming harder to live at home. During my final year, I felt as though if I did not leave soon, we might end up physically harming one another. Now, I had always dreamed of a church wedding with its elegance and beauty, but as my conflicts with Mom and Dad had become ferocious, I began to worry about survival, not social or religious mores. I went back to school for a Nursing Assistant's Certificate, but even then, I was painfully aware that I could not survive on less than four bucks an hour at full-time status. I knew that there were such luxuries as rent, utilities, and food.

So, after discussing everything with Mike, I began planning to live with him. It was simple enough. He would find us an apartment, make all the arrangements, come up and get me. And I would start collecting all the things that it took to run a home: cookware/utensils, dishes, cutlery, flatware, linens, rugs and bathroom items. But from the moment this happened, I felt as though my spirit was grieved. Everything within me was screaming, *"No!"* but I felt as though I had no choice. I tried to embrace my future while ignoring the spiritual damage that I was inflicting on myself.

Now, I want to make something completely clear. There was one thing that I absolutely refused to give up in the face of it all, and that was my virginity. People always assume that couples live together as an excuse to have wild sex whenever they choose, but that simply was not the case in our situation. I was determined that Michael would have that gift when we married and only then, not before. I was still a product of a devout Christian heritage and deeply allergic to the thought of an unwed pregnancy. Today, kids get pregnant and hardly give a second thought to family honor. I had too much of Nana and the mentality of the Old South within me. Family reputation is everything where I come from. It was bad enough living with my boyfriend, but I would've rather someone order me against a wall and put a bullet in my brain than to have a child out of wedlock. I'm not going to say that we didn't try things and experiment, but my virginity was a non-issue, and Michael respected my feelings. (And it was a good thing too. We did not consummate our relationship until three years into our marriage due to physical condition with which I was born. But that's another story for another time.)

Our first apartment was a little cinderblock edifice in the student slums around Florida State University. For about two hundred a month, it offered a good size living room, bedroom, bathroom, dining niche, and cramped kitchen. We didn't have much furniture, only my bedroom suite, a hope chest, and a card table to eat on. Walls were covered with posters, and window dressings consisted of beach mats made of straw and edged with teal-green cloth. No nice wallpaper here, just plain white walls and the dullest brown tile you can imagine.

Florida has the reputation of being a paradise, but the travel brochures never mention how hot the interior of the state can get. Temperatures can reach up to and even exceed

110 degrees, which actually feels like a 130 due to the high humidity in the air. Various lakes, springs, and rivers- not to mention its close proximity to the Gulf of Mexico surround Tallahassee. In summer, the water in the atmosphere makes it feel as though one is in a sauna. Makeup tends to slide off your face if you spend too long outdoors.

Florida is also the home of a large insect population including some of the biggest cockroaches you'll ever see. These critters are up to three inches long and have wings! There were more than enough mosquitoes, and during a certain period of the year, one would encounter the infamous Florida love bugs. They are called that because they spend a third of their lifecycle breeding while flying in the air. This species is particularly attracted to the smells of car exhaust and gasoline, so veritable clouds of them hang around gas stations and close to highways. They frequently splatter windshields and can actually clog the exhaust system in a car. Slower and more stupid than the average insect, love bugs are God's gifts to old frogs. They are the only species that will hang in mid-air, and let you take another swing at them after you've missed the first time.

Yes, Florida was different from the world I had known as a child, and in many ways, I suffered from another episode of culture shock. I was in a new home in a new state, and the only support network I had ever known was no longer available on a daily basis. I had no family nor friends, just Michael and his network of support that I hoped that I would soon be an accepted part. Now, if everything had gone smoothly, I would have converted to Catholicism, married Michael in a grand ceremony, gone to Florida State for a nursing degree, gotten a good job and lived happily ever after. But there are snakes in every garden. Michael's friends, Miri and Cameron, lived next door to us, and they disturbed me.

These friends were paradoxical people. In one aspect, they possessed a naive idealism over the smallest issues, while completely disregarding the most important elements of life such as God, hard work, and family ties. They grew to view me as narrow-minded. Miri once told Michael that I was a "new soul" while she was more spiritually advanced of course. Cameron was a kind of "yes man" who seemed utterly besotted with his girlfriend to the point of losing his will sometimes. On other occasions, both would engage in caustic arguments that could curl hair.

It is doubtful that Miri ever respected Cameron. When I knew them, they had a beautiful baby girl named Lilly. Cameron doted on the child, even witnessing her birth. I had always assumed that Lilly was his daughter. One time, Miri took special pains to explain that she wasn't sure who Lilly's father was. One the night of conception, she had casual sex with three or four different guys. I was more than shocked, and even worse, she said this in front of Cameron who seemed to hang his head at the revelation. At that moment, I was sad for him, and could only view Miri with contempt, not because of the circumstances of Lilly's conception, but because she had needlessly inflicted pain on someone she was supposed to love.

I have always been a rebel but within certain perimeters. Miri was a throwback to the "free love" counter culture of the sixties and early seventies. I saw her as self-serving with a set of morals relative to what was good for Miri and no one else. Everything that she stood for was completely anathema to what I valued in life. Anyone could guess that both Miri and I were on a kind of collision course when it came to values and spirituality, but there was another kind of struggle going on.

Michael is one of the most generous people I have ever met, donating time, money, and resources to help friends. He was even more so when I first met him. Miri had gotten used to using Mike's money and drafting him into whatever tasks she needed done around her apartment. Now that we had moved in our own place, that had to change. We were starting a life together, and money and labor had to go into that end. Building a family was more important than supplementing the income and needs of friends. At first, Miri and Cameron played us against one another. When I was alone, they would often comment on Michael's perceived faults, and when Mike was by himself with them, it would be time to set about destroying his image of me. But it wasn't working fast enough.

A couple months after I had moved to Florida, Mike and I were at the local mall called Governor's Square. We stumbled into a jewelry store and were looking at different engagement sets. I fell in love a particular set that looked like a cocktail ring. The engagement ring set into and locked with the surrounding wedding ring. It was made of two double swirls of diamonds around a center stone- very unusual, just like us.

We bought it, and I was so pleased and proud. It was going to be wonderful to be married to Michael Gunn. After a celebratory dinner, we came home. Miri and Cameron were home, so we wandered over and announced the happy news. I was beaming when I showed my ring. It glittered and glinted as the light caught fire in the tiny stones. Miri smiled and acted pleased, but her eyes betrayed her true feelings. I caught a glimpse of something cold, almost reptilian, flitting away; leaving a strange kind of uneasiness that could not be dispelled.

It's one thing to say I love you, but to pair that statement with an expensive engagement ring is something else. When Mike awakened the next morning, he was a little jittery. (I suppose that's natural after giving your favorite girl a hunk of gold and diamonds.) I tried to reassure him, but he made small little remarks about me marrying him for money. Of course, that made no sense at all. He worked full-time at a service station and his parents, while solid middle class, were nowhere near the label "mega rich." Mike sounded unsure of everything as we wheeled into my employer's parking lot, but I dismissed it as pre-wedding doubt and worries. I told him that I wanted a long engagement, so that we could plan everything properly, and that I was in no particular rush. So, I left Michael, still looking apprehensive in his Mustang II.

Most of the day, I basked in happy pride. My coworkers crowed when they saw the ring. (Some were even quite envious.) Around four-thirty that evening, I answered a phone call from Mike. I'm not sure that I remember the words, but he said something like this: ***"My car is broken down around Waukeenah. We're planning to fix it tomorrow. I can't come home tonight."***

His voice was seemed distant, even flat, as if he were giving some planned message. I asked exactly where he was; Michael gave me some sketchy details and hung up. I then telephoned John Gunn at his home in Monticello, explained the situation, and asked for help. John knew a lot about cars, and could probably fix it and get Michael home that night. But something about this did not sit well with me. My "little voice" was insistent that our relationship was at the base of this problem and not the car.

After a few hours, I called Monticello again. John was furious that I had sent him on a fool's errand. He had searched the area that I spoke of and found neither Michael nor the Mustang! Mr. Gunn had driven as far as Capps and had no luck. He slammed the receiver down, and left my head spinning. Michael had to be out there somewhere, and it was getting dark. If John couldn't find him, I was determined that I would.

So, I called Wayne, a college buddy from Michael's FSU days, and begged for help. We spent hours looking for my boyfriend who seemed to have dropped off the face of the planet. Coming home to a quiet, empty space, I drifted aimlessly about the rooms, eyes swollen with tears and a dreadful fear in my heart that left me silent. Sleep, if any that night, was fitful. I would have given anything to hear Michael's voice, and dreamed of waking from this horrific nightmare. I was startled from sleep many times- witnessing a deafening silence that only mocked me.

The next day was even more surreal. I dressed and caught the bus in a daze as if drunk and separated from my senses. I felt like a zombie cut off from life, and as the word implies, I rarely drank any liquids and ate nothing. During the day, I stumbled into the hospital chapel. Some black Pentecostals were there. They were very kind. Forgetting their own problems, they set about anointing me in fervent prayer. It helped a lot. But when I reached home that evening, I found a note on the door and some of Mike's things missing inside. Apparently, he had lied about the car. After explaining that he was OK, Michael wrote that he needed time away from me and would be away for a few days.

Something was wrong. This was not the Michael I knew who had always been loyal and kind. My suspicious nature latched on to the only person who seemed set against me from the start, Miri. I had no real evidence, but I knew that she could be manipulative. I had witnessed her power over Cameron, and knew Michael enough to realize he could be influenced as well given the right pressure at the appropriate time. Like a dark spider, she had waited and carefully made use of Mike's own doubts and fears, a little poison from a dear friend instead of the reassurance he needed. I think that part of me was wise to the whole scheme from the beginning. It's common to know a truth within one's heart and openly reject it as if to naively declare, *"I refuse to believe!"* Psychologists call it denial.

I felt that I could break her spell, but I had to get Michael to talk and quickly before it was too late. There was a distinct urgency about the situation that said, *"Miri's planning something else. You may never see Michael again."* So, I called Mike's dad. John was still angry and blamed me for the whole affair. I cried and tried to explain, begging for his help. But my tears incurred scorn not sympathy. I guess John saw me as an overly emotional, clinging vine instead of a terrified individual, far from home, stranded in an environment with no one to turn to for solace and help.

That day, I also contacted Wayne who had helped me look for Michael the first night. But suddenly, Wayne absolutely refused to help anymore in any way. He didn't want to get involved. I said that was fine, and all that I was asking from him was to forward a message for me to Mike. But even that small request seemed to fall on deaf ears.

Now I had no one. I knew that I had to stand and fight alone, and I was determined that if I went down, it would be a costly victory for my enemies. After another sleepless night, I decided that I had one chance to change everything. Michael had been off from work, but now, it was time to come back. For the first time in three days, he would be in a particular place at a particular time. I wrote Mike a letter that reminded him of his promise to look after me and keep me safe. If Michael welched on this agreement, he would have no honor in my eyes and would be unsuitable to marry. I asked a friend to deliver the letter in person along with my beautiful ring. Taking the lovely creation off my hand was one of the hardest things that I have ever done. If Michael were indeed worthy, he would put it back where it belonged.

Otherwise, I would cash my last paycheck, pack what I could take home, and leave Tallahassee for good. I was sure that I could talk my parents into letting me stay until I could move to some college campus. While I would lose all my furniture and household knick-knacks, they would only remind me of a ruined relationship, something I did not need. Perhaps Miri could make use of my new china plates and the flatware with its stylish "G" engraved on each handle. In any case, I was determined that I too would disappear. And no matter how hard Michael looked for me in the future, he would never see me again.

A few hours later, I called the service station and asked for Michael. His voice was shaky when he answered the phone. He definitely wanted to talk. That evening after work, I took the city bus over and met with Mike while his coworker covered his position at the register. Michael took the ring and put it back on my finger, saying, *"Never do that again!"*

To that I replied, *"Come home where you belong."*

Michael left work early that evening with me. As we were going out the door, Cameron showed up with supper. Mike pulled him aside and informed him that we would be going back to our apartment together. In response, Cameron hissed an angry comment that I couldn't really hear.

It had been kind of strange how I had seen so little of Miri and her consort during those three hellish nights, but shortly after we reached home, they were back. From that moment, the "Bobsie Twins" made no attempt to disguise their anger and contempt for me. According to them, I had broken some agreement that I had made saying that when and if Mike and I did meet, we would see each other on neutral ground. I don't recollect making such an agreement. Besides, Miri and Cameron weren't people to take the moral high ground considering the fact that they made their own rules and then broke them when it suited their cause. Miri used people and discarded them like worn shoes. But I decided to let them say their ugly comments and declarations and avoid being overly critical. Something told me that their actions and words would reveal their true nature to Mike, and then, he would see who and what they really were. And that's exactly what happened.

Michael began to understand that it was not my ambition for money that was at fault, but the need to control and dominate on the part of Miri. My fiancé discovered that I was the same girl he'd met at MOC I, not the gold-digging fortune hunter that I was portrayed to be. From that moment on, Miri and Cameron no longer held any influence, and Michael drifted away from their grasp.

After awhile, I began to learn the details of those three days. The truth was that Michael had never left Tallahassee. Instead, he had been just blocks away from our home. Miri and Cameron had never let him have a moment alone. Mike had mirrored my behavior, eating and drinking very little. He, too, had experienced a kind of fugue state, complete with the sleeplessness and emotional trauma of being separated from my side. Miri had even tried to seduce Michael to relieve this lovesickness, but to no avail. What was another concubine in her harem?

My fiancé also revealed that Miri and Cameron had entertained plans to leave Tallahassee and take up with a traveling renaissance fair, and of course, they wanted Michael to go with them. "Ren fairs" follow routes all over the Southeast and are much like the old circuses and carnies of the nineteenth and early twentieth centuries. Had Miri had her way, John and Jean might not have seen their son for years afterward. In which case, Michael might have turned out a very different person from who he is today. Miri and Cameron had a hardened criminality about them that would surely have affected him. But the nightmare ended when Mike received my engagement ring set. He would tell me later that it was as if a cold hand had reached out and slapped him back to consciousness.

I could not believe my luck; I had fought a major battle and won. But it was a bittersweet victory. Those three days had left a heavy mark, and I fell into a depression that I couldn't shake. I remember crying uncontrollably at the least provocation. Everything might have been different had Michael's friends and family been more supportive, but they seemed resentful that I remained in Mike's life despite the revelation that Miri had planned to take my love faraway from all of them. I alone had thwarted her scheme, but no one wanted to even give me that credit. There was not one ounce of sympathy or even outrage at what had happened.

Because of this, I grew to distrust and fear the friends and family that I had wanted so much to be part of. Yes, Miri had failed to separate us, but she had succeeded in driving wedge and placing hard feelings between the Gunns, Michael's friends, and me. I began to see them all as complicit in the attempted destruction of my home and the life that I was building with my fiancé.

Dawn's Palest Rays

In the midst of the turmoil and darkness and despite living in a "sinful" state, God remained at my side. A good friend had given me a Sandi Patti tape before I left for Tallahassee. I found myself listening to her voice and remembering how good it felt know Christ. And more than anything, I longed for my separation from Him to end.

From the very beginning, my soul was wounded with the knowledge that I was offending God by living with Michael outside of the sanctifying grace of marriage. I had been raised in a Christian home, and I knew that what I had done was wrong. Looking back at everything, I am sure that we could have done something else to solve my problems at home. Since I came to live in Florida, I had seen myself as Michael's wife, not a girlfriend. Why not make it a reality? Michael must have been conscious of my struggle. He understood that it had to be resolved and soon.

One year after I had received my engagement ring, we were driving around town. He looked at me and asked rather casually, *"So when do you want to marry?"* I was a little surprised, considering his mindset the previous year. But we both knew that this was the right thing to do. The fact that we share the same birthday has always intrigued us and everyone else we know, so we decided to make that date our wedding day as well. It felt natural and fitting that we should officially start a new life on the day that we were both given life.

Now, I had always dreamed of a grand marriage ceremony in a church. For months, I had drooled over the latest designs in the magazines and planning the ceremony, even the menu. But I gradually realized that a large affair might not be wise, considering my relationship with John and Jean Gunn and the rest of the family. For a while, I had been just a romantic interest from three states away, hardly worth worrying over. But my moving down conveyed the message that our relationship was serious. Michael's parents had to have realized that marriage was being considered, and that was totally different in their eyes.

I was a Southern Baptist at the time, and didn't really understand their feelings. Recently, one of Michael's sisters remarked that some of the Gunn family had actually been in fights for being Catholic. Others had suffered derision from non-Catholic Christians. Now, here was a Baptist of independent stock attempting to marry into their clan, and they were less than enthusiastic. In a small town where Catholics were portrayed as little more than pagans, the Gunns had suffered years of persecution and prejudice. Mike's family did not understand the fact that a Protestant like me could be not only fair, but friendly as well. To worsen matters, the three eldest children had married spouses outside the Church and by that, were no longer in full communion with it. I'm sure that the Gunns felt that they and the Church were about "lose" another child to an outsider.

And Michael was a special child. I would later learn that they had wanted Michael to completely devote his life to the priesthood. Because Jean had had a particularly rough pregnancy while carrying him, they had given Mike back to God in a special way. But God had other plans. Michael had fallen in love with me and had chosen family life over a clerical calling just as his father had so many years before.

I also felt our families might clash and turn a lovely service into a disaster. My family members were all strict Protestants while Michael hailed from a family of "cradle Catholics." So, considering all of these circumstances, we decided to elope, and then, sometime in the future, get the marriage blessed by a priest. Hopefully, when the dust settled, we could still have the ceremony we wanted, but after everyone had gotten used to the idea of our marriage.

So, we applied for our license in the nearby town of Quincy. A few days before a wedding, the courthouse will post the marriage bans, publicly declaring the intention of marriage. This is the governmental way of trying to prevent fraud and bigamy. Tallahassee was not a good choice as John and Jean were well known, and someone might have commented that a "Gunn" was about to marry. We did not want a confrontation.

At this time, we came into a small amount of money. This we used to get a new apartment in a nicer, quieter section of town. We also took in Lee, another friend from Mike's FSU days, as a roommate. If you remember, I first met the guy at the Atlanta Fantasy Fair. Quiet and very solitary, Lee was (and still is) a talented artist with an unusual ability to recall a lot of musical/pop culture trivia. He is a powerful opponent in the game of Trivial Pursuit. For a while, he had lived in Valdosta and worked at a local radio station as a DJ. But the job had folded, and Bainbridge wasn't known for its ability to employ. Most people worked elsewhere and just lived there. Lee needed a place to relocate, so he came to live with us. (We also hoped that this might actually lower our cost of living once he got a job in Tallahassee.)

The extra money also helped pay for our wedding. I bought a tea length dress of white chiffon, elegant lace over satin pumps with a matching purse, and a pink silk bouquet- hardly what I had spent months pining for, but it was a nice outfit. And I could use it for other occasions. Few people knew about the upcoming ceremony. Lee and Wayne, Michael's closest friends were the only one's who were in on what we were planning. In fact, Lee was our witness at the courthouse. Our marriage wasn't even performed by a Justice of the Peace, but by an Assistant Clerk of the Court. We still laugh about that.

Marrying my husband was as stress-free as breathing air, no doubts or worries. I can still see us standing in the empty courtroom, saying those vows. It felt good to formalize the commitment, which had been there all along. That night, we celebrated at our favorite Chinese restaurant, dining on Peking duck with plum wine sauce and sautéed vegetables. The owner, a personal friend, furnished a bottle of champagne to toast to our happiness.

A Distant Call from a Familiar Place

My first Christmas as a married woman was leaner than the previous year, but we did manage to get a Christmas tree. Everything on it was white, gold, silver, and crystalline- a tradition I still observe. We may not have had presents, but we made the apartment look beautiful. In addition to the tree, there were large white candles that burned a jasmine fragrance and gold foil on the door. Michael and I raided the local library for Christmas music, took the records home, and dubbed them onto tapes. There was no money, but lots of atmosphere.

Of course, our marriage was not that warmly received, and there seemed to be a wall between Michael's family and friends that I could not breach. With the exception of Lee (who is still like a brother to both of us), we were alone. Most of that holiday was spent in seclusion- listening to the old carols in the darkened living room with only the lights from the tree and the candles. At one point, Lee joked that I had turned the apartment into a monastery.

The only things that gave an air of normality to my life were my cats, Sugar and Midnight, who were fond of drag racing through the apartment and around the tree. Sugar was a beautiful cinnamon-gray tabby with gold eyes. Midnight, an American short hair, was jet black with tiny little white hairs mixed into her coat. They were my babies and would often curl up beside me on my second hand couch and beg for attention. They kept me from brooding too much, and made the whole house laugh with their comic relief.

The year before, both Michael and I had gone to my home to spend time with my folks, but this year, it all seemed impossible. Determined to see me in spite of my financial situation, my parents sent a plane ticket, and I got the chance to be with them during the month of December. That time was bittersweet. Mom and Dad could only afford one ticket, so I was away from Michael for the first time in over a year.

Being home was like listening to an old song. For a while, I could forget my finances and that life was hard. I could also surround myself with my Baptist friends who were all about everyday spirituality. No devious friends and relatives here- just ordinary folks singing hymns, decking the halls and eating well. I was spiritually drained and needed a vacation from Florida.

My parents' home was suddenly like a warm blanket, and I, a child shivering in cold, wet clothes. When it was time to leave, I didn't want to go back. I did not belong in some foreign place, but in the town I had known as a child with people I understood who accepted me without question. Here, I had a sense of belonging cultivated from years of involvement in the community and real friends who did not campaign against me. Despite my love for Michael, Florida had been a cold, dispassionate state that seemed to suck my spirit dry and give me nothing in return. I was still wounded and "soul sick," a bird with broken wings. Daddy knew it, though I said nothing. I suppose he saw it in my eyes. We both cried on our way to the airport. The sun was setting as we hugged an emotional good-bye. It felt so good to be wanted and missed! His last words were: *"If you ever want to come back, I'll help you find a place and get started."*

Those words seemed to embed themselves in my mind for the rest of December. But I was also aware that moving back meant a lot of aggravation. There was the actual move. We had doubled the amount of possessions that would have to be packed away, then unpacked. Michael and I would also have to land new positions quickly in order to meet monthly expenses. And what would happen to Lee or my cats. It seemed a lot of trouble; and once I came home, homesickness gave way to reality. I wanted to put the whole idea out of my head- until the end of the month.

There were instances when I was sure that Michael's parents and siblings accepted me, but at other times, they seemed distant. I believe now that it would have been completely different had I announced my intentions of becoming a Catholic from the first moment they knew me. I had started to take classes in the faith, but I wanted this to be a surprise- a kind of added bonus after they had grown to appreciate the person that I was. I did not want their approval for something I was about to do.

I was still willing to persevere and fight for a place in Florida and in the hearts of Michael's family. But, something unforeseen forced the issue. At the end of December, our car broke down, and we needed the funds to fix it until payday. The bill was a small amount of only one hundred dollars, but no one had it until the end of the week. It was our only car, and we needed it for work and errands around town. Tallahassee isn't known as a pedestrian's city. It sprawls, and unless you live on the bus route, losing your car can be tantamount to losing your job and even your home (if you can't pay your bills). Michael turned to his parents for a small loan against payday. He did receive the money, but only after a lot of harsh words were said.

Outwardly, much of their anger was over economics. But I could feel that it was much deeper than that. They were angry with me and were using this problem to vent their collective frustration. This nasty argument ended with me asking to make a long distance call. I talked with my father, inquiring about his offer to help us resettle in my hometown. They heard my words; I let them know that I was considering going back home. During my time on the phone, I wanted John and Jean to make peace and tell me not to be hasty, that we could work it out. I was silently pleading, **"Don't let me leave!"** But all I witnessed were stony faces. I had stolen their son, and the sooner I left the better. At that moment, my heart broke. So, this was how they felt.

Some people have life's treasure handed to them. They are born with charm, grace and good looks and a natural ability to gain wealth and the attentions of the opposite sex. I was never that fortunate. I have had to fight, scratch, and claw for everything that God has given me. I guess that Michael was no exception to that rule. First, it had been Miri, now it was the Gunn family itself. They picked the wrong adversary.

My return home had a price tag. If I were leaving, then Michael would surely go with me. And as a result, John and Jean would be lucky if they got to speak with Michael on the phone or even see him every few years, not out of spite on my part, but as a matter of logistics. Traveling to see the Gunn family would take planning, time off from work, and money. We would no longer be a half-hour up the road. But, if that was their choice, then let them count the cost.

Rejected, I turned away from everything that I had originally wanted so much to be a part of, including the Catholic faith. I put my books away and stopped attending catechism classes. After all, my conversion would have been seen as a vain attempt to please them. The dreams that I had for Florida were dead and burying them, I mourned for what might have been. A month later, we loaded up a moving trailer and left Tallahassee for my home in the North.

Voyage to Another World: Sunrise on the Water

When I came back home, it was as if I was stepping into daylight after languishing in two years of darkness, with just an occasional flash of light. What did I learn from my long dark night? Well, I learned that the spiritual realm is nothing to be tampered with. Trying to manipulate it with divination, séances, incantations, potions, and spells will only end in disaster.

And my spiritual trial taught me that my faith was priceless in the face of shifting pop culture and changing values. Even though I had wandered away from my roots, Jesus had never left me. In all my meandering, I had only to turn around and find Him waiting for His errant lamb, His arms outstretched, reaching to encircle me.

I still grieve for my "lost" wedding. Even my tenth anniversary renewal ceremony could not completely blot out the guilt and shame. Living with Michael before marriage took a heavy toll. Maybe, these painful memories are meant to remain with me as a reminder that situational ethics can cause a loss of integrity and a lapse of judgment. For me, this was the worst offense that I have ever committed because of the length of time in which the sin occurred. Hopefully, this book may offer a penance for my colorful past, so that I may continue to grow and learn in Christ.

But some things did not change. I still love science fiction and fantasy. I suppose that this interest has kept me young at heart because its best elements always challenge individuals to explore the human condition with all of its nobility and failings. And after nearly twenty years, I still look at the universe with childlike wonder and enthusiasm. Even role-playing games have found a reason for being in my life.

My husband and I are now in the on-going process of developing a Christian role-playing game, set in the Roman Persecution, where Christians must live and propagate the Christian faith in secret or face death in the Roman Coliseum. Characters may also encounter mythic creatures from Greco-Roman, Norse, and Celtic folklore. But a character cannot use magic or divination, break the Christian code of conduct, or use fighting skills for anything other than defensive purposes. Ignoring the rules means a loss of spiritual gifts, forcing the wayward Christian on a quest or campaign as a way of penance for sins committed against God. We're calling this game, **Spiritus Gladius** or **The Sword of the Spirit.**

Remember how I've compared life to a tapestry or mural as it weaves unrelated elements into a larger picture. Neither Mike nor I would have ever guessed that we would channel our love for gaming into such a project. We specifically designed it to bring enjoyment to teens that are cut off from the gaming culture because it conflicts with their Christian faith. It's amazing how God can use a role-playing game to further His objectives.

By now, it should be clear that people become who they are through pain, struggle, and conflict. Perhaps, it was all those talks with Father Leo or the mystic beauty of my first Midnight Mass. Whatever had impressed me so had worked because I remained drawn to Catholicism. Despite all the misery of Florida and my safe return to my family and familiar surroundings, it was simply not enough to go back to my old Baptist church.

I tried for a year or so to fit in, but Michael and I seemed to be on a different level than they were. Our spiritual life at church was dry and unfulfilled; home was more like church than going to the sanctuary in town. We would have long, deep conversations about God, theology and the scriptures that would have made any Sunday school teacher proud. Michael fostered something within me, which longed for a richer spiritual life that my church could not provide.

In fact, my church's environment was really not what I was looking for. Most of the time, everyone was nice to Michael, but there were moments when a few of the congregation made little comments about his spiritual heritage. Then, there was the fact that many of the friends I had known had grown up and left for college. Of course, I had seen them during the holidays, but then, kids come home to visit family around Christmas. I guess I had the illusion of belonging, but once I moved back up, it seemed to dissipate. As a result, I lost my identity, becoming known as my mother's daughter and Gwyneth's sister even to the point of people forgetting my name. I was a stranger with a borrowed persona, hardly what I wanted to be at church.

I once knew a priest whose favorite saying was, **"You don't learn Catholicism; you "osmose it"**(meaning that an individual actually absorbs the faith over time.) I think that Florida changed me in that I no longer saw myself as a Baptist. While I had put my Catholic books away, I had also opened the door to a larger world, and try as I might, I could not seem to completely close it.

The first step in my conversion was the growing awareness that having a civil marriage outside the Church had placed my husband at odds with his faith. Michael could not legitimately receive the sacraments until a priest had properly blessed our marriage. After much thought and soul searching, I contacted Father Leo. I expected the usual fare of running to classes, but Leo seemed more than satisfied that Michael and I belonged together. We made an appointment and signed the papers.

I will never forget our marriage ceremony. The sanctuary was dimly lit except for the candles glowing brightly around the altar. Mina, my maid of honor, was there to witness the occasion. I wore the dress I had worn a year earlier at the courthouse, and I carried the same pink silk bouquet. Father Leo's homily was so moving that, when I looked up at Mina, I saw tears in her eyes. For the first time in three years, I felt as if heaven smiled at us. There was such a feeling of peace. That day, I came to the realization that I belonged in Michael's church.

But that was just the beginning. It would take another two years before I would confirm, and I was not an easy pupil. Long before the confirmation classes, I began to look at the various points of faith and dogmatic views and ask for scriptural proof or the biblical logic behind them. Because I had come from a devout fundamentalist upbringing, listening to what this or that theologian wrote or said was not good enough for me. I had to see it in the Bible or at least, know the logic of different teachings and how they related to the scriptures. Luckily, I married a scholar who had done his own biblical research concerning the Catholic faith. Along the way, I discovered that I have an ancient heart. Though born into Protestant Fundamentalism, my fascination with Catholicism had begun at an early age. Michael offered me the chance to learn and understand Christianity's past: the faith, customs, and traditions that echo back through the centuries. I realized that the Catholic Church is a living key to another place and time, a kind of spiritual puzzle.

Catholics are a mystical people. Protestants have given the word "mystical" a bad connotation with their books on New Age mysticism. But when I say "mystical," I mean it as defined in the most primary way. A mystery is something with no explanation, and mystical simply denotes that which is unexplained. As Christians, we cannot hold God in a test tube; neither can we scientifically explain miracles.

As stated above, becoming a Catholic does not entail a couple sessions with a minister as with most Protestant denominations; one attends classes for months. That person not only learns the tenets of the faith, but also shares feelings and life experiences with the group as they journey together. In the end, classmates become like family, bonded in the most intimate way, though laughter and tears.

This was my catharsis. I began to face the fact that condemning all Catholics for the conduct of the Gunn family was unfair; and that I would be just as guilty in the end as they had been when they had judged my character by the behavior of other Protestants. I'm not sure exactly when forgiveness came, but it did, and with it came a newfound grace.

I was confirmed at Easter, in 1992. After ten years, I can still smell the aroma of the Easter fire. I was reborn in those flames. It was if the old individual lay crumpled in ashes at my feet, and I was a fledgling phoenix. Clad in a white robe and carrying my tall candle, I was anointed with sacred oil, renamed, infused with the living presence of Christ, and sealed with the Holy Spirit. Everything was new and forever changed. Confirmation carries with it an indelible mark on the soul. There is no going back; to return to who you once were is to regress.

Rising Phoenix

For the next four years, I led a quiet existence, and slowly my life became stable. When we first came back, Michael and I had lived in a tiny matchbox of an apartment in the countryside; then Lee came up, and we all relocated to a three-bedroom place in the city. By 1996, we had acquired a succession of roommates who shared living expenses, one of which was Leslie, a divorced lady who would later marry Lee. Her children would often visit on weekends and became unofficial godchildren.

I also managed to adopt a new set of cats. Sugar and Midnight had been lost to me. My original apartment took no pets, and I had asked Martin to look after them at his grandmother's home. One day they just ran off and didn't return. With no children to mother, these felines became my new babies. Having fallen in love with the Celtic culture, each new animal's name reflected that growing affection. Michael kindly, but firmly, put an end to my ever-increasing number of furry roommates after we adopted the fourth kitten.

So, my home was happy, if not a little boisterous, with as many as four adults, three children, and four cats on the weekends. Yes, I know that it was a "three-ring circus," but we managed to handle most situations with a sense of humor. I suppose that I had begun to crave the idea of a large, loving family like that of the Gunns. And if I could not have children of my own, then I would "adopt" strays until I had the appropriate number. But this arrangement could last only so long.

In 1996, shortly before Michael's graduation with an Electronics Engineering Degree, Lee, Leslie and the gang vacated the premises. By now, we were in a two-bedroom house. Staring into vacant rooms, I probably suffered with a bad case of "empty-nest syndrome" after having roommates for seven years. So, I decided to go back to school in the face of this loneliness, to pursue a degree in Psychology. The first part of this new career choice demanded a list of basic core classes of English, foreign languages, math, science, history and a number of basic sociology and psychology courses, which I pursued at my local community college, just as Michael did before me. With the exception of math, most of these courses were a lot of fun. Most people feel depressed when they hit thirty; I felt like I was eighteen.

It was during my college years that I became increasingly aware of a pervasive undercurrent of anti-Catholicism. So far, I had been insulated away from this growing conflict, but college life forced me to learn how to defend my faith. I had always assumed that teachers would be fair and give equal time to both Catholics and Protestants. I was wrong. In addition to the comments and questions of various classmates, which I could usually handle, some teachers portrayed a lop-sided picture of history and culture, which I found intolerable. I would often openly object when they forgot to mention Protestant debacles and the excesses of the Reformation. Even before becoming a Catholic, I had realized that Protestants weren't a gang of choirboys either, having their own faults and collective sins.

It was during one of my final classes for my Associates in Arts Degree that I had another spiritual revelation. I was taking Art Appreciation that summer and having marvelous fun. At the end of the semester, our class took a field trip to a local art gallery. As I drifted through the exhibits, making small talk, I heard, *"All Catholics do is worship Mary!"*

I turned and faced the owner of that voice, and interjected, *"That's a lie!"*

Carla, the young woman who had made the remark, declared that she had once attended a Catholic school and that was how she saw it. I told Carla that she hadn't paid that much attention to her teachers if that was everything that she had come away with. This exchange led to an ugly confrontation. While I had been frequently grilled about my faith, no one had ever been that offensive. I was angered to the point of tears.

Normally, I'm good-natured, and I rarely lose my temper like that. But Carla had gone too far. There are few things that I despise more than being judged and labeled. Ashamed that I had let her get to me, I went to my friends in the class and explained my actions afterwards. I was relieved that most of them seemed to be sympathetic. When I had walked away crying, some had criticized her for her wicked remark. Even so, Carla and another Bible thumper made the last two weeks of school miserable. They made off-hand comments in class and even left a Christian tract on the desk next to me when I was taking the final exam. If it had happened earlier in the semester, I would have informed the teacher, then gone to student services and filed a complaint.

The "Bible Thumper," whom I will call Darien, was once a friend, who had learned that I had a temper when it came to being prejudged. I told Darien that our friendship was at an end because of his actions and that if he wished to discuss my faith or the scriptures in the future, he could speak with Michael who was better versed in the scriptures than I was. That was, if he had the courage to face a scripture-quoting Catholic. Oddly, Darien was not in a hurry to do this.

In the aftermath of this incident, I began to feel extraordinary spiritual pressure to write about and address all the popular myths and misconceptions that Protestants entertain about Catholicism. Demonstrated in both Carla's and Darien's actions was an inherent ignorance that beget prejudice, hatred, and religious intolerance, which is extremely harmful to the Body of Christ as a whole. I finally understood why the Gunn family was so defensive at times when it came to their faith. I suppose it was only natural to assume that I was like the rest of the Protestants in Mike's hometown. How could they have truly known that I would be different?

Now that my religious and cultural identity had been christened in fire, I was inspired write because Michael had taught me that there was nothing to fear from the scriptures when defending Catholicism. He had learned this shortly after his own confirmation when a zealous classmate began proselytizing him, wanting to lead him back to the fold, which he had never left in the first place. Mike made it his business to be well versed on the Bible as well as the history, languages, and culture surrounding the scriptures.

Michael's teachers were a Notre Dame Seminarian, three Baptist ministers, and an Orthodox Jewish Rabbinical student who had converted to the Christian faith during the final phase of his religious studies. I might also add that the Jewish scholar taught Michael the New Testament from a Jewish perspective, which in and of itself is very unusual. My catechism teacher was not "Suzy Homemaker" from the local parish who took a few courses, but a husband whose Catholic education is hard core classical.

When creating this book, I wanted to share my faith as I, myself, had learned it, and with a primary emphasis placed on the scriptures. One of the greatest fallacies, embraced by both Protestants and Catholics, is the idea that Catholicism is not scriptural. Nothing is further from the truth. The scriptures reveal to us the person known as ***Y'shua Hamashiach***, known to most of the world as **Jesus Christ**. Catholic creed and the sacraments come from the scriptures. Our Mass has at least four large readings from the Bible (one from the Old Testament, one from Paul's letters, one from the four Gospels and one from either Psalms or Proverbs), that blend into a common theme for the Mass.

When we look closely, it becomes clear that Catholicism is hardly what one might call "unscriptural." So, the main source of this apology (explanation) will be the Bible. Other elements included are cultural, historical and linguistic data; these aspects help us to see the scriptures in their proper light. It is my fondest hope that upon finishing this volume, you will have a better picture of this sacred land of mystics and miracles, the faraway ancient country called Catholicism.

Part II

CATHOLICISM 101

Before beginning this section, I would like to personally thank the individual(s) behind the Bible Defends The Catholic Church website: www.globalserve.net ~bumblebee/ ecclesia /ecclesia.htm. This site proved invaluable in the creation of this book. I knew Catholicism was indeed biblical before I started, but I had no idea how biblical until I stumbled across this site. Believe it or not, the passages you are about to read are only a taste of the extensive research that was done.

Note: All quotations from the Order of the Mass are taken from the new Order of the Mass, which is effective November 27, 2011, the 1st Sunday of Advent. (USCCB)

A Brief History Lesson

In early times, there were five major centers where Christianity flourished, each governed by a resident patriarch. These centers were situated in Jerusalem, Antioch, Alexandria, Byzantium or Constantinople (now Istanbul) and Rome. Each patriarch ruled his own area, with the Roman patriarch being the leader and spokesman. Rome was the seat of Peter, the first among equals and the leader of the Apostles.

Because the Roman Empire became split into East and West, four of these centers were cut off from Rome and suffered from limited contact and communication with their Western neighbor. It was inevitable that political wrangling would eventually cause a schism within the Church as a whole. Catholicism defines a church as schismatic when it continues to accept Catholic beliefs and doctrines but will not submit to the authority of the Pope. The division occurred in 1054 between the Eastern and the Western portions of the Church. Those churches, which separated from Rome, became known as the Eastern Orthodox Churches. They continue to differ with Rome as to the primacy of Peter and infallibility of the Pope. However, some eastern churches did survive the schism from Rome and remain Catholic today. (Morrow 152-153)

Other issues surrounding the schism concern Purgatory, the Immaculate Conception, Holy Eucharist, and Procession of the Holy Spirit. Some churches denied the need for indulgences, saying that the sacrament of Penance remits all temporal punishment as well as any guilt from sin. Others endorsed the belief that Mary was not conceived free of original sin (the Immaculate Conception), but cleansed of it at the Annunciation. Western devotion to the Eucharist (Communion) is more extensive, with the use of tabernacles, processions and benedictions. Eastern Orthodox Churches concentrate their devotion to Eucharist during the Mass. Another argument concerned the procession of the Holy Spirit. The Orthodox churches believed that the Holy Spirit proceeded from the Father alone and not the Son, while Catholicism teaches that the Holy Spirit processes from them both. However, it should be said that the Orthodox Churches still venerate Our Lady and are rich in monastic traditions. (Morrow 153)

The eastern centers were situated in the Middle East, and consequently fell during the Crusades and the Islamic conquests of the region. In the end, there was only one center left, and that was Rome. However, all five of the original patriarchies still survive today, along with newer offices created as the Orthodox Churches grew.

What Protestants must understand that Catholicism is not another religion; it is deeply Christian. The word "catholic" is one of the oldest words describing the Body of Christ. In his work, Dogmatic Theology, Francis S. Hall (an Anglican priest) writes, **"The term catholic, appears first to have been applied to the Church at large by St. Ignatius of Antioch about 110 AD." (V. VIII 199)**

Ignatius of Antioch was the spiritual protégé of St. John, the Beloved. The words, *ta ekklesia katolika* are ancient Greek and mean *"the universal church."* While the Bible mentions *"churches of God,"* this is strictly a general label and does not refer to the Church of Christ or Church of God denominations which were founded well after the sixteenth century. Big "C" Catholic would later come to describe the Catholic faith after the different splits from the Church during the Reformation.

Modern Christianity has a confusing array of beliefs mainly due to the growing numbers of independent Christian churches. The early Christian Fathers were facing the same dilemma during the first few centuries of Christianity, a time when many heresies were quickly spreading; it became important to know which beliefs were true beliefs and which were heretical. So, the Council of Nicea met in AD 325. The early Church Fathers laid down the foundation for what would become the Nicene Creed (also known as the Catholic Profession of Faith), which defined exactly what Christians do and do not believe. What is the simplest rule of thumb for judging if a denomination is Christian? All Christians embrace the divinity of Christ. So, what do Catholics really believe?

I believe in one God,
   The Father, the Almighty,
   Maker of heaven and earth,
   Of all things visible and invisible.

I believe in one Lord, Jesus Christ,
   The Only Begotten Son of God
   Born of the Father before all ages,
   God from God, Light from Light,
   True God from true God,
   Begotten, not made, consubstantial with the Father.
   Through Him all things were made.
   For us men and for our salvation
   He came down from Heaven:
   And by the power of the Holy Spirit
   Was incarnate of the Virgin Mary, and became man.
   For our sake, He was crucified under Pontius Pilate;
   He suffered death and was buried,
   And rose again on the third day
   In accordance of the Scriptures.
   He ascended into heaven
   And is seated at the right hand of the Father.
   He will come again in glory to judge the living
   And the dead, and His kingdom will have no end.

I believe in the Holy Spirit, the Lord, the giver of life.
   Who proceeds from the Father and the Son.
   Who with the Father and the Son is adored and glorified.

Who has spoken through the Prophets.
I believe in one holy catholic (universal) and apostolic church.
I confess one baptism for the forgiveness of sins.
And I look for the resurrection of the dead,
And the life of the world to come. Amen.

Upon looking closely at the creed, you may notice that there is a little "c" in catholic. Little "c" denotes the universal body of Christ that is all denominations and independents that claim Christ as their Savior. It doesn't matter who you are or what church you belong to; if you are a Christian, you fall into this category.

Catholics do ***NOT*** believe:

-That the Pope is God and can do no wrong.
-That anybody or anything may be worshiped or adored besides the True God.
-That the Blessed Virgin is equal to God.
-That images may be worshiped.
-That indulgences give permission to commit sin.
-That a Mass can be bought.
-That forgiveness of sin can be bought.
-That sin can be forgiven without true sorrow.
-That scapulars, medals, crucifixes, and other sacramentals can give graces without the proper disposition on the part of the user.
-That non-Catholics will all be damned.
-That all Catholics will go to heaven.
-That outward piety is profitable without charity of spirit.
-That all religions are the same.
 (Morrow 117)

What is heresy? Catholicism sees heresy as willfully disregarding revealed truth in favor of one's own personal interpretation of scripture. Heresies abounded everywhere in ancient times. (Morrow 152) Here are just a few:

Montanism- Montanus of Phrygia (AD 170), taught that the "end of the world" was coming and proposed a harsh standard of conduct and morality.

Gnosticism- taught that that reason is better than faith, giving deeper insights into various doctrines and beliefs.

Arianism- propagated by Arius, a priest who lived in AD 280-336, this tenet claimed that Christ was not divine.

Nestorianism- founded by Nestorius (AD 451); he tried to separate Jesus' human and divine natures, promoting the belief that what is true of Jesus as man, may not be said for Jesus as God.

Monophysitism- taught by Eutyches (AD 373-454), this heresy states that Christ had a blended nature as opposed to two distinct natures: human and divine.

Monothelism- promoted by Severus of Antioch and Sergius, Patriarch of Constantinople in 681, this belief claimed that Christ had only a divine will and not a human one.

Donatism- propagated by Donatius (AD 254-257), this tenet held that the sacraments, if administered by heretics and sinners, were invalid.

Jansenism- taught by Cornelius Jansenius (1585-1638), this heresy claims that some humans are predestined to go to heaven, others to hell. He believed that Jesus only died for those going to heaven. Jansenius also embraced a harsh code of conduct and morality. (Morrow 153)

Albigensianism- Albigensian heretics rejected the Old Testament, infant baptism and declared that there were two principles as the source of the universe. The good principle created the spiritual world while the evil principle made the physical one. (Anatolios & Brown 49)

After examining these popular heresies, it would be safe to assume that many still survive in Christianity, though most Christians are unaware of their origins. Now let us look at the Scriptures themselves. The main difference between the Catholic Bible and the Protestant Bible is seven extra books and extra passages in the books of Daniel and Esther in the Old Testament and extra passages in the Gospel of Mark in the New Testament. Protestants collectively refer to these books and passages as the Apocrypha while Catholics know them as the Deuterocanonicals. They contain mostly historical accounts as well as advice on living a saintly life.

Often used by Protestant ministers, the stories of "Susanna and the Elders" and "Bel and the Dragon" are only found in the Deuterocanonicals (the Protestant Apocrypha.) It is interesting to note that the story of Shadrach, Meshach, and Abednego is found in the Protestant Bible where it talks of these three being cast into a furnace where they were unharmed. They glorified God with a song of praise and thanksgiving. But the song itself is not mentioned- unless we look at the extra verses in the Deuterocanonicals.

So, why do Protestants distinguish these books as different, even to the point of rejection? There were four big conditions to making it into the Protestant Old Testament. Each book had to be written before 500 BC, in Hebrew- not Aramaic or Greek. And any books in question had to have been historically used by the Jewish community and accepted by the Pharisees, who were the ruling theologians after Rome took possession of Jerusalem. (Horn 7) Sounds simple, doesn't it?

Well, some passages of Ezra, Daniel and Jeremiah were written in Aramaic. (Horn 7) And even before the Diaspora, the Jewish community extended beyond the borders of Israel. In 320 BC, Ptolemy Lagi, ruler of Egypt, took 200,000 Israelites from their homeland back to his kingdom as slaves. These Jews settled in Alexandria and the surrounding countryside. Because they were out of contact with Israel, these slaves adopted the tongue of their captors: Greek. So, when the Deuterocanonicals were created in Egypt, they were written in Greek, so that the Jews in Alexandria could understand them. (Laux 14) Why speak Greek in Egypt?

Because, there was this young man named Alexander the Great who had conquered the area sometime before all of this took place. He spread the Greek language and culture throughout the Holy Land. Upon his death, Alexander's empire was split between his generals, one of whom founded the last dynasty of Egypt, Ptolemy. By 130 BC, most, if not all, books of the Old Testament were translated into Greek, and this work became known as the Septuagint, from the Latin word *Septuaginta* or "the work of the seventy." Originally, the term referred to the seventy (or seventy-two) Jewish scholars that translated the Books of Moses, but would later extend to all of the books of the Old Testament including the Deuterocanonicals. (Laux 14)

By the time of Christ, many gentiles had already been exposed to the Septuagint. This made it that much easier for the Apostles to evangelize the ancient world. Not only did they write the New Testament in Greek, but they also used the Septuagint because it too was written in Greek as opposed to the Hebrew *Tanak*, which few outsiders could truly understand. In fact, the Apostles quote the Septuagint, not the Tanak, in all versions, Catholic and Protestant, of the New Testament when speaking of Christ fulfilling this or that prophecy according to the Old Testament prophets. Matthew was really big on this as he wrote to specifically convert the Jews. For example, Isaiah of the Septuagint speaks of a virgin conceiving and bearing a son while the Tanak's version of Isaiah says a maiden will conceive. In Jewish culture, a maiden was automatically considered a virgin, but the Greeks made the separation between a maiden and a virgin, believing them not to necessarily be one and the same. This is why the Catholic Bible uses the Septuagint, considering it to be the complete and unabridged version of the Old Testament. (Laux 15)

Officially, Protestant theologians rejected the Deuterocanonicals in favor of the Tanak for the reasons mentioned earlier. The Tanak is composed of three parts: the *Torah*, which is the law or Mosaic Code; the *Nevi'im*, which are the Prophets; and the *Ketuvim*, which are the histories. (Horn 7-8) But the underlying reason for this action was the fact that the second Book of Maccabees extols the virtue of prayer for the dead, which is supportive of the belief in purgatory, which conflicts with Protestantism. (Horn 20) It's interesting to note that modern Jews still use the Book of Maccabees of the Septuagint. The miracle of the Maccabbees is the basis for Chanukah, in which the Temple flame burned even after they ran out of oil during a siege of Jerusalem. This can only be found in the Deuterocanonicals, not the Tanak.

Martin Luther wanted these scriptures removed and achieved this end by adopting the Tanak, which is the basis for the Protestant Old Testament. (Mr. Luther wanted any book removed that did not agree with the teachings that he proponed. This included the Letter to the Hebrews, Revelation [for dogmatic reasons], and most importantly, the Letter of James, which rejects "justification by faith alone," a tenet dearly held by Protestants today.)(Laux 10) This is why we have the discrepancy between the Catholic and Protestant Old Testaments. The Catholic and Protestant New Testaments are virtually identical, with the exception of extra passages in the Gospel of Mark.

Since we're speaking of the origin of the Bible, let me ask you a question: which came first, the New Testament scriptures or the Church? I know that it's easy to say that the scriptures were in existence first, but let's think this through logically. Now, both Protestants and Catholics will usually agree that the Church was founded on the day of Pentecost, when the Holy Spirit came down upon the Disciples, preparing them to minister to the people. But this is some time before Paul's conversion, and the Gospels would not be written until decades later. Remember that Paul's letters are to churches that were already established. Corinth, Ephesus, Thessalonica, Philippi, and Rome had thriving Christian communities. So, it is clear that the Church came first.

Modern day Christians forget that these were the days when biblical books were not knitted together into one massive work. Each book circulated on its own and was carefully copied by hand in the Jewish tradition. Communities rarely had the kind of access to the scriptures that we enjoy today. There was no such thing as mass printing. So, the Church relied upon oral tradition, just as other ancient societies. Make no mistake, they did have the Holy Spirit to guide them, but tradition has always played a major part in Christianity, particularly Catholicism. While both Catholics and Protestants have often criticized tradition, the Apostle Paul endorses it in his second letter to the Thessalonians, saying, *"Therefore, brethren, stand fast, and hold the traditions which ye have been taught, whether by word, or our epistle." (II Thessalonians 2:15, KJV)*

Also, in his second letter, John the Evangelist writes, *"Having many things to write unto you, I would not write with paper and ink: but I trust to come unto you, and speak face to face, that our joy may be full. (II John 1:12, KJV)*

Note that Paul differentiates teaching by "word" and by "epistle", thus separating oral and written teachings. Why do so unless tradition had an important role? The Catholic faith, as we know it, sits upon a kind of tripod: the scriptures, tradition, and the Magisterium. The Magisterium is defined as "the living teaching office of the Church," which interprets the word of God, both in Holy Scripture and in tradition. It is not one of the departments of the Vatican, as so many people believe. The Magisterium assures the Church's fidelity to the teachings of the Apostles in the realms of faith and morals. (Catechism 887)

Those who espouse the tenet of ***sola scriptura*** or Christian teachings based on "scripture alone" need to be aware that there are practical problems that emanate from complete reliance on the scriptures and nothing else. This implies a personal interpretation of the scripture with no spiritual teaching authority to answer to. There are presuppositions that come with such a belief. In order for ***sola scriptura*** to be valid, believers (***at the time of Christ***) would need to:

1) Have all books of the Bible bound into one work
2) Have the printing press- for mass printing of the scriptures
3) Have mass circulation- so everyone could have a
complete copy of the Bible
4) Have universal literacy
5) Have proper nutrition (the mind does not function
well without a good diet)
6) Have a universal education with cultivated critical thinking skills and all the materials needed to achieve that end
7) Have adequate time to devote to the study of the scriptures (Akin 3)

Needless to say, all these conditions were not met by the bulk of humanity until the twentieth century. And even now, there are still places where people are uneducated, illiterate, with inadequate nutritional needs and little time for studying the scriptures. ***Sola scriptura*** is a tenet created by a group of Renaissance scholars, who were lucky enough to *have* most of those advantages listed above.

Finally, the belief of "personal interpretation" of the scripture continues to be the primary reason for the continuing splits and fractures within the Body of Christ. Because there is no final authority in Christian teachings outside of Catholicism, groups continually form when opinions and convictions differ. It's fine to have a personal interpretation of the Bible until one's personal interpretation argues with the position of one's minister or denomination. After which, we have a split. According to the Oxford University Press's latest figures, Christianity has around 20,000 different denominations that it lists in its World Christian Encyclopedia. (Akin 1)

Because all of my readers need to be on "the same page" (so to speak), I will concentrate mainly on scriptural documentation as I wrote this book for the purpose of educating Protestants (particularly independent faiths) about Catholicism. I chose the original King James (1611) Version specifically because of its widespread acceptance and use by Protestants; reaching people means starting with the Bible with which they personally feel comfortable. If you like, you may take out your Bible and follow along with me.

But as you do this, I would like you to consider another important question. How did the Church function the first sixteen centuries without the King James Version of the Bible? Many Protestants will not even look at any other version, considering them all heretical. Did we all just stumble around blindly? Remember that the King James Version is an English translation of a series of books written in three languages. God's Inspired Word comes to us by way of Greek, Hebrew, and Aramaic, not the ornate English that most of us are used to.

The Trinity

The Triune Godhead (also known as the Trinity) is the belief that the Father, the Son, and the Holy Spirit are each a distinct Person, and yet, are all God. A great mystery and a bear to explain to the unschooled, this concept is one of the binding cords throughout the Christian world, mainline denominations and independents alike.

Perhaps one of the best illustrations of the Trinity is found in a simple equilateral triangle. All three sides and all three angles are equal. We might consider the top point to be God, the Father, while the two other side angles represent God, the Son, and God, the Holy Spirit. While each angle is distinct, each angular range fans out until it blends with the others in the center of the figure. Everything within the whole triangle represents God; each point is a distinct personage vital to the complete structure. Three angles link together to make one geometric figure; take one angle away and we have no triangle.

Now, there are those individuals who cannot accept this teaching. Some groups see the Father, the Son, and the Holy Spirit to just be God with no distinct persons. This belief is called "Monism." In their eyes, the concept of the Trinity is wrong, even heretical. But is it? From the very beginning of the Bible, there are indications that the Godhead truly does exist. Let look at *Genesis 1:26, KJV: "And God said, 'Let us make man in our image, after our likeness: and let them have dominion over the fish of the sea, and over the fowl of the air, and over the cattle, and over all the earth, and over every creeping thing that creepeth on the earth.'"*

It may be easy to dismiss this scripture as a kind of royal proclamation just as when an earthly monarch calls him/herself as "our", "us" or "we." But, there is also the way that the Israelites referred to God. According to ***The Living Bible Encyclopedia in Story and Pictures***, the oldest name for God is **Elohim** (its etymology is considered prehistoric), having been mentioned over 2500 times in the Old Testament (611). In fact, names with "el" (its singular form) in them have God incorporated into their meanings.

Here are just a few:

Israel - "He who strives with God and prevails" (880)
Elijah - "Jehovah is God" (582)
Elishah - "God saves" (610)
Ezekiel - "God strengthens" (654)
Samuel - "Name of God or His name is El" (1833)
Daniel - "God is my judge" (472)
Elizabeth - "God is my oath" (610)

The Jewish use of elohim is interesting in that the word is a plural grouping (611). The "-im" ending denotes more than one. Other examples of this are seraph (one) - seraphim (plural) and cherub (one) - cherubim (plural). The Israelites always refer to pagan gods as "elohim are," but refer to the God of Israel as "Elohim is." Here we have a plural name being used with a singular verb. This subtle nuance gets lost in the English translation, but remains noticeable if we go back to the original Hebrew of the Old Testament.

Isaiah speaks of the coming Incarnation when he declares, *"...Behold, a Virgin shall conceive, and bear a son, and shall call His name Immanuel." (Isaiah 7:14 KJV) Immanuel* means *"God is with us."* (Stuttman et al. 840)

Isaiah continues with, *"For unto us a child is born, unto us a son is given; and the government shall be upon His shoulder; and His name shall be called Wonderful, Counselor, The mighty God, The everlasting Father, The Prince of Peace." (Isaiah 9:6, KJV).*

The titles "The mighty God" and "The everlasting Father" are titles strictly reserved for God and yet the prophet speaks of the Virgin birth and her child bearing these titles. The prophet further describes this child in *Isaiah 11:1-2, KJV: And there shall come forth a rod out of the stem of Jesse, and a branch shall grow out of his roots; and the spirit of the Lord shall rest upon Him, the spirit of wisdom and understanding, the spirit of counsel and might, the spirit of knowledge and of the fear of the Lord.*

If monism is correct, then why did the prophet write it that way? If there is only one person in the God of Israel and the Father, Son, and Holy Spirit are just aspects of that person, the spirit of the Lord would not need to rest upon this Messiah. Instead, this spirit would be an intrinsic part of this man. Let's move on to John in the New Testament. He begins his Gospel with: " *In the beginning was the Word and the Word was with God, and the Word was God...And the Word was made flesh, and dwelt among us, (and we beheld His glory, the glory as of the only begotten of the Father,) full of grace and truth." (John 1:14, KJV)*

Again we see togetherness and distinctiveness in the Persons all at once. Because the Word was made flesh, it's obvious that John is speaking of Jesus, but Jesus (the Word) existed with God before His birth. John calls Jesus the only "begotten of the Father." Not being disrespectful to the scriptures or even to the monists, but how does one beget oneself?

If we have any questions about the identity of the Word or how He is conceived, they are easily put to rest with the scripture associated with the Annunciation. *Then said Mary unto the angel, 'How shall this be, seeing I know not a man?' And the angel answered and said unto her, ' The Holy Ghost shall come upon thee, and the power of the Highest shall overshadow thee: therefore also that holy thing which shall be born of thee shall be called the Son of God. (Luke 1:34-35, KJV)*

Here is an excellent example of the three Personages of the Trinity. Mary is told that God, the Father will preside over the conception, the Holy Spirit participates in the actual act, and the end result is Jesus, who is the Son of God. We have three Persons. This is illustrated again in Christ's baptism: *"Now when all the people were baptized, it came to pass, that Jesus also being baptized, and praying, the heaven was opened, and the Holy Ghost descended in a bodily shape like a dove upon Him, and a voice came from heaven, which said, 'Thou art my beloved Son; in Thee I am well pleased." (Luke 3:21-22)*

Both of the preceding passages show the three Persons of the Godhead. In each, we have the Persons in different locations, taking different forms, and doing different things, though they always act together, in concert. Even Jesus Himself gives evidence of the Trinity with His descriptions and prayers to God, the Father. He calls the Father ***"Abba"***. The English translations of the Bible translate this into "Father," but that translation is not quite correct. ***Av*** was the Hebrew word for ***"Father"*** and was very formal. But the word

abba translates into a familiar, affectionate term and is closer to the modern day word ***"Daddy"*** or ***"Papa"***. (Gross 85) This probably got more than its share of raised eyebrows from the Jewish religious leaders as it denoted a loving relationship between parent and child. If Jesus were just an aspect of God, the Father, then why would He constantly refer to Himself in the third person, pray to Himself, or call Himself by such a term as "abba?"

It becomes even more complicated when Jesus speaks of the Holy Spirit. Scripture tells us that Christ became filled with the Holy Spirit. Was He full of Himself? I don't think so. Jesus talks of going away, so that His followers may receive the Holy Spirit as a comforting presence. Then, we have a very serious edict that Jesus gives us regarding our treatment of the Holy Spirit.

> *Wherefore I say unto you, all manner of sin and blasphemy shall be forgiven unto men: But the blasphemy against the Holy Ghost shall not be forgiven unto men. And whosoever speaketh a word against the Son of Man, it shall be forgiven him: but whosoever speaketh against the Holy Ghost, it shall not be forgiven him, neither in this world, neither in the world to come. (Matthew 12:31-32, KJV)*

Notice that Jesus makes a distinction between offending the Son of Man (Himself) and the Holy Spirit. This passage cannot make sense from the monist's point of view if all three are just aspects of one being and not three distinct Persons.

Now, I have heard the argument that because Christ "was in the flesh," He was temporarily split from the other aspects of God, but that after His visit to earth, He rejoined the whole again.

St. John disagrees with this stance when he writes, *"For there are three that bear record in heaven, the Father, the Word, and the Holy Ghost: and these three are one." (1 John 5:7, KJV)*

Jesus is now in heaven, and we still see distinctiveness between the Three Persons of the Godhead. This continues to be the case when we look at the Book of Revelation:
Behold I stand at the door and knock: if any man hear my voice, and open the door, I will come into him, and will sup with him, and he with me. To him that overcomes will grant to sit with me in my throne. Even as I also overcame, and am set down with my father in His throne. (Revelation 3:20-21, KJV)

So, even after death, the Resurrection, and the Ascension, we still have distinctive differences in heaven. Where does Christ sit but on the right hand of the Father. Does it make sense to have multiple thrones for a God with multiple aspects- or multiple personages? And Christ continues to refer to God in the third person, even beyond the veil of flesh into the spirit world.

The other side of the doctrine of the Triune Godhead is, of course, the concept that although distinct Persons, the Father, the Son, and the Holy Spirit of the Trinity are all God, thus we have the phrase, "three in one" which is where the words "Trinity" or "Triune" come from. This oneness is illustrated in the following passage:

> *And it came to pass, that He went through the cornfields on the Sabbath day; and His Disciples began as they went to pluck the ears of the corn. And the Pharisees said unto Him, "Behold, why do they on the Sabbath day that which is not lawful?"*

> *And He said unto them, "Have ye never read what David did, when he had need, and was an hungered, he, and they that were with him? How he went into the house of God in the Days of Abiathar, the High Priest, and did eat the shewbread, which is not lawful to eat but for the priests and gave also to them which were with him?"*
>
> *And He said unto them, "The Sabbath was made for man, and not man for the Sabbath. Therefore, the Son of Man is Lord also of the Sabbath." (Mark 2:23-28, KJV)*

The title "Lord of the Sabbath" is a title that the Jews reserved for God. When Jesus uses this title, the implication is very clear to these religious men. This idea is affirmed when Christ says: *"My sheep hear my voice and I know them, and they follow me. And I give unto them eternal life; and they shall never perish; neither shall any man pluck them out of my hand. My Father which gave them me is greater than all; and no man is able to pluck them out of my Father's hand. I and my Father are one." (John 10:27-30, KJV)*

Jesus restates this again with His words in *John 14:7-9, KJV*:

> *If ye had known me, ye should have known my Father also; and from henceforth ye know Him, and have seen Him. Philip saith unto Him, "Lord sheweth us the Father, and it sufficeth us."*
>
> *Jesus saith unto him, "Have I been so long time with you, and yet hast thou not known me, Philip? He that hath seen me hath seen the Father: and how saith thou then, shew us the Father?"*

Jesus calls Himself the great "I am" when He is cross-examined by the Pharisees in an earlier passage, which reads:

> *Then said the Jews unto Him, "Now we know thou hast a devil. Abraham is dead, and the prophets, and thou sayest, 'If a man keep my saying, he shall never taste death.' Art thou greater than our father Abraham, which is dead; whom makest thou thyself."*
>
> *Jesus answered, "If I honor myself, my honor is nothing: it is my Father that honoreth me; of whom ye say that He is your God. Yet ye have not known Him; but I know Him: and if I should say, 'I know Him not," I shall be a liar like unto you. But I know Him and keep His saying. Your father Abraham rejoiced to see my day, and he saw it and was glad."*
>
> *Then said the Jews unto Him, "Thou art not yet fifty years old, and hast thou seen Abraham?"*
>
> *Jesus said unto them, "Verily, verily, I say unto you, before Abraham was, I AM."(John 8:52-58, KJV)*

This passage is extremely important as it documents that Jesus is God Incarnate. He is speaking of His relationship with Abraham that could not possibly have been unless He was God. Abraham was the root of the Israelite nation and lived at a time incompatible with the age of Rome, the time that heralded the birth of the Messiah and the dawning of the Christian faith. And when, Christ declares Himself as *"I am"* He is calling Himself

God. This harks back to God's declaration to Moses at the burning bush on Mt. Sinai. God calls Himself **Yahweh** or **YHWH**, which means, *"I am who I am."* (Catechism 904)

Notice that Jesus uses the phrase *"****Verily, verily, I say unto you****"*. This is prophetic language as the Old Testament prophets would often say, *"****Verily, verily, thus saith the Lord your God.****"* But Christ says, *'**I say**'* instead of *'thus saith the Lord your God.'* He doesn't see the need. In effect, He is saying that He is God.

These passages are but a fraction of the scriptures that support the doctrine of the Trinity. But the idea that there are three Persons but one God is a vivid reminder that we as humans can only accept the mystery that we call the Triune Godhead; we cannot completely explain it. We, with childlike faith, embrace God in three Persons: God, the Father, who created the universe and everything within it; Jesus, His Son, who purchased eternal life with His very blood; and the Holy Spirit, who communes with God's followers on a daily level, the spiritual fountain from which we receive a never ending flow of God's grace and love. There is no "how" or "why." The Triune Godhead just is- existing before man and time itself, eternally.

Understanding the Sacraments through Protestant Eyes

Before we begin this section, I would like to ask a question: what exactly is a "ritual?" Many people conjure up images of secret gestures and exotic ceremonies, even witchcraft, when this word is uttered. But this view is hardly realistic or accurate. You see, a ritual is simply a prescribed way of doing something. The business and political world might call this same term a "protocol." If something were not done or handled the proper way, it would be considered, "against protocol."

Truth is that humans have dozens of routines that they do on a daily, weekly, or monthly basis. We bathe and brush our teeth daily, buy groceries every week, and pay monthly bills, and we all have a certain way that we carry out each activity. Most of these routines are unannounced and really unplanned, but we do them at intervals and usually according to a preset procedure. And while these simple routines are anything but sacred, they are still rituals because of how they are done.

I have heard it said that the Catholic Church is ritualistic and, therefore, wrong in its practices. But what other faiths fail to realize is that they themselves are ritualistic as well. I know of no church that does not conduct its affairs in an orderly, prescribed fashion.

For example, what would you think if a church had no specific meeting times; people just came and went whenever? The minister preached whenever and however he chose, with no regard to when the congregation was there to listen or what the best way to convey his/her message was. People just sang hymns whenever and however they wanted, without regard for anyone else in the congregation or the minister conducting the "service." Worse yet, can you imagine a communion supper, symbolic or not, where the bread and wine (or grape juice) were unceremoniously placed on the altar, with someone yelling out, **_"Come and get it!"_**

That last description should make any Christian cringe, but that's what the religious world would be like without rituals. Any church that says that it doesn't have them is lying to itself and its congregation. Call them anything else, but these procedures are rituals in the purest sense of the word. Catholicism contains an elaborate set of rituals with regard to conducting almost any form of business, whether secular or sacred. When a church is as large as we are, nothing will get done unless it is well organized. The Catholic Church has its own government with a law-making body, a judicial system, and a ruling head of state. Yes, we're bureaucratic, but we have to be. However, in spite of its cumbersome size, Catholicism still stresses the simple joy of communing with Christ. We celebrate the presence of God in our lives in a variety of ways such as music, scripture, homilies (somewhat like sermons), and the sacraments.

So, what is a sacrament? It comes from the Latin word **_sacramentum_**, which means, **_"to make holy."_** This harks back to the Baptismal vows that are first made by parents on a child's behalf, but later, continually renewed on the individual's part. Sacraments are spiritual events that occur within the life of the Church as well as the lives of individuals where the presence of God is invited, acknowledged and welcomed. Some Protestants frown on the use of the word "sacrament", but I know of no church that does not celebrate significant events that are blessed by God.

But a sacrament is different from a non-sacramental ritual. First of all, sacraments are specific events instituted or sanctified by Christ Himself. The act of a sacrament is not just symbolic, though it has many symbolic elements. Sacraments blend faith and works together into life changing events, making Christ present in the lives of the faithful. There are many Protestants who believe in "justification by faith alone." This position does not hold water in the scriptures because no matter how strong a person's faith is, they must show it through works of love and mercy in Christ's name. Just believing is not enough; one must act on one's belief. Listen to the words of St. James:

> *But be ye doers of the word, and not hearers only, deceiving your own selves. For if any be a hearer of the word and not a doer, he is like unto a man beholding his natural face in a glass: for he beholdeth himself, and goeth his way, and straightway forgetteth what manner of man he was.*
>
> *But whoso looketh into the perfect law of liberty, and continueth therein, he being not a forgetful hearer, but a doer of the work, this man shall be blessed in his deed. (James 1:22-25, KJV)*

James continues his admonishment regarding faith and works in Chapter 2:

> *What doth it profit, my brethren, though a man saith he hath faith, and have not works? Can faith save him? If a brother or sister be naked, and destitute of daily food, and one of you say unto them, 'Depart in peace, be ye warmed and filled;' notwithstanding ye give them those things which are needful to the body, what doth it profit?*
>
> *Even so faith, if it hath not works, is dead, being alone.*
>
> *Yea, a man may say, 'Thou hast faith, and I have works: shew me thy faith without thy works, and I will shew thee my faith by my works.' Thou believe that there is one God; thou doest well: the devils also believe and tremble.*
>
> *But wilt thou know, 'O vain man, that faith without works is dead. Was not Abraham our father justified by works, when he had offered Isaac his son upon the altar. Seest thou how faith wrought with his works and by works was faith made perfect? And the scripture was fulfilled which saith, 'Abraham believed God, and it was imputed unto him for righteousness: and he was called the Friend of God.*
>
> *Ye see then how that by works a man is justified, and not by faith only. Likewise was Rahab, the harlot, justified by works, when she had received messengers and had sent them out another way. For as the body without the spirit is dead, faith without works is dead also. (James 2:14-26, KJV)*

So, justification by faith alone does not work. With scripture like that, you can see why some Protestants shy away from the Book of James. Remember that Martin Luther pushed to have the Book of James removed from the Bible during the Reformation. Bibles usually have non-scriptural descriptions about what takes place in a chapter, put there by editors to help the reader find what he/she is looking for. When working with one edition of the King James Bible, I was shocked to see that someone actually wrote that Abraham was justified through faith alone in an earlier non-scriptural description when James emphatically declares that he was not in the passage mentioned above. (Personally, I'd be afraid to do that for fear of eternal damnation, but maybe God will understand that they are simply blind to their mistake.)

Now, Protestant theologians often confuse works that reflect one's faith with the works of the law when they offer the Apostle Paul's commentary in Galatians as proof of justification by faith alone. Paul writes:

> *Knowing that a man is not justified by the works of the law, but by the faith of Jesus Christ, even we have believed in Jesus Christ, that we might be justified by*

> *the faith of Christ, and not by the works of the law: for by the works of the law shall no flesh be justified.*
>
> *But if, while we seek to be justified by Christ, we ourselves also are found sinners, is therefore Christ the minister of sin? God forbid. For if I build again the thing which I destroyed, I make myself a transgressor. For I through the law am dead to the law, that I might live unto God.*
>
> *I am crucified with Christ: nevertheless I live; yet not I but Christ liveth in me: and the life which I now live in the flesh I live by the faith of the Son of God, who loved me, and gave Himself for me. I do not frustrate the grace of God: for if righteousness come by the law then Christ is dead in vain. (Galatians 2:16-21, KJV)*

Notice that Paul is talking about freedom from the needless legality of the Mosaic Code, saying that trying to adhere to it frustrates God's redemptive plan. He also adds that if it were possible to be redeemed by the law, then the Crucifixion was unnecessary in the first place. Remember that the Jewish leaders were more concerned with a strict adherence to the law that gave the appearance of spiritual virtue and less interested in actually cultivating a real relationship with God. In the Jewish mindset, works could stand alone. Paul understood this mentality more than anyone else.

But the Apostle's commentary does not undermine the importance of works as a reflection of one's faith. Faith cannot stand alone either. It must be supported by actions. If we look at the life of Christ and the miracles He worked, many times He says that someone's faith has saved them, but if we read the preceding passages to those words, actions are linked with faith. The person acts first, and then is rewarded with that declaration, even if it is something as simple as going out to meet Him or touching Christ's robe. To be Christian, we must admit that we're sinners, confess those sins, be sorry for them, and turn our lives over to Jesus. The words "admit", "confess" and "turn" are verbs, words that imply some action. It's ironic that every Protestant tract says this, and yet justification by faith alone is against the very nature of those words.

When Catholics present themselves before God and embrace the sacraments with loving, humble hearts, they are justified by their acts, blending faith with works as James tells us to do. Sacraments are acts that confer graces upon the recipients through the work of the Holy Spirit. These events can be as plentiful as Holy Eucharist or as solitary as Baptism or Confirmation. There are seven sacraments: Baptism, Reconciliation, Holy Eucharist, Confirmation, Marriage, Anointing of the Sick, and Holy Orders.

Baptism

The first sacrament that we will cover is Baptism, mainly because of the fact that this sacrament is administered to infants (preferably under eight days old). Infant baptism dates back before the age of science when there were very high death rates. The Church worried for the state of a child's soul should death occur. Of course, after Vatican II, theologians came to trust the fate of unbaptized newborns to the mercy of God. Believing in Christ's love for children, we give them full funeral rites and bury them in consecrated ground, remembering His words from the Book of Luke: *"...Suffer the little children to come unto me, and forbid them not: for such is the Kingdom of God. Verily I say unto you, whosoever shall not receive the Kingdom of God as a little child shall in no wise enter there in." (Luke 18:16-17, KJV)*

This is illustrated again after Jesus delivers one child from demonic possession. He declares, *"... Whosoever shall receive this child in my name receiveth me; and whosoever shall receive me receiveth Him that sent me; for he that is least among you all, the same shall be great." (Luke 9:48, KJV)*

It is in remembering those words that Catholics believe that their children must be returned to God and consecrated to His kingdom as soon as possible; otherwise, they are hindering their children's spiritual growth. Baptism is a gift, given without concern to human merit. It is the gateway to Christian life and the starting point from where an individual will begin journeying with Christ.

While there is little argument over adult baptism, infant baptism has always been a hot point with some Protestant groups who argue that there is no free will exercised on the part of the child. But Christ's words from these passages suggest that the Savior is not concerned with a child's age or cognitive abilities. We hear no specific stipulations, just His directive to receive children in His name. The real conflict lies not in age differences and cognition, but in warring concepts behind the practice itself. Certain Protestants believe in the symbolism of the act, believing it to be an outward sign of an inward change. If a child is too young, they are incapable of making a rational choice to follow Christ, so the symbolism is lost.

But no one knows for sure when cognition begins. Science has documented fetal reactions to various stimuli outside the womb. The Psalms agree that we can believe in the womb. Listen to the words from *Psalm 22, verses 9-10, KJV: "But thou art he that took me out of the womb: thou didst make me hope when I was upon my mother's breasts. I was cast upon thee from the womb: thou art my God from my mother's belly."*

The most powerful Biblical example of pre-birth cognition deals with John the Baptist. Consider this passage. *"And it came to pass, that, when Elizabeth heard the Salutation of Mary, the babe leaped in her womb; and Elizabeth was filled with the Holy Ghost: And she spake with a loud voice, and said, "Blessed art thou among women, and blessed is the fruit of thy womb. And whence is this to me, that the mother of my Lord should come to me?" (Luke 1:41-43)*

John the Baptist isn't even born yet, but he still reacts strongly to the sound of Mary's voice. He senses the presence of God Incarnate. Just because man cannot completely gauge cognition does not mean that it does not exist. Mystics have a term for being "conscious in the womb;" they call it being *"preborn."*

The Bible speaks of whole households being baptized. Let's look at the following passages:

And when she was baptized, and her household, she besought us saying, "If ye have judged me to be faithful to the Lord, come into my house and abide there." and she constrained us. Acts 16:15, KJV

And Crispus, the chief ruler of the synagogue, believed on the Lord with all his house; and many of the Corinthians, hearing believed, and were baptized. Acts 18:8, KJV

And I baptized also the household of Stephanas: besides I know not whether I baptized any other. 1 Corinthians 1:16, KJV

Even today, referencing a household means all people who dwell within it including infants. When filing taxes or applying for governmental aid, individuals must identify all relatives, even their smallest ones. In Biblical times and into the Common Era, members of a household extended to the servants, their spouses, and children. Children, no matter how innocent, are still sinners, nonetheless. The Book of Psalms records: *"Behold I was shapen in inequity; and in sin did my mother conceive me." (Psalm 51:5,KJV)*

The Apostle Paul writes: *"For all have sinned and fall short of the glory of God." Romans 3:23, KJV*

Furthermore, Paul admonishes: *"Wherefore, as by one man sin entered into the world, and death by sin; and so death passed upon all men, for that all have sinned...For as by one man's disobedience many were made sinners, so by the obedience of one shall many be made righteous". Romans 5:12, 19, KJV*

In his letter to the Colossians, Paul also notes that Christian baptism now replaced the Jewish circumcision, a ceremony generally reserved for infants. He states: *"In whom also ye are circumcised with the circumcision made without hands, in putting off the body of the sins of the flesh by the circumcision of Christ: Buried with Him in baptism, wherein also ye are risen with Him through the faith of the operation of God, who hath raised Him from the dead." (Colossians 2:12, KJV)*

Catholics see baptism as not only symbolic, signifying a rebirth in Jesus, but also believe that the act itself bestows certain graces upon the recipient. Catholic baptism confers forgiveness of all sins, original sin and personal sins as well as their spiritual punishment. It is here that an individual is "born again." (This is why most Catholics can't put a date and time on their rebirth. It's hard to remember back that far.) Do the scriptures agree that the act of baptism confers the remission of sin? Well yes, they do. Jesus tells Nicodemus, *"Verily, Verily, I say unto thee, except a man be born of water and of the Spirit, he cannot enter into the Kingdom of God." (John 3:5, KJV)*

Peter also reiterates this in the Book of Acts. *"Then Peter said unto them, 'Repent and be baptized everyone of you in the name of Jesus Christ for the remission of sins, and ye shall receive the gift of the Holy Ghost. For the promise is unto you, and to*

your children, and to all that afar off, even as many as the Lord our God shall call".
(Acts 2:38-39, KJV)

Notice that in both passages, water and spirit are separate. They are not incorporated into one event. First we have the spiritual seal of baptism, then the reception of the Holy Spirit (which happens during the sacrament of Confirmation.) These statements illustrate the gravity of Baptism as being bound with salvation itself. The sacrament of Baptism is a spiritual imperative issued by Christ Himself when He tells His Disciples: "*Go ye therefore, and teach all nations, baptizing them in name of the Father, and of the Son, and of the Holy Ghost: teaching them to observe all things whatsoever I have commanded you: and lo, I am with you alway, even unto the end of the world. Amen."* *(Matthew 28:19-20, KJV)*

The problem with Baptism as a purely symbolic ritual is that Holy Scripture links Baptism with Salvation. Baptism conveys spiritual purity and makes the soul clean Peter tells the faithful: *"...In the days of Noah, during the building of the ark...a few... were saved through water. Baptism, which corresponds to this, now saves you. (1 Peter 3:20-21, KJV)*

Mark says: *"He who believes and is baptized will be saved." (Mark 6:16, KJV)*

Titus 3:5, KJV, **states***: It was for no reason except His own compassion that He saved us by means of the cleansing water of rebirth and by renewing us with the Holy Spirit."*

So, we see that Salvation comes through actions joined with faith, echoing the scripture passages from Book of James. The Book of Acts also stresses the importance of actions blending with faith in Chapter 2, verse 38: *"You must repent," Peter answered, "and everyone of you must be baptised in the name of Jesus Christ for the forgiveness of your sins, and you will receive the Holy Spirit."*

And this passage: *"And now why do you wait? Rise up and be baptized, and wash away your sins, calling on His name."*

Baptism is not just symbolism to be accepted or dismissed on a whim. And if baptism confers God's forgiveness upon the baptized, then it must also make the person totally and completely new. As a new creature or neophyte, the individual is sanctified by the Trinity with the grace of justification which allows the person to believe, hope, and love God through the theological virtues; gives the ability to live and act under the guidance of the Holy Spirit through His gifts; and allows spiritual growth through moral virtues. (Catechism 322)

Catholicism also teaches that the sacrament of baptism grafts the individual into the Church, the body of Christ. As such, that individual becomes part of a chosen race, a royal priesthood, and a holy nation. This is illustrated in the First Book of Peter:

As newborn babes, desire the sincere milk of the word that ye grow thereby: If so be ye have tasted that the Lord is gracious. To whom coming, as unto a living stone, disallowed indeed of men, but chosen of God, and precious. Ye also, as

> lively stones, are built up a spiritual house, an holy priesthood, to offer up spiritual sacrifices, acceptable to God by Jesus Christ.
> But ye are a chosen generation, a royal priesthood, an holy nation, a peculiar people; that ye should shew forth the praises of Him who hath called you out of darkness into marvelous light. (1 Peter 2:2-5, 2:9 KJV)

As such, membership in God's family entails certain responsibilities and grants special rights. The baptized are expected to serve, obey and submit to the Church's leaders, granting them their deepest love and respect. And neophytes are expected to profess their faith openly before men and participate in the Apostolic and missionary work of the Christian faith (also known as the Great Commission). Rights and privileges include access to the sacraments, nourishment through the scriptures, and other forms of spiritual aid from the Church. This sacrament is the binding cord for all Christians everywhere, even those who are not in complete union with the Catholic Church. Catholicism will accept baptisms celebrated in other churches when adult catechumens enter the Church (though documentation is usually required). (Catechism 323)

A baptism leaves an indelible mark upon the soul, the seal of the Lord or **_Dominicus Character._** (Catechism 324) We are sealed with Holy Spirit until the "day of redemption." The Apostle Paul states this in _Ephesians 4:30, KJV, saying, "And grieve not the holy spirit of God, whereby ye are sealed unto the day of redemption."_

This seal can never be removed, even if the individual rejects Christianity for a life of sin. Though broken, the mark on the soul will remain. However, if the baptized keeps the covenant with God that the baptismal vows entail, he or she will depart from earthly life embossed with the sign of faith and receive everlasting life. Because this is the seal of the Lord, it cannot be duplicated. Whether Protestant or Catholic, there is but one baptism for each Christian. (Catechism 324)

Obviously, there is a vast difference between how many Protestants view baptism as opposed to Catholics. But what about free will? This argument, though at first compelling, has no real substance. As stated from the beginning, the word sacrament comes from sacramentum, which calls to mind the Baptismal vows. Every time Catholics witness another baptism or any other sacrament, they recall and embrace the baptismal vows once made for them so long ago. Even the blessed water that we mark ourselves with reminds each of us of our own sacred birthday when we were reborn in Christ.

Other Ways

When we think of baptism, we think of pouring water on the head or submerging the candidate completely, and the invocation of the Trinity, but there is another form of baptism- a baptism of blood. This is the domain of martyrs. If a person dies for Christ without the benefit of ordinary baptism, he/she is baptized by his/her death for and with Christ. (Catechism 321)

A catechumen who dies before baptism can also be forgiven and granted salvation, providing that the individual sought God in earnest and faithfully tried to fulfill His will. Those who never had the chance to hear the Gospel of Christ and embrace His Body, the Church, but still tried to seek God and do His will as much as they could understand it, may be saved. It is understood that they would have explicitly desired baptism if they had known of its necessity (Catechism 325).

Who Can Baptize?

Baptism is generally performed by bishops, priests and deacons within the Roman Church. However, in cases of necessity, any person (even one who is unbaptized) may administer this rite as long as their intention agrees with the Church's when her servants baptize. Simply pour water over the person's forehead and declare, ***"I baptize you in the name of the Father, and of the Son, and of the Holy Spirit."*** I have even heard of healthcare personnel being especially trained to do this in situations where someone, particularly a newborn, is near death. (Catechism 325)

But baptisms are generally happy affairs, featuring parents, godparents, and the attending congregation. Some of the elements of this ceremony include: a white garment, signifying that the baptized has "put on Christ," a lit candle representing illumination by the "light of the world", blessed and scented oil (also called chrism oil) for anointing, and blessed water. (Catechism 217-318) Some Protestant groups balk at the idea of pouring water over the head and strictly promote total water immersion. Catholicism has been known to do both; however, in most situations we favor pouring water over the head. The main idea is consecration to God, not how much of the body gets wet.

The parents embrace solemn vows to teach their children the Nicene Creed, rejection of Satan, and Christian virtues. Godparents are responsible for providing good examples of everyday Christian life, and in earlier times, were also responsible for looking after the child should tragedy befall the family and the parents become unable to perform their duties. The congregation stands in support and welcome, renewing their baptismal vows as they are sprinkled as well.

So, Catholic baptism is given to an individual without consideration of age, cognition, or deeds, and is the inauguration of a Christian's life with Christ. The sacrament confers the forgiveness of all sins upon the recipient and grafts him/her into the family of God with all the titles, duties, and responsibilities that entails. Initial consent really doesn't enter into it because at some point, the individual will willingly embrace the baptismal vows while participating in the other sacraments; every sacrament is based upon the baptismal vows.

There is the baptism of blood, when martyrs who were never baptized die for Christ before it can be done. We also hold that those who love and follow Jesus may still attain redemption without baptism and believe that they would have sought it had they been aware of its importance. This is also true for those who have joined with the Church in their faith journey, with intent of being baptized, but die before it is done.

Baptism is the universal binding cord for all Christians and as such, leaves an indelible mark upon the soul which can never be removed, even if the baptized rejects God, so there's no need to be baptized over and over again. Catholicism accepts baptisms that occur in other Christian denominations whether the person's preceding faith considered the act a sacrament or not.

Penance

The second sacrament is that of Penance, also known as Confession or Reconciliation. It is called Penance because it demands atonement for the wrongs committed against one's neighbor, God and His Church. The Sacrament of Penance has four essential elements: contrition, confession of sins, satisfaction or reparation, and absolution. (Catechism 357-358) Penance is one of the most criticized practices in Catholicism today. The main problem for Protestants is the idea that a priest is supposedly needed for the forgiveness of sin when Christ is our High Priest and we need no intercessor. This assumption about confession is an inaccurate reflection of this sacrament.

Why should we confess our sins to one another in the first place? When we actually say what we've done wrong to another human being, we are acknowledging and taking responsibility for our sins. Voicing our offenses takes them out of the shadowy corners of our souls and gives them form and shape. When we do this, we are opening ourselves to the Lord and freeing ourselves from the snares of sin. We feel clean, refreshed. To admit to is to be released.

And darkness and sin always prosper when they are ignored, glossed over, and generally left alone. Humans are like houses; no matter how clean they may start out being, they always need a periodic cleaning. We sweep away the dust and cobwebs that have quietly accumulated and throw open the windows and the door. God comes in and cleans away the dirt and grime, and we are completely His once again.

Catholics believe that anyone can receive forgiveness without a priest, providing that there is risk of death before an attending priest may be found or if there are not enough confessors to serve a large crowd of penitents properly and within a reasonable space of time. (Catechism 372) We also participate in a general penitential right during the Mass itself where the congregation is asked to recall any recent sins, mistakes, faults, or failures that would hinder full communion with Christ. The cantor will sing an invocation, and we sing back.

Mass Penitential Rite Prayer
You were sent to heal the contrite of heart:
Lord, have mercy.
   -Lord, have mercy.
You came to call sinners:
Christ, have mercy.
   -Christ, have mercy.
You are seated at the right hand of the Father to intercede for us:
Lord, have mercy.
   -Lord, have mercy.

(The priest finishes the invocation.)
May almighty God have mercy on us,
Forgive us our sins,
And bring us to everlasting life.
Amen. (Celebremos 8)

The previous prayer is also known as the ***Kyrie***, which is the Greek translation of the rite:

Kyrie eleison (Lord, have mercy.)
Christe eleison (Christ, have mercy.)
Kyrie eleison (Lord, have mercy.)(Worship 319)

Besides the public rites, we are always encouraged to rededicate our lives to Christ and ask His healing forgiveness on a daily basis. This is for simple mistakes such as losing one's temper and mouthing off, forgetting to hand back that pencil someone loaned you, forgetting to take out the trash after you were asked by your parents, etc. We call these sins *venial* because they are the simple transgressions. But there are instances when we commit *mortal* sins, which put the soul in danger of eternal damnation and require the services of a priest. **Mortal sins are serious in nature, must be committed with full consent of the will and full knowledge of the sinfulness of the act.**

Protestants tend to believe that sin is sin and that there is no classification of lesser (venial) sins and grave (mortal) sins, but that position is not supported in the following passage from the First Letter of John:

> *And this is the confidence we have in Him, if we ask anything according to His will, He heareth us: And if we know that He hear us, whatsoever we ask, we know that we have the petitions that we desired of Him. If any man see his brother sin a sin which is not unto death, he shall ask, and He shall give him life for them that sin not unto death. There is a sin unto death: I do not say that he shall pray for it. (1 John 5:14-17, KJV)*

In the preceding passage, we hear of sins that do not place souls in immediate jeopardy. And if we pray for those who make those simple mistakes, those people are forgiven for they receive "life" from Christ without even asking God themselves. However, in the case of grave offenses, which jeopardize a sinner's hope of eternal salvation, we may not intercede on someone's behalf. That individual must present themselves before the Throne of Grace, personally.

In many ways, our sinfulness is like a physical illness. Seeking daily forgiveness of small infractions is like curing the occasional headache with a couple of tablets from the aspirin bottle in the bathroom cabinet. But when it's a life threatening disease such as cancer, heart disease, or diabetes, the bathroom cabinet will not do the job. Mortal sins are not life threatening as much as they are "soul threatening." We must present ourselves before the "Great Physician" and submit to His instrument, the priest.

Repeated sinful behavior may also be a "symptom" of a deeper problem. Many times, if the underlying problem is addressed, then the sinful behavior stops or is significantly reduced. For example, let's suppose that a husband has abused his wife and children due to alcohol and drug use, which in turn, may have been nurtured by abuse in his own childhood. Until he faces the pain from his own life, he will never stop abusing drugs and be the loving husband and father that he should be. Another example is the teenage girl who engages in sex to feed a low personal self-confidence and self-esteem, which in turn, is caused by some other form of abuse. She must face the fact that her sin only plunges her further into depression and abuse. She is looking for love and validation in wrong places and will never find it in the outside world, but only in the arms of Jesus. Complex problems demand intensive treatment whether they are physical or spiritual. Priests are trained to be counselors. Is it any wonder that most Catholics don't see a therapist or psychologist for everyday problems? Instead, they meet with their parish priest.

Yes, Jesus is the "Great Physician," and we can call on His help at any moment. But a priest is Christ's hands and feet, the physical practitioner of His healing grace. Humans crave physical interaction with other humans; they need to be consoled, counseled, and reassured from time to time. And when we come to the throne of grace ourselves without the spiritual aid we need, we have a tendency of not forgiving ourselves, even though God has certainly forgiven us. A priest provides a way to help us to let go and continue our journey with Christ completely reconciled with God and His Church.

So prompts the burning question: "Can a priest forgive sins?" Actually, yes, they can. **Only God forgives sin, but Christ "by virtue of His divine authority," gave His Apostles this power to exercise in His name.** (Catechism 362) In the Gospel of Matthew, Jesus addresses Peter, saying, *"And I say unto thee, that thou art Peter, and upon this rock I will build my church; and the gates of Hell will not prevail against it. And I will give unto thee the keys to the kingdom of Heaven: and whatsoever thou shalt bind on earth, shall be bound in Heaven: and whatsoever thou shalt loose shall be loosed in Heaven." (Matthew 16:18-19, KJV)*

The power to loose and bind is very important because it confers the ability to forgive sin, through the power and authority of Christ Himself. It also gives the power to declare what is and is not a sin. Peter and his spiritual descendants are the gatekeepers of heaven itself. Someone with a key to a gate has the power to admit or turn away those who might enter. Those who are excluded from communion with Peter and his descendants will be excluded from communion with God, but those who are welcomed back, are reconciled and embraced by God. Reconciliation with the Church is inseparable from reconciliation with God. (Catechism 363) Jesus also reiterates this in the Gospel of *John 20:23, KJV*: *"Whose soever sins ye remit, they are remitted unto them; and whose soever sins ye retain, they are retained."*

But this power cannot be used as some form of spiritual blackmail. The Church is constantly called to bring sinners back to the fold, forgiving them and restoring the ruptures caused by sin because her collective redemption is linked to her ability to forgive. Christ also admonishes*: "For if ye forgive men their trespasses, your heavenly Father will also forgive you: but if ye forgive not men their trespasses, neither will your Father forgive your trespasses." (Matthew 6:14-15, KJV)*

So, how does a priest absolve the penitent at the end of the confession? He declares:

God, the Father of mercies,
Through the death and the resurrection of His Son
Has reconciled the world to Himself
And sent the Holy Spirit among us
For the forgiveness of sins
Through the ministry of His church.
May God give you pardon and peace,
And I absolve you from your sins
In the name of the Father, and of the Son, and of the Holy Spirit
(Catechism 364)

Believe it or not, many Protestant churches, especially independents, have a cousin of the sacrament of Penance. This is called **"the Altar Call"** where people come to front of the church to pray and ask Jesus for His forgiveness and His Lordship over their lives. Those who come are usually attended by the pastor/evangelist as well as other experienced elders in the Church. Though they are not ordained Catholic priests, these people *also* console, counsel, and reassure the individual. Most pastors and church elders would cringe if they realized that they behave in a priestly manner when they do altar calls.

But listen to the words of James:

Is any sick among you? Let him call for the elders of the church; and let them pray over him, anointing him with oil in the name of the Lord: And the prayer of faith shall save the sick, and the Lord shall raise him up; and if he have committed sins, they shall be forgiven him. Confess your faults one to another, and pray one for another, that ye may be healed. The effectual fervent prayer of a righteous man availeth much. (James 5:14-16, KJV)

There are critical differences between an altar call and the Sacrament of Penance. First of all, an altar call is not a sacrament, which reinforces all the Baptismal vows as discussed earlier in the last chapter. And an altar call is a public event while reconciliation is extremely private. No one save the penitent may ever reveal what took place. Any priest who breaks the seal of the confessional is immediately defrocked and excommunicated in the eyes of God. It is a damnable offense of which only the Pope may absolve. (Morrow 333)

And while the offending priest may be welcomed back into the Church after recanting, and reconciling himself to her, he can never serve a congregation in any capacity again. He cannot be a lay minister, serve in the choir, head up committees, etc. Betraying a penitent is the worst sin that a priest can commit and demands a lifetime of penance and denial of leadership roles. Men have been imprisoned, even killed, rather than break the seal.

One Hispanic martyr, Father Correa Magallanes, died at the hands of the Mexican government on Feb. 5, 1927. At a time when the Mexican authorities persecuted Catholic clergymen, Father Magallanes was ordered to hear confessions of other prisoners, then commanded to reveal the details of those confessions to the authorities. After Magallanes heard the confessions, he adamantly refused to violate the sanctity of the confessional and was immediately shot to death by a firing squad. *("Our Glorious Story," 6, Columbia, 7/04)*

Unfortunately, other churches do not have the kind of stringent rules that we have regarding counseling their flocks. The congregation must rely on the honor of the pastor, and some ministers are less than honorable.

Another advantage of penance is that it is considered a normal, healthy thing to do on a regular basis whereas altar calls are generally reserved for "sinners or backsliders." Many times, witnesses to an altar call may wonder what the person did if they see a seasoned Christian at the altar. Catholics see a regular parishioner leaving the confessional and tend to examine their own hearts for problems in their faith. Going to Penance periodically has a preventive effect, much like getting that physical from your general practitioner. Confessing small, everyday faults helps to create a stronger conscience, reinforce resistance to sin itself, open us to God's healing grace, and progress into a deeper spiritual communion with the Holy Spirit.

Here is some actual commentary from our Catechism:

Whoever confesses his sins...is already working with God. God indicts your sins; if you indict them, you are joined with God. Man and sinner are, so to speak, two realities: when you hear 'man'- this is what God has made; when you hear 'sinner'- this is what man himself has made. Destroy what you have made, so that God may save what he made...When you begin to abhor what you have made, it is then that your good works are beginning, since you are accusing yourself of your evil works. The beginning of good works is the confession of evil works. You do the truth and come to the light. (366)

Some myths about Penance are that of the Sunday Catholic who runs to the priest for forgiveness, then proceeds to break every commandment through the week or the criminal who visits the priest after an illegal act has been committed and feels free to escape earthly punishment for his misdeed. Sunday Catholics are no different than those Protestants who feel that they have the freedom to commit whatever sins they wish due to making a one-time profession of faith. Real Christianity involves an effort to change one's sinful habits. We must remember that true forgiveness demands true sorrow for one's sin along with the fervent desire that with the help of the Holy Spirit, never to commit that sin again. This is called contrition. ***Imperfect contrition, or attrition,*** is contrition born from the revulsion of one's sinful acts and fear of eternal damnation and other penalties associated with sin. Perfect contrition is always desirable above simple attrition because it is born out of a love that seeks perfect harmony with God. (Catechism 364) The Sunday Catholic is more concerned with avoiding punishment than developing a rich faith in the Lord. That said, any person with the ***"I'll do what I want to"*** mentality does not have a real relationship with Christ because they lack true remorse for the evils that they commit.

Satisfaction

According to the Catechism of the Catholic Church as promulgated by Pope John Paul II, **"Penance requires... the sinner to endure all things willingly, be contrite of heart, confess with the lips, and practice complete humility and fruitful satisfaction." (364)**

Satisfaction means that the penitent must make amends for wrongs done against his/her neighbor. Some examples are paying for or returning stolen goods and restoring a slandered reputation. While we are always forgiven, that is only part of the equation of penance. We must still pay for what we have done. An example of this is like throwing a baseball through a neighbor's window. After the neighbor forgives you for breaking the glass, the damage still needs to be paid for. Satisfaction may mean giving the monetary equivalent of the window to the neighbor or going to the store, buying the glass, and replacing the window yourself. (Catechism 366-367)

This idea is evident in criminal law. While the convicted may demonstrate a deep sorrow for the crime committed, he/she must still pay the debt owed to society. Ever wonder why prisons are called "Penitentiaries" or why the system is known as the Penal system. These words come from the Catholic concept of Penance. This is man's justice; how much more demanding is God's just punishment? While forgiveness takes away a sin, it does not remove all the problems and maladies that the sin caused. Delivered from sin, the penitent must still recover full spiritual health by "making satisfaction for" or expiating the sin. (Catechism 366)

And how does the Bible feel about satisfaction? Well, consider the following verses:

Therefore if thou bring thy gift to the altar, and there rememberest that thy brother hath ought against thee; leave thy gift before the altar, and go thy way; first be reconciled with thy brother, and then come and offer thy gift. Agree with thine adversary quickly, whilst thou art in the way with him; lest at any time the adversary deliver thee to the judge, and the judge deliver thee to the officer, and thou be cast into prison. Verily I say unto thee, thou shalt by no means come out thence till thou hast paid the uttermost farthing. (Matthew 5:23-26, KJV)

I suppose that one could argue that the judge mentioned up above is an earthly judge, and not God, the Father. But there is no name mentioned, and Jesus is speaking about gifts left on the altar. Sacrificial gifts on the altar are generally intended for God. It could also be argued that this warning is meant for just the Jews; however, most churches that I've ever attended, Catholic or Protestant, had an altar- either as an ornate place for the sacrifice of the Mass or a simple place at which to kneel and pray. Notice that Jesus says that we must pay the "uttermost farthing." Can you imagine the debts of those who never give a thought to making restitution for all the wrongs that they have done? While they may be forgiven, the acts themselves must be paid for. And if satisfaction is not given for one's sins in this life, then penance will be given in the afterlife.

Paul supports this idea in his second letter to the church at Corinth, when he writes, *"For we must appear before the judgment seat of Christ; that every one may receive the things done in His body, according to that he hath done, whether it be good or bad." (2 Corinthians 5:10, KJV)*

Catholics call these physical acts of penance "sin offerings" and remember the words of Peter, when he declares, *"And above all things have fervent charity among yourselves: for charity shall cover a multitude of sins." (1 Peter 4:8, KJV)*

Most importantly, our Lord Jesus Christ endorses the use of sin offerings in the Gospel, stating, *"For whosoever shall give you a cup of water to drink in my name, because ye belong to Christ, verily, I say unto you, he shall not lose his reward." (Mark 9:41, KJV)*

Here is an action that secures a reward. What is the reward? Well, consider that Christ came to earth to give us the ultimate gift, eternal life in paradise with our heavenly Father. So, obviously, an act of charity for the love of God helps us to pay to our "uttermost farthing."

Other forms of satisfaction include prayer, fasting, sacrificial giving of time, talent and treasure, public service, acts of spiritual and physical mercy, and self-denial. The degree of satisfaction is dependent upon the gravity of the offense. The scriptures say:

And that servant, which knew his lord's will, and prepared not himself, neither did according to his will, shall be beaten with many stripes. But he that knew not, and did commit things worthy of stripes shall be beaten with few stripes. For unto whomsoever much is given, of him shall be much required: and to whom men have committeth much, of him they will ask the more. (Luke 12:47-48, KJV)

Above all, we are expected to bear our cross and suffer with Christ, so that we may become co-heirs with Him. (Catechism 367) *Colossians 1:24, KJV*, says: *"Who now rejoice in my sufferings for you, fill up that which is behind of the afflictions of Christ in my flesh for His body's sake, which is the church:"*

These spiritual gifts are our sacrifice to God. Our catechism declares:

The satisfaction that we make for our sins, however, is not so much ours as though it were not done through Jesus Christ. We who can do nothing ourselves, as if just by ourselves, can do all things with the cooperation of 'Him who strengthens' us. Thus, man has nothing of which to boast, but all our boasting is in Christ...in whom we make satisfaction by bringing forth 'fruits that befit repentance.' These fruits have their efficacy from Him, by Him they are offered to the Father, and through Him they are accepted by the Father. (Catechism 367)

Indulgences

Sin is a rupture between an individual and God as well as a breach within the Church, herself. As a result, it carries with it a two-fold punishment: grave sins deprive us of communion with God and place our souls in danger of "eternal punishment" while simple mistakes demonstrate an unhealthy attachment to the world and must be atoned for or the individual risks temporal punishment. These punishments do not reflect God's vengeance toward the sinner as much as they are consequences of sin itself due to its very nature. A conversion born out of fervent charity or love can attain complete purification, which leaves no punishment, but generally speaking, when we gain remission from eternal punishment, the temporal punishment will remain.

An indulgence is a remission of the temporal punishment of sins whose guilt has been previously forgiven. Indulgences are partial or plenary, removing part or all of the temporal punishment of past forgiven sins. This is inextricably linked with the sacrament of Penance because it is through acts of penance that we pay for the wrongs that we have committed. When we have atoned, we are granted this remission before God through His trusted ministers of mercy and grace, the Church and her priests. This, again, comes through the Christ-given authority to Peter to loose or bind. (Catechism 370-371)

Indulgences are also gained through the fervent prayers of Mary and the saints on behalf of all the faithful who need indulgences. Unlike the Protestant world, Catholics see creation as an unending continuum where the prayers of the heavenly community can and do intervene for the good of those still on their journey to paradise. The benefits from their prayers are known collectively as the Church's Treasury. (Catechism 371)

Personal Reflections on Reconciliation

Hollywood loves to show the old image of the little black box with a formal, withdrawn priest, but the rite of Reconciliation is more "user-friendly" nowadays. While the anonymity is still preferred among the older, more traditional set, newer converts tend to meet with their priest face to face. You simply sit down and talk.

My first confession was anything but the "black box" experience. My priest was a little Burmese fellow who loved to laugh and joke. The rite took place at the rectory in a warm, comforting room with sunlight streaming through the window, spotlighting tiny little flecks of dust dancing in the air. And there was St. Francis in the corner, tending his injured animals. I didn't have that much to confess, except to say that I would like to be closer to God. The priest sat and quietly listened- his feet propped upon the desk in his office. It was a serious rite accomplished in a calming, relaxed way.

Another confession that I remember vividly was a tumultuous one. A couple of years after my confirmation, a young independent convert started working at my store.

Everything was fine, until she realized that I was a Catholic. Then, it became her sworn duty to bring me "back to the fold." Feeling singled out and attacked, I began to dread walking through the door for the worry of encountering her. When I came to the priest, it was really for comfort and reassurance, as I was a mental shambles. My Christianity had been invalidated, simply because I did not attend her church, nor see every issue the way she did. I remember how understanding and kind the priest seemed, as he told me of similar experiences at work when he had moved to the South. It was so good to share my pain and frustration, and this incident became a bonding experience with my Church. I left the sacrament with a strong sense of resolve and solidarity with other Catholics who were suffering as well.

As I have said, human beings have trouble letting go and forgiving themselves when they commit a grievous offense against God, even though it is certain that God has released them from their sin and washed its stain away. There is that horrible feeling of guilt that will not go away. I understand this all too well.

For close to fifteen years, I suffered from the guilt and shame of my long dark night, specifically my excursion into the occult and living with my husband before marriage. Having been free of these sins for over a decade, I simply could not leave my offenses and their guilt with God, although I felt that He had forgiven me. One morning Michael walked into our study and found me crying over my keyboard as I was writing this book. I still remember his reaction: ***"That's it. You need to talk to Father about this."***

I don't understand why people are so slow to go to the Sacrament of Penance. Every priest that I have ever been to for this rite has been generously merciful and never overly punitive. After all the tears and painful recollections, the priest gently, but firmly, separated me from my past. I cannot tell you how good that felt, to see the guilt, which had wounded me for so long, evaporate and disappear, like a nightmare in the face of the morning sun.

When I first became a Catholic, it was difficult to entrust a priest to my innermost thoughts and feelings. I wanted to believe that I did not need Penance on the level that it is proponed by Catholic theologians. However as I have begun maturing in my faith, I have learned the importance of this sacrament. The Sacrament of Penance is like a bath for the soul. You feel so clean inside that you spiritually squeak. Catholics aren't reborn just once, but every time they go and confess their sins to the listening ear and loving heart of a priest.

Unfinished Business

Before we begin this chapter, I would like to give my readers an interesting spiritual puzzle: As Christians, we must believe that embracing Jesus is how we reach heaven. This is a given and cannot be disputed as it comes directly from Christ who said that no one can come to the Father but by Him. Ok, what about those individuals who, through no fault of their own, never got the chance to make that decision? They lived and died with no knowledge of the scriptures? For that matter, what about the prophets and early heroes in the Old Testament? While they communed with God, the Father, they had no knowledge of Christ because Christ was not born yet. How can a loving God send millions to hell because they never had the chance to know Jesus?

Say you're a virtuous pagan (they do exist), and you never had the chance to hear the Gospel and come to know Christ as one of His Disciples. However, you embody all that is good and noble about humanity; you even seek God out in your own limited way. When you die, you expect to be received into Paradise, knowing that you have done your utmost to make a difference in this life. Does the Judeo-Christian God condemn you to hell, understanding that you were born, lived, and died, never having a chance in the first place? Does He say, **"You did your best, but were unfortunate never to hear the Gospel and convert. You didn't live in the right place and time. I'm sorry my son. You still must go to hell"?**

Humans would call that horribly unfair, and we often run short on mercy. God is infinitely just and infinitely merciful. Knowing what I have learned about His mercy, I doubt that He'd let that happen, but that's the position that many Protestant ministers hold. Never mind the fact that the person was honorable and just, even deeply spiritual, they still go to hell anyway.

Let me complicate things further by asking another question: Do you believe in ghosts? That question is a lot like asking someone if they believe in God. For the most part, there is no evidence that will convince a skeptic, or sway a believer. But ghosts are a part of almost every culture and race known to man. Ghost stories are universal in their power to enthrall and fire our imagination.

In many ways, these questions lay at the heart of our concept of the afterlife. They particularly boggle the Protestant mind. Now many ministers want us to believe that there's only just heaven and hell, and have gone so far as to declare that there is really no such thing as a ghost, that all "ghosts" are actually demons bent on trickery and leading God's people astray. While there should be no doubt in the existence of demons, to label all ghosts as demons in disguise is also wrong as it conflicts with biblical scripture. Why? Because, the Bible mentions at least one ghost by name:

> *Now Samuel was dead, and all Israel had lamented him, and buried him in Ramah, even in his own city. And Saul had put away those that had familiar spirits, and the wizards, out of the land.*
>
> *And the Philistines gathered themselves together, and came and pitched in Shunem: and Saul gathered all Israel together, and they pitched in Gilboa. And when Saul saw the host of the Philistines, he was afraid, and his heart greatly trembled. And when Saul inquired of the Lord, the Lord answered him not neither by dreams, nor by Urim, nor by prophets.*
>
> *Then said Saul unto his servants, 'Seek me a woman that hath a familiar spirit, that I may go to her, and enquire of her.'*
>
> *And his servant said to him, 'Behold, there is a woman that hath a familiar spirit at Endor.'*

> *And Saul disguised himself, and put on other raiment, and he went, and two men with him, and they came to the woman by night: and he said, 'I pray thee, divine unto me by the familiar spirit, and bring me him up, whom I shall name unto thee.'*
> *And the woman said unto him, 'Behold, thou knowest what Saul hath done, how he hath cut off those that have familiar spirits, and the wizards, out of the land: wherefore then layest thou a snare for my life, to cause me to die?*
> *And Saul sware to her by the Lord, saying, 'As the Lord liveth, there shall no punishment happen to thee for this thing.'*
> *When said the woman, 'Whom shall I bring up unto thee?'*
> *And he said, 'Bring me up Samuel.'*
> *And when the woman saw Samuel, she cried with a loud voice: and the woman spake to Saul, saying, 'Why hast thou deceived me? For thou art Saul.'*
> *And the king said unto her, 'Be not afraid: for what sawest thou?'*
> *And the woman said unto Saul, 'I saw God ascending out of the earth.'*
> *And he said unto her, 'What form is he of?'*
> *And she said, 'An old man cometh up; and he is covered with a mantle. And Saul perceived that it was Samuel, and he stooped with his face to the ground and bowed himself. (1 Samuel 28:3-14, KJV)*

Now, I want to make something absolutely clear. I am not trying to endorse witchcraft nor the conjuring of spirits. These practices are wrong and extremely dangerous; this I know from personal experience. It was wrong of Saul to consult the witch in the first place. However, conjured or not, we ***still*** have the spirit of Samuel the prophet appearing before Saul. He is clearly a ghost. The Bible does not say that this was a demon in the guise of Samuel. Instead, scripture declares Samuel dead from the beginning, then proceeds to describe Saul's ghostly encounter with the dead prophet.

Notice that the woman asked **"*Whom shall I bring up unto thee?*"** If the only spirit were that of Samuel, there would be no need to ask, would there? The obvious implication of those words is that there is a number of spirits loosed from their mortal bodies. And what is Samuel doing roaming around anyway? He was deeply devoted to God, a great holy man. He should be in heaven, but he is not. Here we have concrete scriptural evidence of what many Protestant ministers cannot accept: a soul trapped between heaven and hell, a ghost.

Ok, if we have ghosts, then where do we put them in the Christian universe? While they are tied to the earth, they are no longer living on the material plain. Heaven and hell are exclusive places, so it's extremely unlikely that people come and go from these destinations as they please. There must be a third state in the afterlife where souls linger before continuing their journey. This is what Catholics refer to as "Purgatory" or a place of cleansing where all traces of sin are purged away.

Why do we need a place of purging? Because many believers die without doing penance for their sins. As stated in the earlier chapter on the Sacrament of Penance, everything that we do wrong in this life has a price tag. Even though we are forgiven, we must still pay for what we have done. This is accomplished by prayer, seeking restitution with the person whom we've done wrong (if possible) or sacrificing our time, talent, and treasure with a loving, contrite heart. Penance is always encouraged in the mortal state to avoid or shorten one's time in purgatory in the afterlife.

Christ alludes to this third state when He speaks of grieving the Holy Spirit:

> *Wherefore I say unto you, all manner of sin and blasphemy shall be forgiven unto men: but the blasphemy against the Holy Ghost shall not be forgiven unto men. And whosoever speaketh a word against the son of man, it shall be forgiven him: but whosoever speaketh against the Holy Ghost, it shall not be forgiven him, neither in this world, neither in the world to come. (Matthew 12:31-32, KJV)*

If there is only heaven or hell, then why say ***"neither in the world to come?"*** Why not simply say that the person will be damned? The above-mentioned phrase implies that there is a place for the forgiveness of sins in the afterlife. No person needs forgiveness in heaven neither can he/she use it in hell. Hell is a place of everlasting torment where redemption is impossible. Yet, Peter tells us that Jesus preached to the dead:

> *For Christ also hath suffered for sins, the just for the unjust, that He might bring us unto God, being put to death in the flesh, but quickened by the Spirit: by which also He went and preached unto the spirits in prison; which were sometime disobedient, when once the long-suffering of God waited in the days of Noah, while the ark was a preparing, wherein few, that is, eight souls were saved by water...For this cause was the Gospel preached also to them that are dead, that they may be judged according to men in the flesh, but live according to God in the spirit. (1 Peter 3:18-20, 4:6, KJV)*

Looking at this passage, we see that this took place between our Lord's Crucifixion and Resurrection. These spirits cannot belong to living people because scripture says that they were around from the time of Noah. It also describes them as being imprisoned. Heaven is anything but a prison, and hell offers no way out. Why would Jesus preach, if not to offer salvation, which would be useless those who were eternally damned.

Catholics have retained the Jewish tradition of praying for the dead as an aid in hastening their time in purgatory. This tradition goes back at least to the time of the Maccabees, two hundred years before the birth of Christ. After a battle, Judah Machabeus found that many of his Jewish comrades to be wearing amulets to pagan gods when they were killed. Because of this, it was believed that God had allowed their deaths. The people were admonished to refrain from all sin, and a large sum of two thousand drachmae was collected and sent to Jerusalem for a sacrifice against the collective sin of Judah's fallen comrades:

> *For if he had not expected the fallen to rise again, it would have been superfluous and foolish to pray for the dead, whereas if he in view the splendid recompense reserved for those who make a pious end, the thought was holy and devout. This was why he had this atonement sacrifice offered for the dead, so that they might be released from their sin. (II Maccabees 12: 44-46, Jerusalem Bible)*

The above passage comes from the Deuterocanonical Books, which the Protestants call the Apocrypha; those extra seven books in the Old Testament which are not in the King James Version. I am not using them as scripture as much as I am documenting the fact that the Jews have prayed for the dead centuries before Christ came into the world.

Even though these events were recorded in Greek, in Egypt, we should note that they took place around Jerusalem. Today, Jews celebrate **Chanukah**, an eight day festival of light commemorating the "Miracle of the Maccabees," when the Temple flame continued to burn, throughout the siege of Jerusalem, even after it was supposed to have run out of oil. This prayer and almsgiving on behalf of the dead occurred after the city was liberated. (Choy 1)

So, by time of Jesus, prayer for the dead was a firmly entrenched belief within the Jewish faith. Yet, our Savior ***never*** corrects this belief. We're talking about salvation and the state of one's immortal soul. If this were a heretical teaching, it is certain that Christ would have directly addressed it as being so. We know that Jesus goes out of His way to show the error of the Jewish religion regarding marriage and divorce, religious hypocrisy, and meaningless pomp and ceremony of the Jewish priests and rabbis. But He says absolutely nothing negative about this practice, which was a palpable part of Judaism.

It still is today. Jews have ***shiv'a***, a seven-day period of mourning in which the bereaved do nothing but completely explore the grieving process. They remember, weep, and reflect over the life of the deceased, completely divorcing themselves from the world and everyday secular activities such as work, school, and housework. This practice harks back to when Joseph mourned his father Jacob for seven days and is required under Jewish law. The Hebrew word ***shiv'a*** means *"seven."* (Diamant 1)

Today, Jews still pray for departed souls. They celebrate the life of the individual and pray for that person's eternal peace. Here is an actual prayer for the dead, the ***Eli Malei Rachamim***:

God of compassion,
Grant perfect peace in Your sheltering Presence,
Among the holy and pure, who shine in the brightness of the firmament.
To the soul of our dear_____, who has gone to his eternal rest.
God of compassion, remember all his worthy deeds in the land of the living.
May his soul be bound up in the bond of everlasting life.
May God be his inheritance.
May he rest in peace.
And let us answer: Amen. (Beliefnet.com 2/04/03)

The Apostle Paul endorses the practice of prayer for the dead when he prays for his friend, Onesiphorus in the second book of Timothy:

> *The Lord give mercy unto the house of Onesiphorus; for he oft refreshed me, and was not ashamed of my chain: but when he was in Rome, he sought me out very diligently, and found me. The Lord grant unto him that he might find mercy of the Lord in that day: and in how many things he ministered unto me at Ephesus, thou knowest very well. (2 Timothy 1:16-18, KJV)*

If we analyze the way that Paul is speaking about Onesiphorus, he is talking about his friend in the past tense, in the same manner as the Jewish prayer mentioned above the scriptural passage. Paul seems to separate the man, Onesiphorus, from the house of Onesiphorus. This is evidence that Onesiphorus is no longer living. The Apostle also asks for God's mercy on behalf of his friend, which hints that Paul does not believe that Onesiphorus died completely cleansed of his sins and their stains. But wouldn't this prayer be in vain if there is only heaven and hell, and no purgatory?

Purgatory and prayer for the dead have left curious traces in the Protestant world. There is, of course, the belief in ghosts that many Protestants have. (Although, some only admit to it on a one to one basis.) We also have the famous "R.I.P." which has been loosely translated "Rest in Peace." Originally, the letters meant **Requiescat in pace** or *"May He/She Rest in Peace,"* an implied prayer. Have you ever heard someone mention a name and then say, *"God rest his/her soul"?* It's not just a saying; it's a prayer. There is a wish for that person's spiritual welfare. Listen to the words and you will hear the silent *"may."*

And just as Paul does in the previous passage, Protestant ministers, who would ordinarily reject the belief in purgatory, can often be heard praying for the dead at funerals. Witness comments like *"Lord, please accept your servant...."* or *"Father, look with kindness upon our brother/ sister..."* This is a powerful example of praying for the dead. Any minister who believes that there is only heaven or hell should refrain from saying those words. Pray for the family and the community, but that person has already gone to wherever they were headed. Lay flowers on the casket, throw dirt on the grave, and walk away.

Catholics believe that prayer for the dead is a good and honorable thing. This is often accompanied with the sacrifice of the Mass (Holy Eucharist). When the bread becomes the Body of Christ, all kinds of mercies to the spiritual realm are released. Heaven comes down, and we have a real encounter with Christ, who is truly present. When attending Mass, the congregation will often hear it is being held for the repose of some believer's soul. This is usually accompanied by a sacrificial donation of funds to the Church by that person's family or a part of the faith community. However, anyone can ask for the congregation's prayers for a dead loved one without a donation when the congregation voices its petitions in the Mass, whether aloud or in silence. And when Catholics attend Mass every November 2nd, All Souls Day, they set aside time to pray and honor departed love ones without excessive giving.

How powerful are prayers for the dead and the Mass? Well, let's consider one famous ghost story. According to legend, the small town of Wizard's Clip (also called Cliptown or Middleway) in West Virginia was named after the antics of a particularly nasty poltergeist. It was once called Smithfield until a man, Adam Livingstone, settled within the region in the late 1700s. Adam hated and feared Catholics. So, when a stranger lay dying in his home, begging for a Catholic priest for "Last Rites," he refused to let any member of the Catholic clergy enter his home. That action had an awful price tag.

First of all, Livingstone's animals died mysteriously with no trace of injury or disease. Then, his home became the scene of smashed windows, broken dishes, fires, and damaged fences. But what earned the town its name was the ghost's snipping and cutting of all clothing and fabric in the house, leaving crescent-shaped holes and gashes. This misery continued for seven years despite the best efforts of ministers and folk magicians.

Desperate, Livingstone contacted a local Catholic priest named Father Dennis Cahill. The priest came, blessed the house, and offered prayers for the dead. This made the poltergeist much quieter; but when Mass was finally said at Livingstone's home, the ghost left completely- taking the family's cutting shears and leaving a sum of money that had been "mislaid." Mr. Livingstone was so impressed that both he and his family became Catholic and gave thirty-five acres of land to the Church. "The Chapel of the Poor Souls," a sanctuary dedicated to the repose of the dead, would later be built in 1923. While some dispute the origin of the poltergeist, saying that the trouble followed Livingstone from his original home in Pennsylvania, it's interesting to note that it was prayer for the dead and the Mass that brought peace to the Livingstone home. (Spaeth 221-225)

I learned long ago that it is dangerous to call or conjure spirits; however, there are things that a Christian can legitimately do to help souls who are trapped between heaven and hell besides the normal avenues of prayer, alms giving and the Eucharist. Nana always said that ghosts had unfinished business with God, and it was our duty to help them settle their accounts. I've heard of specters that were tied to their homes and possessions because they were so fond of what they had once had that they were unable to let go. Others were connected to lost treasure that was never used, but hoarded away. Many spirits like these find peace when they realize a possession is in good hands or the treasure has been found and put to good use.

Then, there are ghosts of conscience, restless because of the injustice and cruelty inflicted upon them. Of this, I have firsthand experience. For the most part, my heritage is deeply devout and dedicated toward the service of humanity in one way or another. However, we, like everyone else, have events and people that we're not that proud of. One of the darkest chapters in our familial history occurred over two hundred years ago with the torture and death of an African slave. Since then, she has haunted our family. Often dehumanized and maligned in books and on TV, few people actually know her origin.

As one who is privy to who she was and how she died, I have sought to correct the popular myths and folk-tales by sharing her legend with as many people as often as possible. It is my firm conviction that she will continue to haunt our family until the crime is acknowledged, and her humanity is restored. This blends beautifully with Catholicism. As a Protestant, I had no place to put my family ghost in the Christian universe, but Catholic doctrine endorses a third state in the afterlife, which could very well be the spectral realm. Today, I pray for Katya's soul, sacrificially give in her name, and promote her true identity.

There are other agendas that tie the spectral world to us. Apparitions have been known to warn the living of impending danger, even reach out, from beyond the void to save lives. But for every good spirit, there are troubled and confused souls who can harm. And let us not forget demons that enjoy misleading and harming humans. This is why channeling and ouija boards are so problematic. Besides being anathema to God, channeling allows spirits to take over the body, mind, and soul. What happens when and if the spirit refuses to leave or worse, if a demon takes seat? This is called possession.

Exorcism

Science states that for every reaction, there is an equal and opposite reaction. Religions everywhere have always embraced a close cousin of that law, the belief that good is balanced with evil. The law of inverses is a universal axiom that transcends all barriers and is present in all cultures.

While most Christians have no problem believing in angels, some have trouble with their opposites. But we must remember that Satan and his minions are the "fallen" versions of the angels that we love so much. And just as heavenly messengers and protectors seek to promote God's Kingdom, so the demonic world's objective is its perversion and ultimate destruction. Theologians have often seen a possessed person as Lucifer's "ultimate weapon" in this conflict.

Exorcism is the expulsion of an evil spirit or demon from an individual. A variety of Christian faiths have different methods, many of which are performed in special services or informally within someone's home. Some other names for Protestant forms of exorcism are "deliverances" or "pleading the blood of Jesus." The latter term is often used as a cleansing ritual for homes and buildings as well and was the common term used in my father's old church. But all Christian rites originate from Christ, who not only cast out demons, but also gave His Disciples the authority to do likewise in His name. Perhaps the most powerful example of exorcism in biblical times comes from the Gospel of Luke:

> *And they arrived at the country of the Gadarenes, which is over against Galilee. And He went forth to land, there met him out of the city a certain man, which had devils long time, and ware no clothes, neither abode in any house, but in the tombs. When he saw Jesus, he cried out and fell down before him, and with a loud voice said, "What have I to do with thee, Jesus, thou Son of God most high? I beseech thee, torment me not."*
>
> *(For He had commanded the unclean spirit to come out of the man. For often times it had caught him: and he was kept bound with chains and in fetters, and he brake the bands, and was driven of the devil into the wilderness.)*
>
> *And Jesus asked him, "What is thy name?"*
>
> *And he said, "Legion": because many devils were entered into him.*
>
> *And they besought Him that He would not command them to go out into the deep. And there was a herd of many swine feeding on the mountain: they besought Him that He would suffer them to enter into them. And He suffered them. Then went the devils out of the man, and entered into the swine: and the herd ran violently down a steep place into the lake, and were choked.*
>
> *And when they that fed them saw what was done, they fled, and went and told it in the city and in the country. Then they went out to see what was done; and came to Jesus, and found the man, out of whom the devils were departed, sitting at the feet of Jesus, clothed, and in his right mind: and they were afraid. (Luke 8:26-35, KJV)*

So, we see that exorcism has a very biblical history. However, the Protestant Reformation frowned upon this practice. (Martin Luther linked it with the power of Rome.) This aversion, coupled with the birth of modern science, brought skepticism that the practice was needed at all, even questioning the belief in the devil as personified in the New Testament. Today, most psychologists (and many theologians) dismiss possession as a form of mental illness that science has yet to fully explain.

While there is no doubt that much of humanity's aberrant behavior can be classified as mental illnesses or conditions, there remains a number of unexplained cases that continue to frustrate those who completely rely on scientific reason and logic to explain all psychic phenomena. There are two well-documented instances of exorcism, which occurred during the twentieth century.

The first, which happened in 1906, concerned an orphan at the St. Michael's Mission in Natal, South Africa. The account, written by a nun, tells of a young girl named Clara, being able to speak languages that she had no previous knowledge of and demonstrate clairvoyance by revealing the most intimate secrets and transgressions of people with whom she had contact. Clara could not bear to be around blessed objects and seemed imbued with extraordinary strength and ferocity, often hurling the nuns about the convent rooms and beating them up. Her cries had a savage bestiality that astonished those around her.

An attending nun wrote, ***"No animal had ever made such sounds. Neither the lions of East Africa nor angry bulls. At times, it sounded like a veritable herd of wild beasts orchestrated by Satan had formed a hellish choir."***

Two priests were chosen to perform the exorcism, which lasted for two days. Clara's first response was to knock the Bible from the priest's hands and grab his stole from his shoulders and attempt to choke him with it. But, in the end, the demon was forced out and the girl was healed.

The second account is probably the most famous of all cases concerning exorcism and is believed to be the basis for William Peter Blatty's best-selling book, **The Exorcist**. In January, 1949, a thirteen-year-old boy, living in Mt. Rainier, Maryland became involved in satanic possession after trying to contact his deceased aunt (with whom he had been very close) via an ouija board. His home became the scene of many alarming events. Whenever the youth was at home, unexplained noises would reverberate from the attic, furniture would move of its own accord, objects flew, and witnesses reported hearing the sound of marching feet. Once, a portrait of Christ fell off the wall. Forty-eight witnesses would later come forward to substantiate this case and the unbelievable incidents that occurred. The boy was examined by both medical and psychiatric doctors, who could offer no valid explanation for these disturbing events. Then, the frightened parents turned to their Lutheran minister for spiritual aid. At a loss, their clergyman told them that there was nothing that he could do, that there was evil at work in the teen, and their best solution would be to seek the help of a Catholic priest because Catholics knew about that sort of thing.

The first exorcism was conducted by Father Albert Hughes at Georgetown University Hospital, a Jesuit institution. Within five minutes of beginning the ritual, the boy stabbed the priest, inflicting a wound that took stitches. Thus ended the initial attempt to rid the demon. The youth was released and sent home to be with his family. A few days later, the teenager began screaming hysterically while in the bathroom. The parents rushed into the room to find the words "St. Louis" written in blood upon the boy's chest. St. Louis was where the dead aunt had lived. The family then moved to St. Louis to stay with relatives. At this time, the case came before Father William Bowdern, pastor of St. Louis University- another Jesuit institution. After obtaining permission from his bishop, Bowdern would finally succeed where his predecessor had failed.

After Bowdern's initial exorcism, the teen was checked into another hospital run by the Alexian Religious Order. This began an ordeal that would continue for six weeks. Father Walter Halloran, SJ, who assisted, remembers time periods that lasted as quickly as a few hours or as long as most of a day. Halloran recalls that the hospital bed began shaking violently as holy water was sprinkled on the youth and that at one point, a bottle of holy water went sailing in mid air, just missing his head. Another vivid memory the Father Halloran has was of the word "evil" appearing on the teen's body during one prayer session, saying that it was a definite word, not some phenomenon up for personal interpretation.

The demon, when asked when it would leave, told Bowdern and Halloran that it would only do so when the boy uttered the proper words. At last the teenager said, **Christus, Domini** or **"Christ, Lord."** At that moment, the whole hospital echoed with a thunderclap. Then boy told them, *"It's over. It's over."* And it was truly over. The family, now at peace, relocated to their home in Mt. Rainier, and the youth returned to normal life. After over fifty years, this man (whose identity remains a closely guarded secret) has no memories of his possession.

While most psychologists would like to dismiss both these cases as that of mental illness, they cannot fully explain why both people never had a relapse. Clara and the Maryland youth went on to lead normal, healthy existences, whereas schizophrenia and other dissociative disorders are often lifelong and require extensive psychiatric treatment. In the early to middle part of the twentieth century, people were committed to sanitariums for these conditions. Yet, in both cases, there seems to be no recorded residual effects. Full-blown mental illness rarely (if ever) goes away on its own.

We have explored the circumstances surrounding two of the most documented cases of exorcism; now let's look at the Catholic rite of exorcism itself. Catholic exorcism is covered in the **Rituale Romanum**, which was instituted in 1614. This ritual has specific tests to discern whether the individual is truly possessed or not. For instance, the exorcist's assistant closely observes the person's behavior during various prayers.

Few people know that the Latin prayers are often punctuated by pieces of secular Latin texts such as **The War Diaries of Julius Caesar**. As few people speak fluent Latin and can tell where one starts and the other ends, those "possessed" will assume that everything that the priest is saying is a prayer and react appropriately if they are mentally ill or trying to get attention.

However, a truly possessed individual will relax, even if only for a split second. You see, demons cannot bear to hear prayer or the name of Jesus. They cause their prey to writhe in agony, and cannot help but ease up when the torture temporarily subsides. The person who assists is watching for that sign which is a dead give away that evil is truly at work. The use of prayer, holy water and blessed objects is designed to goad the demon into a confrontation and to make it so uncomfortable that the evil will have to flee.

Another important part of exorcism is getting the entity to reveal its name through the use of prayer and the power of Christ. This is important as knowing the demon's name places it at a spiritual disadvantage. In the ancient world, learning a name implied gaining power over its owner. Then, the unclean spirit is forced out by the power of faith and prayer.

Exorcism is a deadly battle of wills, which should never be left to the untrained. Even most priests are unprepared for such a toe-to-toe confrontation. So, the Roman Catholic Church has specially trained people to conduct the Rituale Romanum. Exorcisms are a team effort that no priest may attempt alone. This ensures a greater degree of success as each person's individual faith increases and strengthens the whole collective faith of the group.

It may be interesting to note that in this Catholic bashing age, no form of Christian exorcism is as old, or thoroughly binding as that of the Roman Catholic rite. Indeed, when people think of exorcism, they immediately associate Catholicism with it. If we are the supposed "whore of Babylon," then this would be a severe conflict of interest, would it not? Consider that the Satanic Church is a dark reflection of the Roman Church. It has a "black" (Satanic) pope and a similar structure to Catholicism. Satanists do not concern themselves with creating an unsavory imitation of any of the Protestant denominations.

__Special Note:__ All information regarding both of the cases of exorcism mentioned in this chapter as well as the information on the Rituale Romanum can be found in the History Channel's segment, Exorcism, directed by Joel Rizor and produced by Charlie Maday for Weller/Grossman Productions in 1999, which aired September 5, 2002.

Addressing a Famous Protestant Myth

Before we begin this section, I want to make it clear that it is not my intention to single any particular group or denomination out for ridicule. I attack concepts and beliefs, not people. I love my fellow believers in Christ and acknowledge that they are Christians, no matter what denomination they hail from. Anything I write is always meant to instruct.

As I have said at the beginning of this book, I am writing these pages for release, not to win some popularity contest. And this chapter will assure me that I will never be popular, especially where I live. But I feel that I would be remiss if this matter were not properly addressed because its very nature conflicts with the sacrament of Penance.

Over the years, I have often been cross-examined as to whether I embrace the concept of "once saved, always saved." Even as a Protestant, I felt this idea was contrary to what I understood Christianity was about. Christianity involves a constant struggle between good and evil, between our walk with Christ and the snares and temptations of sin. The idea of making a one-time profession of faith, then proceeding to disregard and break every Christian tenet, while believing that everything is just fine, has always been a foolish notion. "Once saved, always saved" is nice because the person feels freed from the spiritual consequences of sin (mainly hell and damnation), but it is an extremely dangerous assumption. What about the laws of cause and effect? What about making restitution for past wrongs? What about God's eternal justice? Penance embraces continual rebirth, reformation, restitution, and justice while "once saved, always saved" does not.

For example, a young man gets "saved" at the age of twelve. He is baptized and set aside as belonging to God. He tries to walk with Jesus for a few years. But Christian standards are very high, and soon he finds himself slipping into a life of sin. His sexual drives are beginning to peak, and he wants to try different thrills. So, sex and drugs enter the picture. His wild life gets crazier in college, where so many kids fall into an abyss of indiscriminate sex and binge drinking.

By his twenties, he feels relieved that he is free of disease or an unwanted child, but now he's jaded. As a businessman, he uses people, and then throws them away like garbage. He is married, but that ring on his hand means nothing. There are perks to being rich and powerful; women gravitate toward him like they're magnetized. He discards them when they stop being entertaining.

He gets older, and his children lose any respect they have for him as he has no integrity. But, they, in their contempt, continue the life he has lived, for they know no better. By fifty-two, forty years after his shining moment, he dies "in the saddle" with his favorite mistress. He has spent the greater part of his life using and abusing others, and he has trained his children to do the same. His life is littered with victims, people like the girl he convinced to get an abortion in college or the business partner that he gleefully betrayed when it suited him. However, as he dies, he is sure that he took care of God and that eternal life stuff at the age of twelve. His minister assured him that he wouldn't have to worry anymore. One profession of faith and he goes to heaven, without a care?

Now, some may argue that this man was never truly a Christian, but that's simply not true. Remember that he gave the Christian life a serious try for at least a few years; he was sincere, but he fell from grace and never got back up again. Even worse, he took his family with him. We often concentrate on God as a being of peace, love, and mercy, but forget that He is also just. And while we belong to Jesus and no one may pluck us from his hand, we, being free moral agents, can, at anytime, "jump ship."

Catholicism teaches that we must constantly repent, confess, and rededicate our lives to Christ. It declares that we must atone for every sin, whether in this life or the next. At the end of his life, this man could've repented, and confessed his sins at the last minute, and been eligible for eternal life- after he paid for all the wrongs he had committed in life in the state that we call purgatory. But for the Protestant who believes that a one-time profession of faith will save him from hell and damnation, that clever delusion will be all that he has.

Delusion? Why such a harsh word for the concept of "once saved, always saved?" The reason that I chose that word is because there are a number of biblical passages that conflict with this idea. First, let's have look at the Gospel of John. Jesus, Himself, declares:

> *I am the true vine, and my Father is the husbandman. Every branch in me that beareth not fruit He taketh away: and every branch that beareth fruit, He purgeth it, that it may bring forth more fruit.*
>
> *Now ye are clean through the word which I have spoken unto you. Abide in me and I in you. As the branch cannot bear fruit of itself, except that it abide in the vine; no more can ye, except ye abide in me.*
>
> *I am the vine, ye are the branches: he that abideth in me, and I in him, the same bringeth forth much fruit: for without me ye can nothing. If a man abide not in me, he is cast forth as a branch, and is withered; and men gather them, and cast them into the fire, and they are burned.*
>
> *If ye abide in me, and my words abide in you, ye shall ask what ye will, and it shall be done unto you. Herein is my Father glorified, that ye bear much fruit; so shall ye be my Disciples. (John 15:1-8, KJV)*

Can any of us truly say that the man, mentioned earlier, bore any spiritual fruit? Maybe he did, once, but bearing fruit must be a life long pursuit. Ask yourself, how could Jesus welcome this person into heaven and call him a "good and faithful servant" when this man spent his whole adult life serving himself, and never God. He left the Christian path and went his own way.

Think of those forty years, wasted and devoid of any spiritual value. Think of the damage that he did to those around him. Whereas he could've been a productive vine for Christ, he became a dead limb. Anyone who has ever pruned a tree or bush knows what happens to dead limbs. They are cut away from the living portion, then burned or ground into mulch. How many of us want that sort of spiritual fate?

Remember that St. James reiterates Christ's words in His attitude toward the relationship between faith and works:

> *What doth it profit, my brethren, though a man saith he hath faith, and have not works? Can faith save him? If a brother or sister be naked, and destitute of daily food, and one of you say unto them, 'Depart in peace, be ye warmed and filled;' notwithstanding ye give them not those things which are needful to the body; what doth it profit?*
>
> *Even so faith, if it hath not works, is dead, being alone. Yea, a man may say,' Thou hast faith, and I have works: shew me thy faith without thy works, and I will shew thee my faith by my works.' Thou believest that there is one God; thou doest well: the devils also believe and tremble.*
>
> *But wilt thou know, 'O vain man, that faith without works is dead. Was not Abraham our father justified by works, when he had offered Isaac his son upon the altar? Seest thou how faith wrought with his works, and by works was faith made perfect? And the scripture was fulfilled which saith, 'Abraham believed God, and it was imputed unto him for righteousness and he was called the Friend of God.'*
>
> *Ye see then how that by works a man is justified, and not by faith only. Likewise was Rahab, the harlot, justified by works, when she had received messengers and had sent them out another way. For as the body without the spirit is dead, faith without works is dead also. (James 2:14-26, KJV)*

Looking at both of these passages, it becomes easy to see that if a person does not live the Christian life, his faith is dead. He bears no fruit, and as such, will be pruned away from the Body of Christ and thrown on the fire. These are not my words, but Holy Scripture. Remember the words of the Apostle Paul, who also spoke of Christians damning themselves:

> *Wherefore whosoever shall eat this bread, and drink this cup of the Lord unworthily, shall be guilty of the body and blood of the Lord. But let a man examine himself and so eat of that bread and drink of that cup. For he that eateth and drinketh unworthily, eateth and drinketh damnation to himself, not discerning the Lord's body. For this cause, many are weak and sickly among you and many sleep. (I Corinthians 11:27-30, KJV)*

No one but the members of the Christian community would celebrate the Lord's Supper, so Paul is addressing Christians when he warns of damnation. But if a Christian can damn him/herself, then "once saved, always saved" cannot stand as a Christian tenet. This belief says that no one, not even the believer in question, can remove him/herself from the hand of Christ. According to Paul, that is simply not true. Paul also warns of a great apostasy or falling away of believers in his second letter to the church at Thessalonica:

> *Now we beseech you, brethren, by the coming of our Lord Jesus Christ, and by our gathering together unto Him. That ye be not soon shaken in mind, or be troubled, neither by spirit, nor by word, nor by letter as from us, as that day of Christ is at hand.*
>
> *Let no man deceive you by any means: for that day shall come, except there come a falling away first, and that man of sin be revealed, the son of perdition: who opposeth and exalteth himself above all that is called God, or that is*

worshipped; so he as God, sitteth in the temple of God, shewing himself that he is God. (2 Thessalonians 2:1-4, KJV)

It is clear that Paul is speaking of the end of time with his description of the Antichrist. He declares that there will be a great falling away first- before this happens. Again, he is addressing Christians in his warning. But how can one fall away, if "once saved, always saved" were true? It would be impossible for the apostasy to occur in the first place if every believer were unable to be separated from God. Another example of Christians in spiritual peril lies in the Book of Revelation, Chapter 3. The church of Sardis is warned when the scriptures say:

And unto the angel of the Church in Sardis write: These things saith he that hath the seven spirits of God, and the seven stars; I know thy works, that thou hast a name, that thou livest, and art dead. Be watchful and strengthen the things which remain that are ready to die: for I have not found thy works perfect before God.
Remember therefore how thou hast received and heard, and hold fast, and repent. If therefore thou shalt not watch, I will come on thee as a thief, and thou shalt not know what hour I will come upon thee.
Thou hast a few names even in Sardis which have not defiled their garments; and they shall walk with me in white: for they are worthy. (Revelation 3:1-4, KJV)

First of all, these Christians (as a whole) are told that they're spiritually dead. How can the spiritual dead enter Heaven? Spiritual death is a condition for eternal damnation. But, a few are acknowledged as being worthy to walk with Christ in white. While the majority has lost its way, there are followers who are steadfast in their commitment to their faith. If the "once saved, always saved" tenet truly holds, then all of the Church of Sardis would be spiritually living and worthy to walk in white. Remember they received and heard God, but this was not enough. Those who have become dead in sin are told that they must repent to become spiritually alive again or face God, unprepared for His righteous judgment.

But Paul's most vehement passage against the tenet of "once saved, always saved" lies in the Book of Hebrews; he condemns those who believe that a one-time profession of faith insures eternal life. Paul writes:

For if we sin willfully after that we have received the knowledge of the truth, there remaineth no more sacrifice for sins, but a certain fearful looking for of judgment and fiery indignation, which shall devour the adversaries. He that despised Moses' law died without mercy under two or three witnesses: of how much sorer punishment, suppose ye, shall he be thought worthy, who hath trodden under the foot the Son of God, and hath counted the blood of the covenant, wherewith he was sanctified, an unholy thing, and hath done despite unto the Spirit of grace? For we know Him that hath said, "Vengeance belongeth unto me, I will recompense, saith the Lord." And again, "The Lord shall judge His people."
It is a fearful thing to fall into the hands of the living God. (Hebrews 10:26-31, KJV)

The Apostle Paul views those who willfully sin as trampling upon Christ Himself and desecrating the very blood by which they were redeemed. Any punishment under the Mosaic Code will pale beside the wrath incurred for this offense.

Peter compares those who fall away to dogs and pigs- animals who were (and still are) despised and seen as unclean to the Semitic world. He states:

For if after they have escaped the pollutions of the world through the knowledge of the Lord and Saviour Jesus Christ, they are again entangled therein, and overcome, the latter end is worse with them than the beginning. For it had been better for them not to known the way of righteousness, than, after they had known it, to turn from the holy commandment delivered unto them. But it has happened unto them according to the true proverb, "The dog is turned to his own vomit again; and the sow that was washed to her wallowing in the mire." (2 Peter 2:20-22, KJV)

Finally, the Book of Revelation confirms that names that are in the Lamb's Book of Life may also be removed.

For I testify unto every man that heareth the words of the prophecy of this book, if any man shall add unto these things, God shall add unto him the plagues that are written in the book: and if any man shall take away from the words of the book of this prophecy, God shall take away his part out of the Book of Life, and out of the Holy City, and from the things that are written in this book. (Revelation 22:18-19, KJV)

Christians have often spoken of the Lamb's Book of Life as being the confirmation of those who are redeemed and those who are not. If a name can be removed from it's pages, then a Christian can lose salvation, fall away, and be damned to hell, and once saved, always saved can never stand as a legitimate tenet of Christianity.

These passages clearly show that Christians can, indeed, damn themselves after a one-time religious epiphany. As stated before, salvation is the goal of a lifetime of journeying with Christ, and our faith does not give us "carte blanche" to do anything we please afterward. Our spiritual walk lasts a lifetime, demanding a disciplined mind and heart coupled with yielding one's will to the power and working of the Holy Spirit. When we stray from the path, we place our souls in spiritual jeopardy and are unfit to "walk in white" as the Book of Revelation says.

You speak to me,
And I hear your words echo in the silence.
You, who conquered sin, death and hell,
Say I am forgiven, and I weep with joyful tears.
Knitted together, whole once more.
-The Author

<u>Salvation: Catholicism versus Protestant Views</u>

The field of nursing is almost "the family business." My dad was a Licensed Practical Nurse as is my sister, and both my mother and I were Certified Nursing Assistants. Over the years, we've collected many humorous stories and anecdotes. One of my father's favorites really stands out. He was doing his clinicals at our local hospital when a young girl in labor was admitted to obstetrics. Dad placed her on a stretcher and left her side, long enough to find a room. Upon returning, he found the child had been born. With the baby out, all that was left were the postpartum procedures. It was an exceptionally quick birth.

Anyone who knows anything about children will agree that the young mother was indeed blessed. Most births involve hours of labor and even tremendous pain. I can remember hearing about my eldest sister, Lela, who suffered for thirty-six hours with her first son. Lela's experience in childbirth was not a quick feat but a long session of pull and strain on her body.

The differences between these two births have a lot in common with the ways that Protestants and Catholics look at salvation and "being born again." Protestants have an instantaneous view of salvation. For many, being "born again" is an event. They are fond of asking, *"Are you saved?"* or *"When did you become a Christian?"* Moreover, some radicals seem more concerned with the time and date of a conversion and care less about the fact the individual may share a belief in Christ with them.

The problem for most Catholics is that they really can't remember an exact time or date to satisfy this question. And sadly, many Catholics have left the Church because someone convinced them that their faith was not genuine because there was no great moment that they could point to and say, *"Yes, that's where it happened!"*

But conversion is really a matter of the heart. There are countless Protestants who go through the motions of their faith and never truly connect with Christ just as there are Catholics who never connect due to lack of attention to their faith at critical moments. Maybe they goofed off in catechism class or their parents were less than devout. Whatever it was helped to warp and twist their childhood image of Catholicism. And in their ignorance, these improperly taught Catholics are vulnerable to doubts planted by other well-meaning denominations.

But properly trained Catholics should know Christ as their Savior, accept His healing forgiveness and acknowledge His lordship. These are the basic conditions for being "saved." Any Catholic who doubts their commitment to Christ needs to go back to the words of the Catholic Mass, which has become a great source of comfort for me when other Christians make me doubt my faith. I dwell on the scriptures and Gospel readings. I focus on the Nicene Creed, Holy Eucharist, and remember the words of the Greater Gloria:

Glory to God in the highest,
And on earth peace to people of good will.
We praise you, we bless you, we glorify you,
We give thanks for your great glory,
Lord God, Heavenly King,
O God, Almighty Father.
Lord Jesus Christ, Only Begotten Son,
Lord God, Lamb of God, Son of the Father,
You take away the sins of the world.
Have mercy on us.
You take away the sins of the world.
Receive our prayer.
You are seated at the right hand of the Father,
Have mercy on us.
For you ALONE are the holy one. You ALONE are the Lord.
You ALONE are the most high, Jesus Christ.
With the Holy Spirit, in the glory of God the Father. Amen.

That says it all. Those words leave the mind and soul cleansed of doubt, and the world and its chaos fade away. Ex-Catholics who seem so convinced that we are non-Christians had better go back and look again. Were they deaf, dumb, and blind through the Mass? The scriptures are there; the Creed is there, and most importantly, we are given the gift of Holy Eucharist, which is the body, blood, soul, and divinity of Christ, a sacred blessing that many of our Protestant brothers and sisters will never know. The only thing left for the individual is to believe. Believe the scriptures. Believe the prayers. Believe in the Divine Presence. Believe in the power of Christ to forgive our sins. Otherwise it's a waste of time and being a Christian can never happen. When a Catholic walks away from the beauty and power of the Mass, I pity them and look upon them as confused. We should never let a battle of semantics drive us from Mother Church.

So, how does Catholicism look at Christian rebirth and salvation? We see it as a lifelong process in which God slowly refashions an individual. While becoming a Christian can happen in a matter of seconds, that person must war with his/her old nature and conquer personal demons with the help of the holy Spirit. Contrary to popular belief, this is the biblical stance.

Let's look at Jesus' Disciples. An angel did not come down, touch their foreheads and make them perfect saints all at once. Instead, they learned from the mouth of God incarnate for three years. Even so, the Disciples' faith did not truly take shape until Pentecost when they were filled with the Holy Spirit. When each man chose to follow Christ, he was initiating the first step in being born again, the first labor pain. But, the Disciples did not truly leave the spiritual womb until their lives were finished on earth. From Pentecost, they grew into the pillars of the Church that we know them to be and continued living, learning, and growing in the Lord, This process was not instantaneous but ongoing. Theologians love to point to the conversion of the Apostle Paul as being instantaneous. Yes, Paul's conversion is quicker than in the case of the Disciples; however, he also describes battling his old nature. Paul says:

I find then a law, that, when I would do good, evil is present with me. I delight in the law of God after the inward man: but I see another law in my members, warring against the law of my mind, and bringing me into captivity to the law of sin which is in my members. O wretched man that I am! Who shall deliver from the body of this death? (Romans 7:21-24, KJV)

This passage does not support the belief in instant salvation. If Paul were beyond the power of his sinful state, there would be only one nature, not two opposing ones. In 1 Corinthians, Paul compares his life to a race and worries about his own possible spiritual failure. He writes:

Know ye not that they which run in a race run all, but one receiveth the prize? So run, that ye may obtain. And every man that striveth for the mastery is temperate in all things. Now they do it to obtain a corruptible crown; but we an incorruptible. I therefore so run, not as uncertainly; so fight I, not as one that beateth the air: but I keep under my body, and bring it into subjection: lest by any means, when I have preached to others, I myself should be a castaway. (1 Corinthians 9:24-27, KJV)

Paul compares the Christian's journey to that of a race. If the prize of eternal life is gained through being "instantly saved," then why use the analogy of a race? Although races are called events, their very nature involves a beginning, a middle state, and a final outcome. In effect, races are processes. And the word "race" implies the possibility of losing. With instantaneous salvation, there is no possibility of failure or loss and Paul's analogy of the spiritual race is improper.

Another example of instantaneous salvation is the dying thief on the cross next to Christ. Yes, he joins Jesus in paradise that very day, but to be fair, the thief's conversion could never be tested and fall prey to temptation.

Even if a person has had a grand epiphany or spiritual conversion in their life that was soul changing, there were events and circumstances (some maybe too small to register) that led up to that conversion. Despite the evils in Western society, it is permeated with Judeo-Christian concepts that weave their way through daily life- even if only in a loose fashion. I don't think that most Christians were raised by pagans in a remote corner of the globe and only heard the word "Jesus" at the time they converted. God slowly works in our lives using diverse elements to prepare us for such epiphanies.

But waiting for the bells and whistles of a grand epiphany can be dangerous. While those moments can provide clarity, real Christianity demands perseverance and discipline. Human nature makes it extremely difficult (if not impossible) to go from being the worst creature ever produced to spiritual perfection in one quick change. The problem with "instant Christianity" is the idea of instant sainthood that goes with it. When (not if) a person falters, there can be humiliation and doubt about their conversion itself. We forget that emotions (or the lack there of) can bedevil an individual. A spiritual "dry spell" can raise questions. Was it real? Did I truly get saved? Or am I fooling myself? People have a tendency of believing that their personal demons will all vanish with one climactic event and it simply is not so. If anything, things usually get worse. After all, the Devil needs to reclaim lost ground.

Christian society wants dramatic change; some congregations even expect the conversion event to be heralded by extreme emotion and may even doubt the sincerity of the participants unless they see the appropriate display. After this profession of faith, there is pressure to be "perfect." New converts are often the targets of close scrutiny by church members where even the smallest infraction is met with harsh criticism or at least the gossip machine. Instead of slowly growing in grace and maturity while acknowledging weaknesses and problems, new Discipleship can mean playing a nasty game of meeting dress and conduct codes. I have seen people lose heart and give up, believing that they'll never make it as a Christian.

Case in point, despite my husband's devotion to God and his faith, he still wrestles with inglorious memories and old problems from his past. Michael was a notorious prankster in both high school and college. As he often suffered under the heel of the "in-crowd," he became a skilled saboteur of cars and other dearly held possessions of bullies and jocks. I often joke that we did without a car for three years as penance for some of the stunts that he pulled.

While vastly entertaining, these pranks were illegal. Mikes' disregard for the law finally caught up with him when he was caught shoplifting at a local mall. It was a foolish thrill, which Michael has paid for a hundred times over. This incident damaged my trust in my husband to the extent that it would take years before I would let him go alone into any store. And while Mike's faith has always called him to sexual purity, he has often been at odds with it due to the pervasive air of promiscuity so present in pop culture. Though he has never been unfaithful (to my knowledge) through all of our courtship and marriage, my love still battles sexual addiction on a daily level.

These incidents and faults are extremely painful to write about. When I think of my husband, I see a loving, generous man who is loyal and hardworking, and for the most part, has been both forthright and honest. But Michael is still human, with all of the frailty that entails. His life, like mine, is littered with mistakes.

Catholicism stresses that believers will falter, fall, stub their toes, skin their knees, and even break a couple of spiritual bones in their life's journey with Christ. Because of this stance, the Catholic faith is generally more positive because it stresses the importance of getting up and continuing rather than condemnation for falling. Michael loves to say that the first thing you do when you fall down is come up on your knees. (A Christian will often pray in the kneeling position.) Standing up, you continue the journey victorious in the face of adversity, reconciled with God. Spiritual perfection is a goal, not a state of being.

I do not believe that I was ever an instant Christian. Since I could reason and think, I have known that Christ was my Savior and that He could forgive my sins. But, submitting to His will has been a continuing challenge that I believe will be life long. I use to fret that I couldn't put an exact date and time on my faith, but I came to the realization that such things are not as important as my faith itself. Looking back, I can see where God has quietly worked behind the scenes to achieve His purpose.

Once upon a time, I believed that God always thundered and roared (and on rare occasions, He still does), but now I understand that He whispers as well. God is not so much a pillar of fire as much as He is that soft still voice that resonates from the recesses of the heart. I grew up watching elders shout and run the aisles of our old church, but now, I seek God in solitude and silence, as did Christian hermits so long ago.

There are no theatrics or fanfare, simply the company of my Lord. Listen to my hymn of praise:

I will come to you in the silence.
I will lift you from all your fear.
You will hear my voice;
I claim you as my choice,
Be still and know I am here.
I am hope for all who are hopeless.
I am eyes for all who long to see.
In the shadows of the night, I will be your light.
Come and rest in me.
I am strength for all the despairing,
Healing for the ones who dwell in shame.
All the blind will see, the lame will all run free.
And all will know my name.
I am the Word that leads all to freedom,
I am the peace the world cannot give.
I will call your name, embracing all your pain,
Stand up, now walk and live!
Do not be afraid, I am with you.
I have called you each by name.
Come and follow me, I will bring you home.

- "You are Mine", words and text by David Haas, © GIA Publications 1991.

"Terribilis est locus iste: hic domus Dei est, et porta coeli..."
(Fearful is this place: here is the house of God, the gate of heaven.)
(Buettner vi)

Holy Eucharist

If there is a dividing mark between many Protestants and their Catholic counterparts, it lies within the third sacrament of Holy Eucharist or Communion. The word **"Eucharist"** comes from the Greek word *eucharistein* and means **"thanksgiving."** (Catechism 335) What sets Holy Eucharist apart from Protestant Communion is the Catholic doctrine of Transubstantiation, which is the act of God whereby the bread and wine becoming the substance of the Body and Blood of Christ with accidents of bread and wine remaining. Just as our spirits inhabit a physical body, so the Spirit of Christ inhabits the bread and wine. When we partake in this sacred feast, we receive the whole of Christ. That's correct. The very same Jesus who was born in Bethlehem, who performed all sorts of miracles, and conquered death and sin, communes with His followers in this most intimate way. Heaven comes down, and we are filled with glory.

Other denominations stress the symbolism of Communion rather than its literal nature, becoming fixated on the sentence **"Do this in memory of me."** rather than **"This is my body... This is my blood."** But the doctrine of Transubstantiation comes from the Book of John. Look at the following passage:

> *There was a man of the Pharisees, named Nicodemus, a ruler of the Jews: The same came to Jesus by night, and said unto Him, "Rabbi, we know that thou art a teacher come from God: for no man can do these miracles that thou doest except God be with Him."*
>
> *Jesus answered and said unto him, "Verily, verily, I say unto thee except a man be born again, he cannot see the Kingdom of God."*
>
> *Nicodemus saith unto Him, "How can a man be born when he is old? Can he enter the second time into his mother's womb, and be born?"*
>
> *Jesus answered, "Verily, verily I say unto thee, except a man be born of water and of the Spirit, he cannot enter into the kingdom of God. That which is born of flesh is flesh; and that which is born of the spirit is spirit."(John 3:1-6, KJV)*

This piece of scripture is called "The Johannine Paradigm" (John's example). In it, we see Christ make a faith statement. Nicodemus interprets it literally; then, Christ gives the proper interpretation. Now, we skip ahead a few chapters where Jesus is speaking to His followers at a synagogue in Capernaum:

> *I am the Living Bread which came down from heaven: If any man eat of this bread, he shall live forever: and the bread that I will give is my flesh, which I will give for the life of the world.*
>
> *The Jews therefore strove among themselves, saying, "How can this man give us His flesh to eat?"*
>
> *Then Jesus said unto them, "Verily, verily, I say unto you, except ye eat of the flesh of the Son of Man, and drink His blood, ye hath no life within you. Whoso eateth my flesh, and drinketh my blood hath eternal life; and I will raise him up on the last day. For my flesh is meat indeed and my blood is drink indeed. He that eateth my flesh and drinketh my blood, dwelleth in me and I in him.*

> *"As the living Father hath sent me, and I live by the Father: so he that eateth me, even he shall live by me. This is that bread which came down from heaven: not as your fathers did eat manna, and are dead. He that eateth of this bread shall live for ever."* These things said He in the synagogue, as He taught in Capernaum.
>
> Many therefore of His Disciples, when they heard this, said, *"This is an hard saying; who can hear it?"*
>
> When Jesus knew in Himself that His Disciples murmured at it, He said unto them, *"DOTH THIS OFFEND YOU?" (John 6:51-61, KJV)*

These are Jesus' words, not mine. The sad thing about this passage is that Jesus loses many of His followers after these statements are made. Mosaic code dictates that humans are not "kosher" or a proper food to eat. Yet, Christ stands there telling people that they must eat His body and drink His blood. Once again, people take His words literally. But this time Jesus does NOT correct them, saying something like, **"Look guys, it's only symbolic. I don't mean my actual body and blood. Just drink this grape juice, eat this bread wafer, and remember me."**

Instead, He declares His body, real food and His blood, real drink- not just one time but over and over again. Let's also note that in the original Greek of the New Testament, the word for "eat" is ***trogein,*** which means *"to gnaw or chew,"* hardly the proper word to use if Christ had meant this figuratively. Additionally, the ancient Greek for the word "meat" in this passage is *"sarx"* which did not mean symbolic flesh, but *"meat that is cooked and eaten."*(Pohle 1-2) I want to reemphasize the point that this dialogue does not occur in the Upper Room, or at Passover, or even in Jerusalem. It happens in a synagogue in Capernaum, miles away from Jerusalem. It also occurs some time before the Last Supper.

When Christ finally presents the consecrated bread and wine to the Disciples in the Upper Room, it becomes very clear that these earthly things made from human hands have changed in nature and substance though the change is hidden from ordinary senses. The words, *"This is my body...This is my blood..."* take on a mystical quality.

Anyone reading this chapter would find it hard to take this passage as figurative, although I have seen people try. It's amazing how many literalists adopt a symbolic stance on this piece of scripture. It's every dot on every "i" and every cross on every "t" until they get to this passage where their posture and position on the scriptures take an unexpected turn. Christ's followers (even the Disciples) could not handle this declaration, and many modern Christians have the same problem. But belief in the real presence of Christ under the outward signs of bread and wine has been taught from the very beginning.

The Apostle Paul mentions this teaching when he writes, *"The cup of blessing which we bless, is it not the communion of the blood of Christ? The bread which we break, is it not the communion of the body of Christ? For we being many are one bread, and one body: for we are all partakers of that one bread." (1 Corinthians 10:16-17, KJV)*

We would do well to remember that to commune means to share and the word communion means "an act of mutual sharing." Paul also warns fellow Christians against trivializing communion in the following chapter:

> *Wherefore whosoever shall eat this bread, and drink this cup of the Lord unworthily, shall be guilty of the body and blood of the Lord. But let a man examine himself and so eat of that bread and drink of that cup. For he that eateth and drinketh unworthily, eateth and drinketh damnation to himself, not discerning the Lord's body. For this cause, many are weak and sickly among you and many sleep. (I Corinthians 11:27-30, KJV)*

The first thing that we need to note here is that Paul references Judaic law when He speaks of being guilty of the body and blood of Christ. This is another way of saying someone is a murderer if they are guilty of the body and blood of an individual. Just as today we would say, **"You have his blood on your hands."**

If we're talking murder, there is no way that the Lord's Supper can be taken symbolically. When I tear up a picture, I'm not destroying the person, but an image of that individual, a kind of symbolic representation. Murder implies the physical assault and destruction of a living, human body. Most importantly, damnation is attached to those who do not discern the Lord's body within the bread and wine. When discerning, one perceives and understands. Why give such an ominous warning if everything is merely symbolic?

This piece of scripture illustrates why Catholics do not allow non-Catholics to partake in the Eucharist. It is not out of spite or snobbery, but out of concern for the non-Catholics' souls, that they aren't damned by their own ignorance. Not only did Paul believe in the Divine Presence, but also John the Beloved of Christ. His star pupil, St. Ignatius of Antioch wrote about, *"those who hold heterodox opinions"* and asked that ***"they abstain from the Eucharist and from prayer, because they do not confess that the Eucharist is the flesh of our Savior, Jesus Christ, flesh which suffered for our sins and which the Father, in his goodness, raised up again."*** (Catholic Answers 4)

This was a pupil of St. John, author of the Fourth Gospel, three letters, and the Book of Revelation. Remember that it is his Gospel that gives us the Johannine Paradigm and documents Christ's words at Capernaum. Was he such a poor teacher that his most notable student would adopt such a belief and teach it as doctrine? If John had seen the Eucharist as figurative, it would have been a terrible offense for the student to reject his teacher in that fashion. Ignatius' declaration is definite proof that John believed in the Divine nature of the Eucharist.

In AD 150, Justin Martyr would later write, ***"Not as common bread or common drink do we receive these; but since Jesus Christ our Savior was made incarnate by the word of God and had both flesh and blood for our salvation, so too, as we have been taught, the food which has been made into the Eucharist by the Eucharistic prayer set down by Him, and by the change of which our blood and flesh is nourished, is both the Flesh and the Blood of that incarnated Jesus."*** (Ibid. from *First Apology* 66:1-20)

In the mid-300s, Cyril of Jerusalem would also state, ***"Do not, therefore, regard the bread and wine as simply that, for they are, according to the Master's declaration, the Body and Blood of Christ. Even though the senses suggest to you the other, let faith make you firm. Do not judge in this matter by taste, but be fully assured by faith, not doubting that you have been deemed worthy of the Body and Blood of Christ."*** (Ibid. from *Catechetical Discourses: Mystagogic* 4:22:9)

And Theodore of Mopsuestia could have been addressing contemporary Protestants today when he gave a homily in the 5th century, saying, ***"When [Christ] gave the bread, He did not say, 'This is the symbol of my body,' but, 'This is my body.' In the same way, when He gave the cup of His blood, He did not say, 'This is the symbol of my blood,' but, 'This is my blood.'"*** (Ibid. from *Catechetical Homilies* 5:1)

So the Doctrine of Transubstantiation has both biblical and historical roots that come directly from Jesus Himself, through the Apostles, and Early Church Fathers. The idea that the Real Presence is "a late Roman invention" is not valid.

The symbolism/reality conflict is also why Catholics are not supposed to participate in the Lord's Supper in non-Catholic churches. To do so in certain churches would be to admit that the meal **IS** symbolic. And belief in the real presence is why Catholicism teaches that anyone with a grave sin on their conscience should not receive communion because they are spiritually unfit to do so. They should seek the Rite of Reconciliation (Confession) first to make sure that they are properly prepared to take the Body and Blood of our Lord into their bodies. It is also why we prepare to celebrate this sacred mystery by participating in the Mass Penitential Rite, where we admit to even our smallest infractions against God and ask His forgiveness, so that we may be as pure as possible for our meeting with Christ. (Catechism 350)

Many coworkers used to love to ask my husband about his beliefs at work. The topic of Eucharist came up on a regular basis. Once, Mike shared the earlier passages from Paul with a Protestant (I'll call him Jeff) whose minister had just given a long sermon about how Catholics were such pagans for their belief in the divine presence in the hosts. Jeff's preacher had gone on and on about how Catholics were duplicating the process used by Babylonian priests in their worship of Baal, the sun god, making the comparison of letting sunlight fall upon the food to asking the spirit of God to inhabit the bread and wine.

Of course, the minister had overlooked both Christ's and Paul's words in his zeal to sway his congregation. After Michael shared the passages above, Jeff had a crisis of faith. My husband encouraged him to show his minister these scripture verses and ask for an explanation. Jeff felt that this would do no good as the preacher was stubborn in his beliefs and in the end, decided to leave his church and look for one that embraced the divinity of Christ through the bread and wine. To which Michael informed Jeff that only one church teaches transubstantiation as doctrine, and that is the Catholic Church, both the Western or Eastern Rites. Other churches and denominations leave the belief of transubstantiation up to the religious convictions of various congregations or individuals. And still others reject Paul's warning all together and teach as doctrine that communion is only a symbolic meal.

Finally, symbolism of the bread and wine flies directly against the Bible itself. Both the Old and New Testament equate the symbolic eating of flesh and drinking of blood as physical assault and even murder. Isaiah 9:18-21 says:

> *For wickedness burneth as the fire: it shall devour the briers and thorns, and shall kindle in the thickets of the forest, and they shall mount up like the lifting up of smoke. Through the wrath of the LORD of hosts is the land darkened, and the people shall be as the fuel of the fire: no man shall spare his brother. And he shall snatch on the right hand, and be hungry; and he shall eat on the left hand, and they shall not be satisfied: they shall eat every man the flesh of his own arm:*

Manasseh, Ephraim; and Ephraim, Manasseh: and they together shall be against Judah. For all this his anger is not turned away, but his hand is stretched out still.

And Revelation 17: 6, 16 (KJV) speaks of the "whore of Babylon" when it tells us,

And I saw the woman drunken with the blood of the saints, and with the blood of the martyrs of Jesus: and when I saw her, I wondered with great admiration.... And the ten horns which thou sawest upon the beast, these shall hate the whore, and shall make her desolate and naked, and shall eat her flesh, and burn her with fire.

Today, we have a similar phrase, which refers to those who glorify in bloodshed. We call them, *"blood thirsty."* We also speak of being *"chewed out"* or *"biting someone's head off"* for a mistake. These figurative illustrations hark back to the old Jewish viewpoint expressed in the scriptures.

Another argument against the divine presence is the myth that "we are sacrificing Jesus over and over again" with each Mass, during the Eucharist. Of course, those who propagate such an idea forget that time is meaningless to God. He sees everything at once: the past, the present, and the future. When we partake in the glory of the Eucharist, time falls away and we are present on Golgotha's hill to witness Jesus' sacrifice and are enjoined to it. All the grace and merits that were gained through the sacrifice of the Cross are applied to us through the sacrifice of the Mass. (Morrow 286) So, when the old hymn asks *"Where you there?"*, we can, through our faith, resolutely say, *"Yes, I was! Yes, I am! Yes, I will be there!"*

Why are Catholics so metaphysical? Why do we tend to accept the unexplained so easily? Because we witness a miracle each time we attend Mass. The priest lifts the gifts of bread and wine heavenward and asks the Spirit of God to come upon them so that they may become for us the Body and Blood of Christ. Listen to the words from a Eucharistic prayer:

(Words in bold denote the congregation's part in the rite while rest of the prayer is said by the attending priest.)

> Blessed are you, Lord, God of all creation.
> Through your goodness we have received this bread we offer you:
> Fruit of the earth and work of human hands,
> It will become for us the bread of life.
> **Blessed be God forever**
> Blessed are you, Lord, God of all creation.
> Through your goodness, we have received the wine we offer you,
> Fruit of the vine and work of human hands,
> It will become our spiritual drink.
> **Blessed be God forever.**
> Pray, Brethren, that my sacrifice and yours
> May be acceptable to God, the almighty Father.
> **May the Lord accept the sacrifice at your hands**
> **For the praise and glory of His name,**
> **For our good and the good of all His Holy Church.**

The Lord be with you.
>**And with your spirit**

Lift up your hearts.
>**We lift them up to the Lord.**

Let us give thanks to the Lord our God.
>**It is right and just.**

God of power and might, we praise you through your Son,
Jesus Christ, who comes in your name.
He is the Word that brings salvation.
He is the Hand you stretch out to sinners.
He is the Way that leads to your peace.
God our Father,
We had wandered far from you,
But through your Son, you have brought us back.
You gave Him up to death so that we might turn again to you.
And find our way to one another.
We celebrate the reconciliation Christ has gained for us.
We ask you to sanctify these gifts by the power of your Spirit,
As we now fulfill your Son's command.
While he was at supper on the night before he died for us,
He took bread in His hands, and gave you thanks and praise.
He broke the bread, gave it to His Disciples, and said:
Take this, all of you, and eat it:
This is my body, which will be given up for you.
At the end of the meal, he took the cup.
Again he praised you for your goodness,
Gave the cup to His Disciples and said:
Take this, all of you, and drink from it:
This is the cup of my blood,
The blood of the new and everlasting covenant,
It will be shed for you and for all so that sins may be forgiven.
Do this in memory of me.
Let us proclaim the mystery of faith:

>**We proclaim your death, O Lord,**
>**And profess your Resurrection**
>**Until you come again**

Through Him, with Him, in Him;
In the unity of the Holy Spirit,
All glory and honor is yours, almighty Father.
Forever and ever. Amen.

Most people have their First Holy Communion as children. This occasion is one of the great celebrations within the life of a Catholic- marked by classes and their first sacrament of Reconciliation. It is also an event that calls for frilly, white dresses, elegant veils, new suits, cakes and parties. Why dress in a white veil or a new suit? It is customary to wear "wedding clothes" to one's first marriage supper with the Lamb.

The Use of Wine Versus Grape Juice

Many Protestants question the use of wine during Catholic masses, and often associate the use of alcohol in general with various social ills and domestic problems. My childhood church even embraced the ludicrous notion that Christ drank grape juice instead of fermented wine. Of course, deep down inside I rejected this opinion out of hand.

Being a student of world culture, I understood that water in the Old World was often too dangerous to drink. Yes, one could bathe in it or cook with it, but drinking it outright was often a gamble. Americans are spoiled creatures, having some of the cleanest and best tasting water in the world. We often forget that the rest of the planet is not so lucky. What's the number one rule for a seasoned traveler: *"Don't drink the water!"*

That advice calls to mind the image of nasty little microbes that cannot only cause a bout with diarrhea, but can kill as well. Before the chemical treatment of water, ugly visitors like cholera used to wreak havoc on local populaces. Even today, it is inadvisable to drink water in a foreign country as every region has its specific bacteria that are usually harmless to the locals but can easily sicken a stranger. This is why most Europeans think nothing of drinking alcohol. Alcohol, by its very nature, has an antiseptic quality, and kills bacteria and other undesirables. Even as late as the nineteenth century, people even cleansed wounds with "drinking alcohol" as a precaution to infection.

Speaking of medicine, there are a variety of medical uses for wine and spirits. For example, some people drink wine to slow the neural impulses of Parkinson's Disease. Small amounts of alcohol taken with food also keep the human cardiovascular system healthy. In the days before cough syrup, a little whiskey and honey was often used to quiet a cough. Today, alcohol is still used as a carrying agent for various medications because it is absorbed into the bloodstream more quickly. Recently, both my husband and I have taken to drinking one glass of wine daily to keep our cardiovascular system healthier as we age. Health experts cannot completely explain it, but tiny amounts of alcohol can retard aging.

Alcohol is also a great cooking tool, particularly for meats. It is a tenderizer, breaking down the muscle fibers. And just as in the case of medications, alcohol carries the taste of spices and flavorings deep into the meat for a more even seasoning. Cooking sauces such as soy, teriyaki, and Worcestershire, famed for their flavor and versatility, also contain alcohol.

And let us not forget the various uses of vinegar. Yes, vinegar is a form of wine, albeit undrinkable wine. Waste not, want not. Vinegar originates from wine that was unacceptable to drink. Rather than throw it out, wine producers would often use vinegar in cooking and cleaning. Many religious folks cringe at wine but have no problem using vinegar, oblivious to its very origin and alcoholic nature.

The watchword should always be moderation. We have Paul's advice that a little wine for the digestion is good. Having a glass of wine is perfectly ok, but drinking the whole bottle is not. This was the idea that my parents passed onto me. They communicated the sentiment that the occasional glass of something was fine, but becoming drunk was foolish and unacceptable. Not only did it ruin one's health, but it also put an individual at the mercy of predators. I can honestly say that I have never allowed myself to get to the levels of intoxication that beget bed spins, worshipping at the porcelain altar, and incredible hangovers, and I have had many different alcoholic concoctions. Indeed, I'm quite fond of daiquiris and mud slides.

What many Christians fail to realize is that practically everyone drank wine in ancient times. The cultivation of plants, particularly olives and grapes, was a mark of civilization. All people grew grapes, from the richest king to the lowly village worker. Grapes furnished food and fermented drink. Grape juice did not become popular until the Prohibition Era of the 1920's when wineries started selling the juice of grapes in order to stay financially afloat. Unfermented juice was the idea of Dr. Thomas Welch, an avowed prohibitionist, who came up with the use of "unfermented wine" in 1869. He felt that ministers were contradicting themselves by offering wine in church and backing the temperance movement at the same time. His idea was rejected at first, but would later be adopted by his son, Charles Welch in 1875, who began selling it as grape juice. (BRI 274)

The problem with America is that it is a land of extremes. Americans have a tendency of fostering a kind of double standard. We both glamorize and demonize a substance that, in and of itself, is neither good nor bad. Worse yet, we are sending the wrong messages to young people, equating drinking with being adult, then forbidding its use, which creates a powerful attraction to kids who both want to be "grown up" and do the forbidden. It's no wonder that we have teens dying from the effects of binge drinking. Alcohol has no conscience and cannot make decisions. It is humanity that has the power of higher reasoning, not some liquid in a glass. Moderation and responsibility are the most important virtues when alcohol is involved.

The American government and media have the tendency of focusing on "drunk drivers" while ignoring other dangerous hazards to drivers. For example, we seem to have a silent epidemic of sleepy drivers. It is a fact that a sleepy/tired driver can be just as dangerous as a drunken one. For example, I used to work with a sweet girl named Serena. She was a smart and pretty African American girl whose smile could light up a room. One Sunday evening on the way home from the shop, a local man crossed the median line and ploughed into her vehicle in a head-on collision. Her car was so crumpled that it took almost a half-hour to remove her from the wreckage. After clinging to life for over a month, our Serena succumbed to her injuries at just 20 years old.

I remember going to the funeral home and kissing her goodbye. All I that I could say was, *"Why?"* The driver had not been drinking; he was just sleepy. But the effect was the same. Why do we think that we can cure social problems with laws? Handling America's obsession with alcohol is more about attitude than legislation. Catholicism endorses moderation rather than the "don't touch" mentality of certain Protestant denominations. It recognizes that the real fault lies not in the substance, but in the heart and soul of the drinker.

When I think of wine used in church, two images come sharply into focus: the wedding feast at Cana where Christ turned the water into wine (His first miracle) and the Last Supper. For me, these passages offer a picture of life as it was in biblical times, and they speak of joy and remembrance. Because the wine is blessed and consecrated in a Catholic Mass, it is considered improper to take in more than a tiny sip of communion wine, hardly enough to give more than a warm feeling as it goes down the throat. In fact, people get more alcohol from a glass of orange juice than in taking Catholic Eucharist. And Catholics must use wine when they observe the Eucharist.

Drinking grape juice is not truly following the example set down by Our Lord Jesus Christ, who drank wine. And if wine were not a fit Eucharistic host, then why sanctify its use in the Last Supper? Now, I've heard Protestant ministers try to argue that the wine of today is different than biblical wine. Yes, the method of fermentation has been modified with modern techniques, but it is still essentially the same as that which the ancient world employed. (We should not confuse winemaking with distilling various liquors. Wine and spirits are two different things created by two different methods.)

Catholics use a common cup, which is a unifying part of Communion. A side benefit in the use of wine is that antiseptic quality I spoke of earlier. Grape juice does not have the ability to kill everyday germs. It is necessary to keep the contents sanitized as much as possible as each person comes and drinks. The lip of the vessel is even wiped between people. However, individuals suffering from contagious conditions should not drink from the communal cup, but receive the body (bread) instead or have the priest dip the bread in wine and place it on their tongues. This is called ***intinction***, and only the priest may intinct the bread into the wine.

Each communal cup is carefully wiped after the attending priest has consumed all vestiges of the blood following the sacrament of Eucharist. Then, every implement and the cloth will be washed in a tiny sink in sacristy. This sink is special as it does not empty into the common sewer system of a city or community but directly into the ground. Therefore, the ground on which the church is built becomes literally holy ground as it is infused with the living presence of Christ.

The Church makes a stringent effort to prevent any possible misuse or mishandling of the blood at all times, so the use of multiple glasses (as is popular in Protestant churches) is not employed because it cannot guarantee the same degree of prevention. There are simply more handlers, and the wine has a much greater chance of being spilled or inappropriately used and disposed of. Because we believe in the Real Presence, the wine, once changed into blood, cannot be unchanged. As long as it remains wine, it remains blood.

Confirmation

While some Protestants consider Baptism an outward sign of inward change in adults, the Catholic outward sign that bears witness to the heart is the sacrament of Confirmation. It is one of the three Sacraments of Initiation, the other two being Baptism and Eucharist. (Bete, Confirmation 8) Confirmation completes initiation in the Catholic Church for those already baptized in the Church while Holy Communion completes initiation of converts who are new to the faith. So, those confirming enter "full communion" with the Church, with all the privileges and responsibilities of an adult member of the Church. This sacrament transfers responsibility for continuing your walk with Jesus from your parents who were charged with your daily spiritual instruction to you alone.

Baptism is a new birth by water and the Holy Spirit, but confirmation completes the grace of baptism. Remember Christ's words to Nicodemus, *"Verily, verily, I say unto thee, except a man be born of water and of spirit, he cannot enter the kingdom of God." (John 3:5, KJV)*

Traditionally, cradle Catholics have been confirmed at Pentecost, the time when the Disciples were filled with the Holy Spirit. *"Then said Jesus to them again, "Peace be unto you: As my Father hath sent me, even so send I you." And when He had said this, He breathed on them, and saith unto them, "Receive ye the Holy Ghost." (John 20:21-22, KJV)*

Although this passage is linked with the ordination rites of the priesthood, it also shows the gift of the Holy Spirit, a blessing expected to be imparted to all other believers. In the Book of Acts, we read: *"Then Peter said unto them, "Repent, and be baptized every one of you in the name of Jesus Christ for the remission of sins, and ye shall receive the gift of the Holy Ghost. For the promise is unto you, and unto your children, and to all that are afar off, even as many as the Lord our God shall call." (Acts 2:38-39, KJV)*

Now, many Protestants believe that all of this can be done at once, and see no need for a separate sacrament. But this belief conflicts with the scriptures:

Now when the Apostles which were at Jerusalem heard that Samaria had received the word of God, they sent unto them Peter and John: who, when they were come down, prayed for them, that they might received the Holy Ghost: (for as yet He was fallen upon none of them: only they were baptized in the name of the Lord Jesus.) Then they laid their hands on them; they received the Holy Ghost. (Acts 8:14-17, KJV)

In the preceding passage, we have a group of people who had been baptized, but still needed Peter and John to lay hands upon them to complete their inauguration into the body of Christ. We see this again when Paul comes to the city of Ephesus:

And it came to pass, that, while Apollos was at Corinth, Paul having passed through the upper coasts came to Ephesus: and finding certain Disciples, he said unto them, "Have you received the Holy Ghost since ye believed?"

And they said, "We have not so much as heard whether there be any Holy Ghost."

> *And he said unto them, "Unto what then were ye baptized?"*
> *And they said, "Unto John's baptism."*
> *Then said Paul; "John verily baptized with the baptism of repentance, saying unto the people, that they should believe on Him which should come after him, that is, on Christ Jesus."*
> *When they heard this, they were baptized in the name of the Lord Jesus. And when Paul laid his hands upon them, theHoly Ghost came on them; and they spake with tongues and prophesied. (Acts 19:1-6, KJV)*

It is interesting to note that Confirmation's oldest name is "Laying of the Hands," which calls to mind the two previous scripture passages. Catholicism follows the example set down by the Apostles, understanding that membership within the Body of Christ begins with Baptism and is completed with Confirmation. Cradle Catholics are marked with water as children and set aside as belonging to God. They are taught from infancy the importance of accepting Christ, seeking forgiveness, and making Christ the Lord of their lives. Ideally, there should NEVER be a point in a Catholic's life when they do not know Christ as their Savior. The sacrament of Confirmation is a special outpouring of the grace and strength of the Holy Spirit (Bete, Confirmation 15), bringing with it seven gifts: wisdom, understanding, judgment, courage, knowledge, love, and reverence for God. With these gifts come their fruits: charity, joy, peace, patience, kindness, faithfulness, gentleness, goodness and self-restraint. (Bete, Confirmation 5) These gifts and their fruits allow Christians to fully develop and mature in their faith.

Confirmation is really a process. Unlike many churches, people interested in Catholicism are expected to attend six to eight months of weekly classes for adults, and two to three years of instruction for children. They are known as **RCIC (Rite of Christian Initiation in Children)** and **RCIA (Rite of Christian Initiation in Adults)**. While this may sound kind of snobby and hard-nosed, the Church feels that individuals must be spiritually ready for this event. This is the time when many issues and doctrines are explored in-depth. (Bete, RCIA 2)

RCIA or RCIC is really like a spiritual buddy system. In addition to the classes, you gain a sponsor or godparent, who will be there for you to answer questions and share experiences as a Catholic. This is a spiritual mentor who will journey with you toward Confirmation. The practice of sponsoring comes from the Roman persecution of Christians. Because it was very dangerous to be a follower of Christ, converts did not meet in open places. (There was that little problem of Nero and the lions.) So, an individual would slowly enter the Church through another Christian in good standing who would slowly teach and immerse that person in the faith.

There are four steps in RCIA or RCIC toward the objective of confirmation. The first phase is called Evangelization and Precatechumenate, where inquirers hear the gospel, reflect upon God's presence in their lives, and are encouraged to ask questions. Individuals are not expected to commit to anything at this point. This period of time ends with the **Rite of Welcoming the Candidates** (for baptized members of the community) or the **Rite of Becoming a Catechumen** (for unbaptized inquirers). (Bete, RCIA 6)

You must declare before the congregation the wish to be in communion with the church. It is almost like a coronation. Your sponsor introduces you, and you are asked what you want of God's people. Then, you are blessed from head to toe, and marked with the sign of the Cross over each area: head, eyes, ears, mouth, hands, heart, and feet. Having participated in such a ceremony, I can say that the most humbling part was watching my sponsor drop to her knees and bless my feet. The first impulse I had was to scoop down and help her up.

The second section is called the ***Catechumenate*** where the actual preparation begins for Confirmation. This part emphasizes learning and embracing the Scriptures, Catholic doctrines and teachings, and both a solitary and a communal prayer life with other catechumens who are also journeying toward Confirmation. The Catechumenate ends with the **Rite of Calling** (for baptized candidates) or the **Rite of Election** (for the unbaptized). *(Bete, RCIA 7)*

In the beginning, you chose the Church; now the Church must choose you. This is a celebration of "divine election" reminiscent to God's choosing of the Israelites. It recognizes the need to commune with God, a natural part of the human psyche. We crave the intimate bond that is "initiated and sustained by the divine" (Duggan et al, 25). These rites occur on the first Sunday of Lent.

The third portion is called ***Purification and Enlightenment***. It begins with the Scrutinies which are carried out on the third, fourth, and fifth Sundays during Lent. They include readings and prayers. (The whole congregation anoints the catechumens with prayer to strengthen them as they near Confirmation. The ***Presentations*** follow where the catechumens embrace the Apostles' Creed and the Lord's Prayer. Then, the Preparations begin for Holy Week. At this time, the catechumens participate in their first sacrament of Reconciliation as well as devote themselves to prayer in order to completely embrace the sacraments with a clear conscience and a willing spirit. (Bete, RCIA 8)

Modern Catholicism favors confirming individuals at Easter, the high point of the Catholic liturgical year. After the readings in the Mass, baptisms are performed, if needed. This sacrament allows catechumens to share in our Lord's passion and ultimate defeat of death, hell, and sin. Those who have been baptized are called to renew their vows and profess their faith, as the congregation does as it witnesses the sacrament. The bishop or priest will lay their hands on the confirmandi; anoint them with holy chrism oil, making the sign of the cross, saying, ***"Be sealed with the Gift of the Holy Spirit."*** (Bastini, Worship 536)

Then, he will end the rite by giving a sign of God's peace, such as a handshake or embrace. Each of the confirmandi will to choose new names after various biblical or historical saints, and it is those names that the priest will use to address them by during the sacrament. Renaming is a long-standing custom in Christianity dating back to the Old Testament. Remember Abraham was once Abram; Sarah was Sarai, and Jacob became Israel after wrestling with an angel before his reunion with Esau. In the New Testament, Christ renames Simon as Peter and Levi as Matthew, and Saul of Tarsus renamed himself as Paul.

So, Catholics rename themselves upon confirmation after saints with whom they feel a special kinship. Saints are usually exemplary Christians (some are angels) who have led the faithful through their devotion and sincerity to Christ. For example, my husband prizes truth and knowledge; his saint is Saint Michael, the archangel. My saint is Saint Paul, the Apostle, because I have a very "Pauline" nature and wish to share my faith with others. One of my godchildren is a health care worker, so she chose Saint Elizabeth of Hungary who lost her life due to constant ministering to the sick and dying.

The Mass will continue after the sacrament of Confirmation with Holy Eucharist, where the neophytes will commune with Christ through sacred meal of bread and wine. (Those who were not born into Catholicism and did not take First Holy Communion classes as children will have their First Holy Communion at this time.)

After the Sacrament of Confirmation

The final phase of RCIA/RCIC is called ***Post Baptismal Catechesis*** or ***Mystagogia.*** The new Catholics are encouraged into a deeper spiritual life with Christ by celebrating special Masses aimed at neophytes. They are invited to share the Eucharist, further examine the scriptures, lead lives of prayer, and follow Christ's example. Mystagogia also stresses the importance of donating time, talent, and treasure to the family of God as well as participating in community outreach programs. (Bete, RCIA 9)

Besides fulfilling the evangelical and missionary requirements that Jesus set down for His Church, Confirmation and RCIA/RCIC are enriching to the community of faith, calling people to renew and rededicate themselves to God. It is the vindication of beliefs and spiritual convictions, conveying the courage to share one's faith with the world.

Excommunication

To excommunicate means to sever ties with the Catholic Church, so those who are excommunicate cannot legitimately receive the sacraments and are cast out from the Mystical Body of Christ. According to the Catechism of the Catholic Church as promulgated by Pope John Paul II:

Certain particularly grave sins incur excommunication, the most severe ecclesiastical penalty, which impedes the reception of the sacraments and the exercise of certain ecclesiastical acts, and for which absolution cannot consequently be granted, according to canon law, except by the Pope, the bishop or priest authorized by them. In danger of death any priest, even if deprived of faculties for hearing confessions, can absolve from every sin and excommunication. (368)

While various Protestants argue about the validity of excommunication, they would do well to remember that it does have biblical backing. Let me direct the reader's attention to the Book of Acts, where Peter expels the heretic Simon Magus:

And when Simon saw that through laying on the Apostle's hands the Holy Ghost was given, he offered them money, saying, "Give me also this power, that on whomsoever I lay hands, he may receive the Holy Ghost."
But Peter said unto him, "Thy money perish with thee, because thou hast thought that the gift of God may be purchased with money." (Acts 8:18-20, KJV)

Simon believes that he can buy the power of the Holy Spirit, and Peter rebukes and sends this heretic away. It could be argued that rejection of Simon's money conveyed rejection of his membership within the Christian community. Today, there are two forms of excommunication: ***latae sententiae*** (automatic) and ***ferendae sententiae*** (declared.)

Automatic excommunication occurs when the person(s) is/are guilty of: **apostasy, heresy, schism, physical assault on the Pope, absolution of an accomplice in the commission of a sin against the 6th commandment (adultery), violation the sacramental seal, procuring an abortion, or a bishop who ordains a bishop as well as the one ordained when there is no papal mandate for the ordination.** Declared excommunication is rare and requires the action of a church authority, but not necessarily an ecclesiastical court trial. For example, Bishop Bruskewitz, of Lincoln Nebraska, by his own authority publicly excommunicated those Catholics who held membership in the Freemasons or Masonic organizations as well as those who held membership in the civic organization, Call to Action. Catholics may not join any organization that entertains an anti-Catholic viewpoint. This is particularly relevant for me as my paternal aunt was an Eastern Star member, and since I am a blood relative, I could lay claim to her legacy if I wished, but I cannot and be a Catholic in good standing.

The most important thing that we need to remember is that excommunication need never be final. Even Simon Magus could have been received back into the Christian community, had he repented and paid for his mistake. The Catholic Church loves her children and joyfully welcomes them back through the Sacrament of Penance. No matter how grave the offense, those who are excommunicated need only to return, renounce and do penance for their sin. It is only the stubborn heart that will suffer eternal separation from God and His flock.

While Protestants often criticize excommunication, they have similar procedures that they use to correct those Christians who commit grievous offenses against God. The terms of "disfellowship" and "shunning" come to mind. But unlike the penalty of excommunication, disfellowshipping and shunning can often punish the individual's family, unless they also break ties with the offending person. And even after the sin has been forgiven and restitution is made, the person and his/her family may continue to receive amounts of religious discrimination.

This practice is needlessly cruel and actually damaging to the Body of Christ. The lack of forgiveness reflects back upon the congregation, who forget that their own redemption is tied to their ability to forgive and receive God's errant lambs. Hear the words of Christ: *"For if ye forgive men their trespasses, your heavenly Father will also forgive you: but if ye forgive not men their trespasses, neither will your Father forgive your trespasses." (Matthew 6:14-15, KJV)*

So, we know that excommunication is a biblically sound practice and has many Protestant cousins such as shunning and disfellowshipping. Its finality is completely dependent upon the individual's willingness to repent and do penance for a grave infraction. Catholicism tends to be more generous in its forgiving an excommunicating offense than do many Protestant groups who often continue to remind their members of past sins, long after everything has been settled and put to right. This generosity follows the command set down by Jesus Himself.

Marriage

Every religion has provisions for matrimony. In fact, sociologists will tell you that the family is the building block from which society is formed. But Christianity teaches that marriage is a holy estate instituted by God from the very beginning with Adam and Eve. Catholics believe that when Christ turned the water into wine at the Marriage at Cana, it became a sacrament. After all, it was His first miracle, and the honor and holiness of the occasion brought about a dignity to marriage, conferring grace upon those Christians who marry one another in the presence of God. Whereas marriage is often depicted in the Old Testament as both a contract and a covenant, Catholicism looks at matrimony as a covenant. (Bete, Marriage 3-4)

What's the difference? Well, a contract can be abolished, and it involves material goods, rights and duties. Contracted marriage may exclude the rights of children, and it is created in civil law. This is why the Catholic Church frowns on civil marriage as performed by officials such as a Justice of the Peace. A marriage covenant totally unites a man and woman who love each other- emotionally, intellectually, spiritually, and physically. Covenant marriage is enriched by the couple's collective faith, and places an emphasis on children. This position was upheld during the Second Vatican Council and is continually reinforced today. (Bete, Marriage 4)

The Council of Florence formally acknowledged marriage as a sacrament in 1438. As such, sacramental marriage has specific attributes:

1) It totally unifies both partners.
2) It is monogamous- strictly between one man and one woman.
3) It embraces children, who are raised and nurtured
in the Catholic faith.
4) Marriage is sacrificial where both partners are dedicated to each other and the family unit.
5) The couple develops a deep, inseparable bond with one another.
6) Sacramental marriage is redemptive, as the couple grows spiritually, united in Christ.
7) It must be freely entered, without force or restraint.
8) And it is a lifelong commitment, consecrated in an atmosphere
of faith. (Bete, Marriage 5)

Because Catholic marriage is such a serious commitment, engaged couples are expected to attend premarital classes/counseling, also known as **Pre-Cana.** Adequate preparation is incredibly important when approaching marriage. Any couple that does not completely and candidly discuss ideas on money, sex, family, parenting and career issues could be facing major conflicts down the road. Pre-Cana may be uncomfortable at times, but it can prevent needless pain and misery later. The world may place a premium on romantic love, but life demands a realistic look at a future marriage state. All of this is merged with a growing spirituality between the couple and God that emphasizes prayer, studying the Scriptures, and the teachings of the Catholic faith. This foundation is extremely important in creating a marriage that will withstand all the pressures and conflicts that will eventually come. (Bete, Marriage 6)

Even before I was a Catholic, I understood the importance of preparation before marriage. I have seen and heard of too many people entering marriage with little regard or knowledge of how their married life will be conducted. Couples usually don't wish to discuss the "nuts and bolts" of marriage, and that, blended with rushing into marriage, is almost always a recipe for disaster. So, knowing very little about how each person views the married state, they blindly "take the plunge," then complain when things derail later. I hate to say it, but it's all so predictable. Premarital counseling may be unromantic and not very glamorous, but it is the practical and intelligent thing to do.

Besides extensive preparation, other steps to marriage include:

1) The couple will need to contact the parish and determine the amount of time it requires for the ceremony (usually 3 months to a year).

2) They should meet with the priest and build an on going relationship with him. If one partner is non-Catholic, they may have special needs with reference to Pre-Cana.

3) The parish will need to have copies of baptism certificates for each of the people. Remember, both people need to be baptized before a Catholic marriage can take place. The only exception is if the Bishop gives permission.

4) The couple needs to plan the liturgy of the service with the permission and approval of the attending priest. Couples have some latitude concerning music, prayers, readings, etc. to express their love.

5) Any other special needs must be addressed. For example, when a person under the age of eighteen marries, that individual must receive special counseling to adequately prepare for marriage. (Bete, Marriage, 7)

The Ceremony Itself

Though each is different and unique, all Catholic marriages have common elements. There is the Liturgy of the Word where music, scripture, and prayer reflect the hope for a happy and prosperous life for the couple. Then, we have the exchange of vows, a public declaration of fidelity and devotion that each person has for the other. Wedding rings are also exchanged, being an ancient symbol of permanence and abiding love. The prayers of the faithful follow with expressions of joy and hope for the couple, the congregation and the world. (Marriage, Bete 8)

Because the Eucharist is always the centerpiece of the Catholic Mass, the Liturgy of the Eucharist continues the wedding Mass with traditional Eucharistic prayers, praise, and the consecration of the bread and wine. The priest gives the Nuptial Blessing entreating God's favor upon the husband and wife. Mass ends with communion, a physical meeting with Christ.

Special note: When one prospective partner is non-Catholic, the couple can elect to forgo the Eucharistic portion and end with the Nuptial Blessing. (Bete, Marriage, 8)

Married Life

Catholicism considers married life to be a sign of Christ's love, and it mirrors His relationship with the Church. Let's look at the words of St. Paul:

Wives submit to your husbands, as unto the Lord. For the husband is the head of the wife, even as Christ is the head of the church: and he is the Savior of the body. Therefore, as the church is subject unto Christ, so let the wives be to their husbands in every way.

> *Husbands, love your wives, even as Christ also loved the church, and gave Himself for it; that he might sanctify and cleanse it with the washing of water by the word, that he might present it to Himself a glorious church, not having spot, or wrinkle, or any such thing, but that it should be holy and without blemish.*
>
> *So ought men to love their wives as their own bodies. He that loveth his wife loveth himself. For no man ever yet hateth his own flesh; but nourisheth and cherisheth it, even as the Lord the church. For we are members of His body, of His flesh, and of His bones.*
>
> *For this cause shall a man leave his father and mother, and shall be joined unto his wife, and they two shall be one flesh. This is a great mystery: but I speak concerning Christ and the church. (Ephesians 5:22-32, KJV)*

Paul is often picked at for his stance on marriage. But in the passage above, he is balancing authority with love. Pope Pius XI clarified this relationship even further with this statement from his Encyclical on Christian Marriage:

> *This subjection does not take away the liberty which fully belongs to the woman, both in view of her dignity as a human person, and in view of her most noble office as wife and mother and companion; nor does it bid her obey her husband's every request, even if not in harmony with right reason or the dignity due her as a wife... But it forbids that exaggerated liberty which cares not for the good of the family; it forbids that in this body which is the family, the heart be separated from the head, to the great detriment of the whole body, and the proximate danger of ruin. For if the man is the head, the woman is the heart, and as he occupies the chief place in ruling, she ought to claim for herself the chief place in love. (Morrow 357)*

Because it mirrors Christ's relationship with the Church, sacramental marriage stresses the importance of sacrifice, trust, renewal, intimacy, open communication and a positive outlook within the marriage itself. These elements are seen as the ingredients for a happy, healthy union. Couples are expected to grow in Christ together. This begets a deeper union than what the world can provide. Ever notice how transitory marriages can be when Christ is not at the center of them. It's no mystery; they simply lack the solid foundation that Christianity provides.

Growing together in Christ provides a deeper faith and an increased sense of satisfaction and fulfillment in married life, which results in a stronger commitment toward God and the covenant of marriage itself. All of this increases a couple's total peace and happiness within the union itself. A strong Christian family is a witness of Christ's love for all the world to see. It emphasizes the importance of service, worship, and teaching within the Church and the surrounding community. The family leads and inspires by example. Thus, it is made stronger by sharing love and ministering to itself and the other lives that it will touch.

Children

In the age of birth control and abortion, we in western society often forget that the birth of a child in a Christian marriage is a sign of God's favor and love among His people. Children increase and enrich God's Kingdom; they provide new sources of love, build a stronger bond between the married partners, and cultivate more ties with the Church and the surrounding neighborhood. (Catechism 571)

Ideally, children serve another purpose. They become a continuing source of love and support as their parents get older. Nothing is as sad as a person with no one to care for them when they become frail with age. I've seen these folks, locked away in nursing homes with no one to visit them or bring them the excitement of a grandchild. There are no cards or decorations to adorn their walls and no plants for their windowsills. The holidays are lonely with no one to bring them badly needed shoes, toiletries and clothing. Walking into each room, you can tell who has a close-knit family and who does not.

In return for all the gifts that a child can bring, parents are expected to look after that child's total needs, whether they are physical, psychological, or spiritual. The greatest gift that any couple can give a child is a loving Christian home. A good and stable home life provides a foundation for a happy future. It is a psychological fact that children will seek out and duplicate the relationship dynamics that they witnessed on a daily level between their parents, even if those dynamics were destructive. This is a natural inclination and is often subconscious. Don't believe me, and then look at how abuse and cruelty cycle through various families. It is paramount to a child's spiritual and social development to provide a positive daily example of married life.

What is natural family planning?
As most people know, the Catholic Church condemns as immoral the use of artificial forms of contraception, but it does understand the need for specific measures to control the number and spacing of children. This can be done successfully through natural family planning. (Catechism 569)

This method is NOT what people know as the "rhythm method," which is outdated. Instead, a woman learns how her own particular body works, and becomes schooled on the physical signs of ovulation. If the couple wishes to conceive, then this is the optimum time. If not, then they refrain from sex and avoid the possibility of conception.

Believe it or not, natural family planning is beneficial in that it demands a more intimate level of communication and respect than other forms of birth control. Husbands are closer to their wives, and the sexual act is not taken for granted as it is now in popular society. Sex is treated with reverence and restraint when partners engage in natural family planning. (Catechism 570)

Sterilization
Being "snipped" or "having one's tubes tied" to prevent further pregnancies is also wrong in the eyes of the Catholic Church. (Catechism 570) However, if sterilization is the side effect of the treatment of a serious disease or condition, that is different. For example, if a woman had a serious reproductive cancer, which required removal of the ovaries or a complete hysterectomy, her resulting sterility would be considered an unfortunate side effect of the treatment of a life-threatening disease. (Paul IV 36)

Infertile Couples
Infertile couples have a role to play as well within the Catholic Church as well as their respective communities. They minister to one another and to love ones within their extended families. Christian couples can channel their need into community service and becoming more involved within the Body of Christ. They are also free to offer loving homes to foster children, and pursue adoption.

Catholicism does embrace scientific research for the purpose of reducing infertility as long as it is "at the service of the human person, of his inalienable rights, and his true and integral good according to the design and will of God." (Catechism 571) However, just as the Catholic Church feels that artificial means of birth control and sterilization are wrong, it also disapproves of invasive fertility treatments such as artificial insemination and fertilization to conceive children. Catholicism believes that these techniques separate the act of conception from the two spouses and place it in the hands of doctors and scientists. Sperm banks, donated ova, and surrogate mothers are intrusive as they involve the introduction of a third party into the holy sacrament of marriage where there must be only two people, a husband and a wife.

If someone else outside of the marriage donates the sperm or egg, the child's right to know his/her biological parents is impugned. These procedures also undermine the spouses' right to become parents through only their union. Catholicism still sees these methods as morally objectionable, even when all the genetic information belongs to the parents because it isolates the act of procreation from the conjugal act and is disrespectful to the sanctity of human life. (Catechism 571)

Marriage Renewal

Marriage renewal comes in many forms within the Catholic Church. When the partners continually share their faith and love with one another, they are able to meet a multitude of challenges that life gives them. Participating in Mass together provides further bonding and reinforces their lifetime commitment to their marriage.

And like most churches, Catholicism offers numerous marriage enrichment programs and retreats, as well as allowing married couples to help and inspire engaged couples in Pre-Cana. A healthy, Christian marriage can also prove to be a witness to others who lose faith in their marriage and are suffering, offering a call back to the commitment and faith.

Personal Reflections on the Renewal of Marriage Vows

It has become a common practice among many couples to renew their wedding vows, especially if the big church wedding was not possible at the time they married. Although happily married, I pined for the chance to reaffirm our marriage before family and friends. So, on our tenth wedding anniversary, we celebrated a renewal of vows, and for the first time in twelve years, both sides of the family got the chance to truly meet and talk with one another.

Renewal ceremonies can be tricky in Catholicism. Due to the nature of this sacrament, the spouses may only marry one another once. This meant that we had to go out of our way to make it clear that we weren't "getting married again." At first, the whole affair seemed problematic, but we were given a little more latitude, as there was no Mass to be celebrated. Because most members of the congregation (including my family) were Protestant, we elected not to have a Eucharistic service.

In the program that I designed, I explained the importance of not repeating the sacrament. The prayers and scripture readings spoke of unity, faith, and love within our marriage and our collective journey together with Christ. Instead of the expected readings that are in done at weddings, the passages we chose emphasized a sacrament in progress and not its inauguration. I had attendants, not bridesmaids, and while I did wear a gown with all the trimmings, it was a deep ivory, not white, and my husband escorted me down the aisle. My veil did not fall over my face, but was pulled back. These things symbolized the fact that I was indeed a married woman.

But my friends still talk about the beautiful music, which I spent months carefully choosing. There was no wedding march. Instead, our promenade song was **Marble Halls** or **The Dream,** from the nineteenth century Irish Opera, **The Bohemian Girl,** written by

William Balfe, whom Straus once called a "the Master of Melody." (Enya, 44) Hushed and romantic, it spoke of a love echoing from real life into dreams. The rest of the music was religious with hymns like ***Jesus, Like A Shepherd, Lead Us*** (to welcome my family), ***Create in Me A Clean Heart, Angeles*** (a tribute to guardian angels) (Enya, 26), and the benediction song, ***Sent Forth By God's Blessing***, also known as the ancient Welsh hymn, ***Ashgrove***.

In Review

The Catholic sacrament of marriage is actually a primary ministry for the Church. It brings Christ into the home and makes Him present in ordinary daily activities. Catholic marriage cultivates mutual love and respect between the husband and wife and embraces children as the natural fruition of the union. Marriage teaches Christianity by example to children, to the Body of Christ and to the community, at large.

Renewal of this sacrament occurs through participation in the Mass, involvement in various Church activities and enrichment programs, and ministering to other engaged and married couples within the parish and in the community. Renewal ceremonies can be done, but couples must follow certain rules and guidelines because marriage is a sacrament, which cannot be duplicated or have the appearance of being so, especially if an Eucharistic service is done at the ceremony.

Divorce & Annulment

In today's world, divorce is common, and most Christian denominations allow for divorce. The Catholic Church views the sacrament of marriage as lasting for life and therefore, indissoluble. While civil law considers divorce a viable option, Catholicism does not recognize its ability to countermand Divine Law, reaffirmed through the teaching of Christ when he states:

> *It hath been said, whosoever shall put away his wife, let him give her a writing of divorcement: but I say unto you, that whosoever shall put away his wife, saving for the cause of fornication, causeth her to commit adultery: and who shall marry her that is divorced committeth adultery. (Matthew 5:31-32, KJV)*

Jesus addresses the issue of divorce again in chapter 19 of the same Gospel:

> *The Pharisees also came unto Him, tempting Him, and saying unto Him, "Is it lawful for a man to put away his wife for every cause?"*
>
> *And he answered and said unto them, "Have ye not read, that he which made them at the beginning made them male and female, and said for this cause shall a man leave father and mother, and shall cleave to his wife: and they twain shall be one flesh? Wherefore they are no more twain, but one flesh? What therefore God hath joined together, let no man put asunder"*
>
> *They said unto Him, "Why did Moses then command to give a writing of divorcement, and to put her way?"*
>
> *He saith unto them, "Moses because of the hardness of your hearts suffered you to put away your wives: but from the beginning it was not so. And I say unto you, whosoever shall put away his wife, except it be for fornication, and shall marry another, committeth adultery: and whoso marrieth her which is put away doth commit adultery." (Matthew 19:3-9, KJV)*

These are hard words for many people to read and embrace, but we need to understand why Jesus so decisively rejects divorce in the first place. Under Mosaic Code, Jewish men could divorce their wives with impunity for even the most trivial of excuses. As a result, wives could find themselves begging in the streets, with no way to earn a living of their own. Because women were cut off from direct contact with the Jewish faith, they also had no way of seeking atonement, since that came through the men in their respective families. Marriage and children were a Jewish woman's main sources for protection and security, both socially and spiritually. Jesus knew that when he condemned the Jewish religious leaders for their flippancy regarding the holy estate of marriage.

So, what is an ***annulment***? It is the nullifying or voiding of an attempted marriage. This should never be confused with divorce, as divorce concedes that the marriage did, at one time, exist. An annulment is a ruling that declares that a sacramental marriage never occurred in the first place. This comes through the careful investigation of a marriage by a Marriage Tribunal.

There are three reasons for an annulment:
1) Lack or defect of canonical form
2) An impediment to the marriage
3) And defect of consent

Lack or Defect of Canonical Form

This deals with the marriage ceremony itself. The Catholic Church recognizes the validity of marriages performed outside its borders between non-Catholic Christians and non-Christians whether performed in a church or a civil ceremony, as long as it's legitimate. However, those baptized into the Catholic faith or were received into the Catholicism after baptism in another Christian church must have their wedding officiated by an attending priest. If a Catholic enters a civil marriage or the rite is conducted in another faith without the needed permission from the local bishop of the diocese (dispensation), then the marriage is considered invalid in the eyes of the Church, and can be annulled. This problem can be easily rectified if the Church blesses the union as in the case with my own marriage to Michael. The catch is that most couples are expected to go to Pre-Cana classes to avoid rushing into the sacrament.

Impediments

An impediment can be defined as particular circumstances surrounding the marriage that keep the union from being a valid one. Individuals below the minimum age (14 for females and 16 for males) may not lawfully wed under canon law.

Marriages conducted between people in the same family (whether by blood or marriage) are considered invalid unless dispensation is given. (Dispensation will never be given in the case of siblings or parents marrying their own children.) At one time, godparents were not permitted to marry their godchildren, because of their mentoring and parental roles in the relationship.

Then, there is the impediment of ligamen or prior bond that means that the Church will not accept a remarriage if one or both of the spouses are still living. This can be rectified if the previous marriage is nullified or dissolved by the Pope. (This comes from the Pope's authority to loose and bind, a power given by Christ Himself). Afterward, the spouses are free to marry or have their marriage blessed if it was conducted outside the Church.

Defect of Consent

This is the most common reason for annulments. In Catholicism, it is the priest or attending deacon who will officiate at the marriage, acting as a witness and representing the Church in the ritual. But the partners actually marry one another. Therefore, both people must totally and absolutely consent to the marriage. They must be ready, willing and able to say "yes" to everything that a marriage entails.

Readiness means that one must have the mental capacity and have spent sufficient time reflecting on the sacrament of marriage. Certain psychological illnesses and conditions may make it impossible to make the commitment of marriage because of impaired cognition. Immaturity, whirlwind courtships and quick marriages can be nullified IF the partners were not truly ready for marriage.

Willingness involves total acceptance of the married state, with all of its challenges and conflicts as well as the rewards. Getting married to please the family or society does not fulfill this requirement. "Shot gun" or forced marriages are invalid because of the lack of will on the part of the individual. Consent may be overshadowed by guilt and shame as with an unplanned pregnancy or fear and isolation as is the case when a grieving spouse seeks a life partner too early without considering the consequences.

Ability to agree to the sacrament entails the personal aptitude to carry out and fulfill the wedding vows themselves. Some people enter the married state with consuming psychological problems that dominate their lives. In his pamphlet, The Catholic Teaching on Annulment: Preserving the Sanctity of Marriage, Father Becket Soule, O.P. comments:

> *The sense of alienation or inadequacy, self-depreciation, hostility, sexual problems, impulsiveness or selfishness can be pervasive and chronic. It is most unlikely that such a psychologically burdened individual can establish and maintain the close, empathetic, cherishing relationship with a spouse who provides for the mutual growth and the proper rearing of children. To put it briefly, a marriage can be annulled if the person entering marriage does not "have what it takes" to develop the community of life and love that is the substance of the marital pledge. (16)*

Personality disorders that feature "ingrained maladaptive patterns of behavior" (Soule, 16) can also make it impossible to properly consent to the marriage vows. These patterns often trace their origins back to childhood and adolescence and are associated with drug, alcohol, and domestic abuse. Consent would bind the married partners in a lifelong union that can turn into a nightmare, and as such, would not fit the Church's vision of marriage as a healthy, loving state. Finally we have full-blown mental illnesses such as severe bipolar disorder (manic depression) or schizophrenia that can impair the thought processes to the degree that consent to marriage cannot truly occur. In which case, the marriage is invalid despite all the best intentions and sincerity on the part of the couple involved.

Another form of lack of consent comes in the form of simulation, which often manifests itself in the refusal of a person to embrace an essential part of marriage. Common examples of this are the refusal to have children, believing that one can "divorce if it doesn't work out," and the refusal to stay monogamous. Total simulation means that one or both individuals entered the marriage for inappropriate reasons (marrying for wealth or to achieve permanent residence in a country) or that the proper idea of marriage was abandoned in favor of an individual's or couple's own idea of marriage.

The Annulment Process

The annulment process is governed by a set of rules found in Book VII (known as "Processes"), Canons 1400-1752 in the Code of Canon Law, and Titles XXIV-XXVI. Exorbitant fees or special treatment for the wealthy is frowned upon. Yes, there is a fee for annulment because of the sheer manpower that it takes to accomplish the work; however, in cases of poverty, the fee is often partially subsidized or waived because of financial hardship. This is a judicial procedure, conducted by the diocese in which the parties live. Unlike other forms of civil and criminal law, Canon Law is non-adversarial and doesn't assign blame for the failure of the marriage.

Those seeking an annulment are petitioners or co-petitioners (if both spouses wish to nullify a marriage). A petitioner will consult his/her parish priest or contact the diocesan tribunal directly. Then, the priest or tribunal will want a summary of the facts and events surrounding the courtship, marriage, and its disintegration. The petitioner either fills out a questionnaire or writes a narrative on the union, supplying as much evidence to support a possible annulment ruling.

Canon Law demands that the other spouse in the marriage be contacted and notified of the annulment procedure and allowed to participate in the process. The other partner has the right to contribute, oppose the action, trust the ruling to the wisdom of the tribunal, or not be involved at all. Respondents rarely seek to slow or stop an annulment proceeding. The Church seeks their input for a more rounded view of the marriage.

As with other legal systems, witnesses are often called and psychologists are consulted to substantiate the petitioner's claim. Children are usually left out of the process, as they are unable to furnish information about the couple's courtship. If they are called as witnesses, it is as adults. Procurators and advocates (both titles usually belong to one person) represent the petitioners. These are trained people, skilled and experienced in the annulment procedure and in dealing with the marriage tribunal. They represent the petitioner(s) interests and monitor the procedure.

Then, we have the defender of the bond. Defenders of the bond have a degree in canon law and are there to see that the rights of all parties involved are protected, canon law is followed, and that any statements in defense of the marriage are made. The case is usually presented before a judge (either a priest or deacon) or a panel of three judges (one of which may be a lay person). At least one judge must also have a degree in canon law. After considering the arguments for and against, canon law, and all other relevant facts, the judge or panel will deliberate and give a ruling.

If the ruling is for nullification, then the case is reviewed for a second time before another panel of three judges. Either side may appeal at that time if they're unsatisfied with the first decision. If the second panel concurs with the first decision, then a decree of nullity is issued, and both partners are free to marry someone else. While this process sounds long and drawn out, it represents the Church's reluctance to tamper with the sacrament of marriage and reverence for that holy estate.

Contrary to popular belief, Catholicism understands the suffering of its children when they attempt a union only to have it fall apart. 80 percent of cases presented in the United States alone have had an affirmative ruling for nullification. This figure includes all cases, even those marriages lasting for over a decade; however, the percentage of unions that old is much smaller than that of younger marriages that are nullified. In certain cases, an admonition called a monitum will be attached to the decree of nullity, warning the individual(s) that they might lack the maturity and proper mindset to form a healthy union in the future.

Other parties interested in an annulment are those who remarry outside of Catholicism and as a result, are unable to legitimately receive the sacraments. Many times, witnessing a significant event in the life of a child such as baptism, First Holy Communion or confirmation calls them back to full communion with the Church, and annulment allows a complete renewal of faith for everyone in their home. And while annulment nullifies a marriage, it does not attach a stigma to any children born into that marriage. Even though this is a popular argument against nullifying a marriage, Catholicism assumes that the spouses entered the sacrament with the intent of honoring the covenant; therefore, any children born from the union will remain legitimate, even if the marriage is nullified in the future.

Despite the legalities involved, the annulment process allows more closure than a simple divorce. Former partners often feel as though they are still married when they leave civil court. Annulment offers a cleansing finality that brings the deep sense of peace that comes from spiritual healing. Because this process usually occurs years after the civil decree is issued, both parties have the chance to explore, learn from their mistakes, and return to the basic values that come with a life devoted to Christ.

There is no such thing as a "Catholic Divorce." Catholicism fully embraces the married state as indissoluble, as Jesus taught us. But there are times when this state was not properly entered into for a number of reasons, rendering the attempted union null and void. Annulment is simply the formal acknowledgment of that invalidity.

***Special Note**: All information regarding Catholicism's stance on annulment and divorce (other than scripture) comes from "The Catholic Teaching on Annulment: Preserving the Sanctity of Marriage," by Father W. Becket Soule, O.P.*

Anointing of the Sick

Every church that I have ever visited or been a part of had healing rites. In my father's church, the elders would assemble around the afflicted, lay their hands on the person, and pray as the minister anointed the individual's head with oil from a tiny bottle. Notice, that in that description, there were both actions and prayer blended together.

Symbolism can only carry the Protestant world but so far. As in the case of marriage, faith and works must go together in anointing the sick because the rite by its very nature is physical. Physical acts accompanied by faith healed the sick in the Old Testament. Here is an excellent example of blending faith and works:

Now Naaman, captain of the host of the king of Syria, was a great man with his master, and honourable, because by him the Lord had given deliverance unto Syria: he was also a mighty man in valour, but he was a leper. And the Syrians had gone out by companies, and had brought away captive out of the land of Israel a little maid; and she waited on Naaman's wife.

And she said unto her mistress, "Would God my lord were the prophet that is in Samaria! For he would recover him of his leprosy."

And one went in, and told his lord saying, "Thus and thus said the maid that is of the land of Israel"

And the king of Syria said, "Go to, go, and I will send a letter unto the king of Israel."

And he departed and took with him ten talents of silver, and six thousand pieces of gold, and ten changes of raiment. And he brought the letter to the king of Israel saying, "Now when this letter is come unto thee, behold, I have therewith sent Naaman my servant to thee, that thou mayest recover him of his leprosy."

And it came to pass, when the king of Israel had read the letter, that he rent his clothes, and said, "Am I God, to kill and to make alive, that this man doth send unto me to recover a man of his leprosy? Wherefore consider, I pray you, and see how he seeketh a quarrel against me."

And it was so, when Elisha the man of God had heard that the king of Israel had read the letter, that he rent his clothes that he sent to the king saying, "Wherefore hast thou rent thy clothes? Let him come now to me, and he shall know that there is a prophet in Israel." So Naaman came with his horses, and with his chariot, and stood at the door of the house of Elisha. And Elisha sent a messenger unto him saying, "Go and wash in Jordan seven times, and thy flesh shall come again to thee, and thou shalt be clean."

But Naaman was wroth, and went away, and said, "Behold I thought, he will surely come out to me, and stand, and call upon the name of the Lord his God, and strike his hand over the place, and recover the leper. Are not Abana and Pharbar, rivers of Damascus, better than all the water of Israel? May I not wash in them, and be clean."

So he turned and went away in a rage. And his servants came near, and spake unto him, and said, "My father, if the prophet had bid thee do some great thing, wouldst thou not have done it? How much rather then, when he saith to thee, 'Wash and be clean?'"

Then he went down and dipped himself seven times in the Jordan, according to the saying of the man of God: and his flesh came again like unto the flesh of a little child, and he was clean. (2 Kings 5:1-14, KJV)

So, even before Christ came, the idea of blending faith with works into a life-changing event was around. Naaman does more than believe; he follows up with actions. But the healing does not result from direct contact with the prophet Elisha. Jesus healed the sick in a more personal way, and by doing so, made healing to a sacrament, making it an integral part of His ministry. In an age where people were very superstitious about sickness and death, Jesus shunned the popular wisdom of the day by actually allowing the sick to touch His physical person.

> *And a certain woman, which had an issue of blood twelve years, and had suffered many things of many physicians, and had spent all that she had, and was nothing bettered, but rather grew worse, when she had heard of Jesus, came in the press behind, and touched His garment. For she said, "If I may touch but His clothes, I shall be whole."*
>
> *And straightway the fountain of her blood was dried up; and she felt in her body that she was healed of that plague. And Jesus, immediately knowing Himself that virtue had gone out of Him, turn Him about in the press, and said, "Who touched my clothes?"*
>
> *And His Disciples said unto Him, "Thou seest the multitude thronging thee, and sayest thou, 'Who touched me?' "*
>
> *And He looked round about to see her that had done this thing. But the woman fearing and trembling, knowing what was done in her, came and fell down before Him, and told Him all the truth. And He said unto her, "Daughter, thy faith hath made thee whole; go in peace, and be whole of thy plague." (Mark 5:25-34, KJV)*

Here is another poignant example of Christ's compassion toward the sick:

> *And He preached in their synagogues all throughout Galilee, and cast out devils. And there came a leper to Him, beseeching Him, and kneeling down to Him, and saying unto Him, "If thou wilt, thou canst make me clean."*
>
> *And Jesus, moved with compassion, put forth His hand, and touched him and saith unto him, "I will; be thou clean."*
>
> *And as soon as He had spoken, immediately the leprosy departed from him, and he was cleansed. (Mark 1:39-42, KJV)*

Just as in the case with Naaman, both of these events are blendings of faith and works; faith inspires actions on the part of the individuals, and then they are rewarded. But, as stated before, the difference between the Old and New Testament examples is the fact that Jesus demonstrates physical contact with sick and afflicted, which was a revolutionary idea in its time.

Many Christians have heard the story of the leper that was healed, but few truly understand the gravity of this passage. Leprosy was so feared that the afflicted were not allowed to be in society. Lepers were kept segregated in small settlements and ministered to from a distance. If they came out at all, they had to announce their presence loudly and call out, "**Unclean!**" While demonic possession is well documented in the Bible, demons were often blamed for illnesses such as leprosy.

As for physical handicaps, those who were blind, lame, or congenitally afflicted were seen as the end result of their parent's sin. Obviously, someone was to blame for such misfortune. In any case, all good Jews were to refrain from too much contact with these "undesirables," lest they be punished themselves. But Christ made ministering to the sick an imperative by instructing His Disciples to follow the example he set. Scripture says: *"Then He called His twelve Disciples together, and gave them the power and authority over all devils, and to cure diseases. And He sent them to preach the kingdom of God, and to heal the sick." (Luke 9:1-2, KJV)*

Peter carries on the mission of ministering to the sick, after the Ascension in the Book of Acts:

And a certain man lame from his mother's womb was carried, whom they laid daily at the gate of the temple, which is called Beautiful, to ask alms of them that entered the temple. Who seeing Peter and John about to go into the temple asked an alms.
And Peter, fastening his eyes upon him with John, said, "Look on us."
And he gave heed unto them, expecting to receive something of them. Then Peter said, "Silver and gold have I none; but such as I have give I thee: In the name of Jesus Christ of Nazareth, rise up and walk." And he took him by the right hand and lifted him up: and immediately his feet and ancle bones received strength. (Acts 3:2-7, KJV)

But healing was and still is a two-fold proposition. There are those who are not only physically ill but "soul sick" as well. Jesus came to conquer the ultimate form of illness, that of sin, from which we all suffer. The sacrament of Anointing of the Sick seeks to treat the whole person, both physically and spiritually. This is illustrated in the Book of James.

Is any sick among you? Let him call for the elders of the church; and let them pray over him, anointing him with oil in the name of the Lord. And the prayer of faith shall save the sick, and the Lord shall raise him up; and if he have committed sins, they shall be forgiven him. Confess your faults one to another, and pray one for another, that ye may be healed. The effectual fervent prayer of a righteous man availeth much. (James 5:14-16, KJV)

In early Christianity, the sacrament included anointing the person with blessed oil coupled with the prayers of attending elders. Somewhere between the ninth and sixteenth centuries, the emphasis of healing was placed on the soul and sin. Anointing of the Sick became known as "Extreme Unction" or "Last Rites" and was seen as a way to prepare a dying person for eternity. (Bete, Anointing 2) Eyes, ears, nose and mouth were anointed, and the prayers used emphasized forgiveness of sins and the journey into paradise.

Vatican II reaffirmed the healing nature of the rite and reinstituted the involvement of the whole faith community, rather than limiting it to the priest and the sick. Today, this rite treats the whole person. Anointing the Sick offers:

1) Protection from despair in the face of life threatening illness
2) Relief from the emotional wounds that sickness brings
3) Trust in God's love and His authority as "The Great Physician"
4) Physical health- if it is God's will
5) Forgiveness of sins- so that the individual may face death (possibly) with a clear conscience

Conditions and Reception of Anointing of the Sick

The three primary conditions for this sacrament are that the individual is baptized, that they are old enough (beyond the age of reason) and that they be living. The rite may be administered if the priest is unsure if the person is conscious and aware- with the condition that they are living. The Church prefers to give this sacrament to people who are conscious and are able to understand what is happening. However, it will anoint those who are unconscious or have lost the ability to reason, providing it believes that the individual in question would've sought the healing rites if they were conscious and in their right mind. (Bete, Anointing 9)

Those who are anointed are usually adults who have life-threatening illnesses, are facing surgery, children who are extremely sick and are beyond the age of reason, and the elderly who live in fragile health. This sacrament may be repeated if necessary if recovery takes place and then there is a relapse or if a condition continues to worsen after the sacrament takes place.

The Celebration of Anointing the Sick

Anointing ordinarily takes place in a church, a home, or a hospital. This sacrament can be abbreviated or changed in cases of serious injury and/or specific situations and conditions. Other sacraments such as reconciliation and Holy Eucharist can accompany Anointing of the Sick to completely administer to the person's total needs. Family, friends, and the surrounding Christian community are welcomed to participate.

The ordinary rite has four elements. After donning his vestments, the priest will greet the individual and any others present, sprinkling all with blessed water (a reminder of the baptismal vows). Then, the sacrament of Reconciliation takes place if the person is alone, or the priest will lead attending family and friends through the Mass Penitential Rite, in which the people are asked to remember their sins and ask for God's forgiveness.

Various relevant biblical readings, prayers, and the laying on of hands by the priest follow this. This follows the example set down by Christ as he healed through touch. Then, the actual Anointing takes place using some plant oil (olive oil is preferred). The forehead and hands are marked with the sign of the cross and prayers for God's mercy, forgiveness, and healing on behalf of the suffering individual. Everyone says the Lord's Prayer, and Eucharist is received (if possible). Finally, the priest ends the rite by giving a parting blessing to all that have attended.

Though the above rite is often what people expect when it comes to Anointing of the Sick, Catholicism actually prefers the communal rite as opposed to the ordinary rite because the sacrament can include the entire, local church family. This makes it possible for several people to be anointed at once, calling the surrounding community to embrace them in the mystery of Christ's healing. It also makes it possible to for other believers to fulfill their responsibility to minister to the sick and aged as Christ taught us. Communal Anointing often takes place in the Mass or in other specialized events.

Special Note: All information provided (other than scripture passages) on this sacrament comes from the pamphlet, "About the Sacrament of Anointing the Sick," by the Channing L. Bete Co., INC.

Holy Orders

Protestants often criticize the Catholic Church as being overly symbolic. This is extremely ironic because many in the Protestant community reject the literal nature of the sacraments in favor of symbolism. This comes from the Reformation's imperative to remove Rome's authority, and Rome's authority is most keenly felt and witnessed through the Catholic priesthood. It is the priesthood that brings the other sacraments to the people. So, the idea developed into extolling the virtues of the common priesthood to which every believer is called rather than acknowledging that God sets aside some of the faithful to be servants of the rest of the flock. These servants are to live apart from the rest and to be solely devoted God with no divided loyalties.

Because the sacraments blend faith and works together, grace comes to us from specific actions coupled with belief. Sacraments have a physical side while the Protestant world concentrates almost solely on belief, often forgetting that works are the fruition of faith. The sacrament of Holy Orders bestows men with the power and grace to administer the sacraments and serve God and His Church. There are three basic orders of the Catholic Church: the Episcopate (bishops), the Presbyterate (priests) and the Diaconate (deacons) (Bete, Holy Orders 2.)

The history of Holy Orders can trace its origin to the Old Testament when men whom we call "prophets" dedicated themselves to God and His people. First, we have a prefiguring of Christ with the mysterious prophet, priest and king known as Melchizedek.

> *And Melchizedek king of Salem brought forth bread and wine: and he was the priest of the most high God. And he blessed him and said 'Blessed be Abram of the most high God, possessor of Heaven and Earth: And blessed be the most high God, which hath delivered thy enemies into thine hand.' And he gave him tithes of all." (Genesis 14:18-20, KJV)*

Then, we have Moses who led the Israelites from slavery to freedom and Aaron who began the priestly line that would serve Israel's spiritual needs. And the Old Testament is resplendent with the likes of Elijah, Samuel, and Isaiah who constantly called this wandering nation back to God from idolatry and spiritual vices.

In the New Testament, we see Jesus as priest, prophet, and king, just as Melchizedek was. This is important because the line of priests and prophets was always kept separate from that of the kings of Israel, as a kind of balance of power. Yes, Israel had good and honorable servants on her throne from time to time, but the prophets were there to choose the kings and serve them. Here, we have Christ blending these two worlds.

All Christians are part of the Melchizedek line. We all have a common priesthood through Baptism, the ability to prophesy, and are members of a royal house, the family of the King of the Universe. However, Jesus chose His Apostles from the larger population of believers to assist Him and carry on His ministry after the Ascension. These Apostles had two primary objectives: to celebrate the Eucharist as often as possible and the Great Commission (converting the world to Christianity).

Future leaders would inherit the powers, graces, and challenges of the Apostles through the laying on of hands. Over time, the leadership was organized into the overseers, who governed various communities, their councils of elders, who assisted them in governing the faithful, and special assistants, who took care of the daily needs of those religious communities. These positions would later be known as bishops, priests and deacons. (Bete, Holy Orders 4)

In the Middle Ages, the growth and spread of Christianity led to the creation of minor orders such as subdeacons, acolytes, lectors, exorcists and porters. By the 12th century, the Order of Deacons was virtually nonexistent as local priests handled all church affairs within their parishes. It would not be until the 20th century that there would be an increasing need for Diaconate to be restored. (Bete, Holy Orders 5)

The Lay Apostolate was created and developed from 1940-1960, calling ordinary individuals into service to the Church without embracing Holy Orders. In effect, this increased the duties of the common priesthood of the Catholic faith. Vatican II reinstituted the Diaconate Order, and in 1968, Pope Paul VI revised the rites for bishops, priests, and deacons. (Bete, Holy Orders 5) In 1972, the modern rites for acolytes (altar servers) and lectors (scripture readers) were created. Today, lay people even serve as Eucharistic Ministers (assistants that distribute the hosts during a Mass). Other members of the Lay Apostolate include monks and nuns, who like bishops and priests, totally dedicate themselves to God, taking the vows of poverty, chastity, and obedience. (Bete, Holy Orders 14)

Now, some Protestants object to the title of "priest" or "bishop," believing that Christianity has no priesthood as defined by the Catholic Church. They often assert that when the curtain of the Holy of Holies was torn asunder, at the time of the Crucifixion, we no longer needed any priests at all. But that contention is against the scriptures. Here is one such passage:

> *(Peter said) "For it is written in the book of Psalms, 'Let his habitation be desolate and let no man dwell therein: and his bishoprick let another take.' Wherefore of these men which have accompanied with us all the time that the Lord Jesus went in and out among us. Beginning from the baptism of John unto the same day that he was taken up from us, must one be ordained to be a witness with us of His Resurrection."*
>
> *And they appointed two, Joseph called Barsabas, who was surnamed Justus, and Matthias.*
>
> *And they prayed, and said, "Thou, Lord, which knowest the hearts of all men, shew whether of these two thou hast chosen, that he may take part of this ministry and Apostleship, from which Judas by transgression fell, that he might go to his own place."*
>
> *And they gave forth their lots, and the lot fell upon Matthias, and he was numbered with the eleven Apostles. (Acts 1:20-26, KJV)*

The word **bishoprick** is defined as ***"the area that a bishop oversees"***, also known as a ***"see."*** Why have bishopricks without bishops? That makes no sense at all. James speaks of the elders in a church in His commentary on healing and confession of sins.

> *Is any sick among you? Let him call for the elders of the church; and let them pray over him, anointing him with oil in the name of the Lord: And the prayer of faith shall save the sick, and the Lord shall raise him up; and if he have committed sins, they shall be forgiven him. Confess your faults one to another, and pray one for another, that ye may be healed. The effectual fervent prayer of a righteous man availeth much. (James 5:14-16, KJV)*

A lot of churches have elders, but few of them understand that the Greek word for ***"elder"*** is ***presbuteros,*** which is the origin of the word ***"priest."*** (Webster's 290)

Call No Man Father?

Many Protestant theologians argue over the honorific title of "Father," often quoting Jesus' words in the Gospel of Matthew. *"And call no man Your Father upon the earth: for one is your Father, which is in heaven." (Matthew 23:9, KJV)*

Looking at this verse, it certainly seems that they are correct. But call no man your father at all? What about Father Abraham, Father David or even biological fathers? Logic and reason say that we should look at the entire passage before taking such a stance. Let's start with verse 1:

> *Then spake Jesus to the multitude, and to His Disciples, saying, "The scribes and the Pharisees sit in Moses' seat: all therefore whatsoever they bid you observe, that observe and do; but do not ye after their works: for they say and do not.*
>
> *"For they bind heavy burdens and grievous to be borne, and lay them on men's shoulders; but they themselves will not move them with one of their fingers. But all their works they do for to be seen of men: they make broad their phylacteries, and enlarge the borders of their garments, and love the uppermost rooms at feasts, and the chief seats in the synagogues, and greetings in the markets, and to be called of men, Rabbi, Rabbi.*
>
> *"But be not ye called Rabbi: for one is your Master, even Christ; and all ye are brethren.* And call no man Your Father upon the earth: for one is your Father, which is in heaven. *Neither be ye called masters: for one is your master, even Christ.*
>
> *"But he that is greatest among you shall be your servant. And whosoever shall exalt himself shall be abased; and he that shall humble himself shall be exalted. But woe unto you, scribes and Pharisee, hypocrites! For ye shut up the kingdom of heaven against men: for ye neither go in yourselves, neither suffer ye then that are entering to go in." (Matthew 23:1-13, KJV)*

The verses above are a clear example of how people twist and manipulate scripture to justify a particular stance or prejudice. If we put the verse in question back into its proper context, it becomes clear that Jesus is neither addressing His Disciples nor His followers. This passage is a rebuke of the Jewish religious leaders and their hypocrisy and abuse of power. If writers wish to attack the religious establishment in Christianity using this passage, they really should look at the Christian faith across the board. We should remember that there are Protestant hypocrites who abuse power just as there are Catholic ones. (I have personal experience of less than honorable ministers, as do other people from the Protestant Christian faiths.)

But do we actual have scripture documenting the title of "Father?" As a matter of fact, yes we do. Let's look at *1 Timothy 5:1-2, KJV: Rebuke not an elder, but intreat him as a father; and the younger men as brethren; the elder women as mothers; the younger as sisters, with all purity.*

Let me remind you that we've just traced the origin of the word "priest" to the Greek word ***presbuteros*** according to Webster's Dictionary. There can be no doubt that the scriptures are speaking of Church leaders and the flock and how we should conduct ourselves. The Apostle Paul refers to his spiritual children when he writes:

> *For though ye have ten thousand instructors in Christ, yet have ye not many fathers: for in Christ Jesus I have begotten you through the Gospel. Wherefore I*

beseech you, be ye followers of me. For this cause have I sent unto you Timotheus, who is my beloved son, and faithful in the Lord, who shall bring you into remembrance of my ways which be in Christ, as I teach every where in every church. (1 Corinthians 4:15-17, KJV)

In his letter to Philemon, Paul asks:

I beseech thee for my son Onesimus, whom I have begotten in my bonds: which in time past was to thee unprofitable, but now profitable to thee and to me: whom I have sent again: thou therefore receive him, that is mine own bowels: whom I would have retained with me, that in thy stead he might have ministered unto me in the bonds of the Gospel. (Philemon 1:10-13, KJV)

And in 1 Thessalonians 2:11-12, KJV, Paul says: *"As ye know how we exhorted and comforted and charged every one of you, as a father doth his children, that ye would walk worthy of God, who hath called you unto His kingdom and glory."*

How could anyone look at these passages and conclude that the Church cannot follow the tradition of spiritual fatherhood as set down by the Apostles who saw themselves in that role? Paul was unmarried with no biological children, and yet he sees himself as father to so many spiritual children.

There's a special kind of comfort in referring to a spiritual leader as "Father." Our Fathers in the faith represent the Father, our creator in heaven, and speak with the voice of Christ when they comfort, teach, and bestow absolution. There have been times when I have personally felt the overwhelming power of the Holy Spirit resting on the shoulders of a priest, the air literally bristling with electricity. That cloak of power is not the same as that of an ordinary minister; it makes the hairs on the back of your neck stand in reverence.

Sacred Vows

Nuns, brothers, religious priests (those attached to a specific order or discipline) and those consecrated to religious life take vows of poverty, chastity, and obedience. Let's look at them from a scriptural perspective.

Poverty

Throughout Jesus' ministry, He endorses poverty for the love of God. Listen to His words to His Disciples:

Therefore said he unto them, "The harvest truly is great, but the labourers are few: pray ye therefore the Lord of the harvest, that he would send forth labourers into his harvest. Go your ways: behold I send you forth as a lamb among wolves. Carry neither purse, nor scrip, nor shoes: and salute no man by the way. And into whatsoever house ye enter, first say, 'Peace be unto this house.'

"And if the Son of Peace be there, your peace shall rest upon it: if not, it shall turn to you again. And in the same house remain, eating and drinking such things as they give: for the labourer is worthy of his hire. Go not from house to house. And into whatsoever city ye enter, and they receive you, eat such things as are set before you: and heal the sick that are therein, and say unto them, 'the kingdom of God is come nigh unto you.'" (Luke 10: 2-8, KJV)

Jesus also reiterates this in the Gospel of Matthew, when he encounters a young wealthy man who has followed the law since his youth. When he asked Jesus what else he needed to do, Christ says:

> *...If thou wilt be perfect, go and sell that thou hast, and give it to the poor, and thou shalt have treasure in heaven: and come and follow me."*
>
> *But when the young man heard that saying, he went away sorrowful: for he had great possessions. Then said Jesus unto His Disciples, "Verily I say unto you, that a rich man shall hardly enter into the kingdom of Heaven. And again I say unto you, it is easier for a camel to go through the eye of a needle, than for a rich man to enter into the Kingdom of God." (Matthew 19:21-24, KJV)*

Jesus also speaks of God's rewards to those who give everything up for Him: *"And every one that hath forsaken houses, or brethren, or sisters, or father, or mother, or wife, or children, or lands, for my name's sake, shall receive a hundred fold, and shall inherit everlasting life. But many that are first shall be last; and the last shall be first." (Matthew 19:29-30, KJV)*

These particular passages illustrate that the Church's leaders are called to rely on the love and good graces of the communities in which they serve. And in keeping with this, it was traditional for the early Christians, who completely devoted themselves to the Christian community, to give all possessions or monies to its service. To do otherwise had grave consequences.

Here is an example from the Book of Acts:

> *But a certain man named Ananias, with Sapphira his wife, sold a possession, and kept back part of the price, his wife also being privy to it, and brought a certain part, and laid it at the Apostles' feet.*
>
> *But Peter said, "Ananias, why hath Satan filled thine heart to lie to the Holy Ghost, and to keep back part of the price of the land? While it remained, was it not thine own? And after it was sold, was it not in thine own power? Why hast thou conceived this thing in thine heart? Thou hast not lied unto men, but unto God."*
>
> *And Ananias hearing these words fell down and gave up the ghost; and great fear came on all of them that heard these things. And the young men arose, wound him up, and carried him out, and buried him. And it was about the space of three hours after, when his wife, not knowing what was done, came in. And Peter answered unto her, "Tell me whether ye sold the land for so much?"*
>
> *And she said, "Yea for so much."*
>
> *Then Peter said unto her, "How is it that ye have agreed together to tempt the Spirit of the Lord? Behold the feet of them which hath buried thy husband are at the door, and shall carry thee out."*
>
> *Then fell she down straightway at his feet, and yielded up the ghost: and the young men came in, and found her dead and, carrying her forth, buried her by her husband. (Acts 5:1-10, KJV)*

Seeking to hold back part of the profits for themselves, Ananias and Sapphira tried to defraud the Christian community and paid for this misdeed with their lives.

Chastity

Even before Christianity, those who choose perpetual chastity have been venerated by the pagan world. For example, ancient Rome prized its Vestal Virgins, who were the guardians of the eternal flame in the temple of Vesta. Received into this sisterhood at the age of ten, a Virgin would serve for thirty years, during which time, she was forbidden to marry. Rome linked its prosperity with these priestesses, believing that they gained the divine favor of the gods who protected the empire. Vestal Virgins always enjoyed the choicest seating anywhere they went and were given various military honors. If any condemned person ran into a Virgin on his/her way to execution, that person was immediately pardoned. Any Virgin who broke her vow of chastity was seen as a betrayer of Rome and the gods; therefore, she was buried alive. (Morrow 377)

If the non-Christian world saw chastity as a venerable sacrifice, then one can only imagine how God feels when a dedicated Christian gives that part of life up for the glory of His Kingdom, in the service of His Son. Jesus speaks of this noble vow in the Gospel of Matthew:

> *All men cannot receive this saying, save they to whom it is given. For there are some eunuchs, which were born from their mother's womb: and there are some eunuchs, which were made eunuchs of men: and there be eunuchs, which have made themselves eunuchs for the Kingdom of Heaven's sake. He that is able to receive it, let him receive it. (Matthew 19:11-12, KJV)*

For those who are unfamiliar with the term "eunuch," this is a man who is perpetually chaste due to the partial or total loss of his sexual organs. This was often done with palace guards who protected the wives and concubines of a king, sultan, or sheik. This made sure that any children born in the harem were the ruler's and not someone else's. But a spiritual eunuch is something special in that he willingly refrains from marriage and sexuality in the interest of spiritual fulfillment. The Apostle Paul also praises chastity in his first letter to the Corinthians: "*But I speak this of permission and not of commandment. For I would that all men were even as myself. But every man hath his proper gift of God, one after this manner, and another after that. I say therefore to the unmarried and widows: it is good for them to abide even as I.*" *(1 Corinthians 7:6-8, KJV)*

Following Christ's example and the Apostle Paul's advice, Catholic priests, brothers, and sisters are bound to lifelong celibacy. Not only was Jesus was conceived of a virgin, but he was also reared in a celibate home. Because Catholics believe that Mary remained a virgin throughout her life, we also believe that Joseph, her husband, was chaste as well. (Morrow 377) In fact, Joseph is often revered as her "most chaste spouse."

There is also the issue of divided loyalty that sometimes occurs between church and family life in the Protestant world. No matter how devoted to God a minister may be, he must balance his life between his calling and his family, which can be problematic at times. Catholicism endorses the belief that a priest must be totally devoted to God at all times. Paul explores this conflict when he writes:

> *But I would have you without carefulness. He that is unmarried careth for the things that belong to the Lord, how he may please the Lord: But he that is married careth for the things that are of this world, how he may please wife. There is difference also between a wife and a virgin. The unmarried woman careth for*

things of the Lord, that she may be holy both in body and in spirit: but she that is married careth for the things of the world, how she may please her husband.

And this I speak for your own profit; not that I may cast a snare upon you, but for that, which is comely, and that ye may attend upon the Lord without distraction. (1 Corinthians 7:32-35, KJV)

So, we see that the New Testament speaks very highly of those who are willing to forsake their sexual natures in order to more fully serve the Kingdom of God. While the sexual drive is a good and natural thing (in the context of marriage), we are also called as Christians to be above our nature and not subjugated by it. The Catholic Church understands that most of its members will marry and have children, but it also seeks out special individuals to leadership and the higher standards of spirituality that go with that honor.

Obedience

Each of us is called to be obedient. Citizens must obey the laws in their respective countries. Workers are subordinate to their employers. Children are subject to their parents. And we must all submit to our spiritual leaders. But perfect obedience demands that we sacrifice our will to God and give ourselves over completely, without reservation. This is the standard of obedience required of Catholic priests, brothers, and sisters. In a world driven by selfish desire, they must give everything that they are and all that they have.

Sacred Promises

Secular priests (those unattached to a specific order or discipline) are bound by the sacred promises of celibacy and obedience. They can own property. Celibacy inplies chastity as these men are unmarried, and any sexual union outside of marriage is a grave sin.

The Sacrament of Holy Orders

This sacrament has twelve steps and is celebrated in a Mass attended by priests and deacons:

1) The candidates are presented, and either a priest or deacon will ask for their ordination.

2) The people are asked for their approval of the candidates, otherwise known as election.

3) The bishop will give a homily on the duties of the priesthood and diaconate.

4) Each candidate is asked about his determination to perform the duties and handle the responsibilities of his respective post.

5) The candidates must promise obedience to the bishop and his successors.

6) The prospective priests and deacons will then lie face down before the bishop while the Litany of the Saints is sung. This position is an ancient one and denotes an attitude of extreme reverence. Both heaven and earth join together in prayer that God will make these men holy.

7) The bishop lays hands upon each individual, conferring sacred grace and power and joining that person to the clergy.

8) The bishop will consummate the ordination through the Prayer of Ordination. When this is done, the candidates are new priests and deacons.

9) The new clergymen are dressed in vestments by attending priest and deacons. This is called investiture.

10) Each new priest's hands will be anointed with consecrated oil. This is symbolic of bestowing the power to bless and consecrate.

11) The bishop then welcomes each individual into the clergy.

12) All the clergy will celebrate Holy Eucharist together with attending Catholics in the congregation. (Bete, Holy Orders 8-9)

The sacrament of Holy Orders can only be celebrated once, and it also leaves an indelible mark upon the soul. Even if he breaks his vows and is stripped of his responsibilities, a priest will forever remain a priest.

The priesthood is a living sign of God's grace, bringing the sacraments to the people and calling them to a deeper relationship with Christ. A priest shares the Gospel and Holy Scripture and shows how Catholic teachings come from the Holy Scriptures. He serves the church community, maintains the governing structure of the church, and continues a life dedicated to studying theology and canon law, so that he might better serve his flock. And because priests are our leaders, they inspire us with lives completely devoted to Christ. (Bete, Holy Orders 10-11)

Catholicism has a number of religious orders and communities; here are some of our better-known groups and the founders:

The Benedictines - St. Benedict (480-547)
The Dominicans- St. Dominic (1170-1221)
The Franciscans- St. Francis (1181-1226)
Jesuits- St. Ignatius Loyola (1491-1556)
The Sisters of Charity- Sts. Vincent de Paul (1581-1660) & Louise de Marillac (1591-1630)
Trappists- Abbot de Rance (1626-1700)
The American Sisters of Charity- St. Elizabeth Bayley Seton (1774-1821)
The Sacred Heart Society- St. Madeleine Sophie Barat (1779-1865)
The Salesians- St. John Bosco (1815-1888)
The Blessed Sacrament Sisters- Bl. Katherine Drexel (1858-1955)
    (Brown & Anatolios 47)

Pedophilia and the Catholic Clergy

Sometimes, it is particularly painful to be a Catholic, as in the sexual abuse scandal, which rocked the Catholic Church in the spring of 2002. I wish to say on behalf of all good and devout Catholics everywhere that we are collectively shocked and saddened that some of our shepherds should harm the tenderest lambs in their care. It breaks my heart, and I am sick that these individuals would use God's holy priesthood in such an ugly fashion.

I believe that the faithful want these people found and removed from the flock as soon as possible, and it is the responsibility of the presiding bishop of each diocese to see that this is done. Our previous bishop demonstrated this principle by removing clergymen and religious and lay people from various parishes and turning the offenders over to the civil authorities in his area, so that each report could be fully investigated and those in question were either released or charged.

Much of this situation could've easily been avoided had the Catholic leadership been more forthcoming to the authorities or at least removed many of these people from the priesthood before any further harm was done. But Catholicism stresses reformation and reclamation. The Church wants to believe that individuals can change with the proper amount of spiritual guidance and psychological counseling.

Catholic leaders have also made the mistake of believing that they could handle the problem "in house." You see, Catholicism, as a whole, is like a large, boisterous family. And how many families enjoy having outsiders delve into their problems, no matter how dangerous or destructive? Ask any social worker, and they'll say that number is small. Catholics, everywhere, are hoping that this scandal, though horrific, will strengthen us and remove the shadowy assumption that the Roman Catholic priesthood is a haven for pedophiles.

My husband has been a Catholic for forty years. Michael was even an altar boy through much of his childhood- until he became taller than the attending priest. His memories of priests are good and wholesome. 2002 marked the tenth anniversary of my Catholic conversion, and I have no personal knowledge of any priest who has behaved inappropriately with a child or anyone else for that matter.

The outside world wants to believe that we have a sexual predator in every parish, just waiting for a moment alone with a vulnerable child. When dealing with an offending priest, the press, as a whole, hints that all priests are predators. Why doesn't this happen in the Protestant community? They see the occasional offending minister or pastor as an aberration in an otherwise good and honorable spiritual calling. Surely, we, as a society, cannot be so naive as to believe that Catholicism has cornered the market on sexual abuse.

Does we see all teachers and workers in the educational field as predatory? Despite the fact that public education offers most kids a safe environment to learn and grow, it is estimated that one in every ten children will suffer from some form of sexual abuse while attending public school from kindergarten through the 12th grade. This goes from unwanted jokes and remarks to outright criminal behavior. (CNN 1)

This figure was submitted by Charol Shakeshaft, a professor at Hofstra University, in a report commissioned by Congress as a part of the No Child Left Behind legislation. Ms. Shakeshaft found that teachers were the most common offenders, followed by coaches, substitute teachers, bus drivers, and teacher's aides. Surprisingly, the percentage of women was 43 percent, and male students composed 44 percent of the victims. (CNN 2) Why do we see offenders in the school system as exceptions to the rule while seeing a predator in every priestly collar? This double standard is horribly unfair to the majority of decent priests who would never dream of doing such a thing.

Some of the most influential people in my life have been priests. One example is a good friend whom I spend hours with over the phone. His nickname is "St. Chocolatus" because chocolate is one of the few chinks in his armor. Chocolatus looks like Santa Claus would with no red suit and acts as a grandfather figure in my life. Close your eyes and listen, and you'd swear that he was Richard Dreyfuss. Wisecracking and even sarcastic at times, I can imagine the kind of conversations he'd have with Nana if she were living. But this is a guy who is deeply devoted to the fringe of society, misfits, and kids in trouble.

And Chocolatus takes a dim view on sex offenders. I'll never forget that he once told me about an incident involving a sexual predator in his hometown. While serving in the Boy Scouts, my friend stumbled across a scout leader who was about to take indecent liberties with a boy in his charge. Angrily grabbing a tent pole, young Chocolatus swung at the man, breaking the pedophile's jaw in multiple places. My adopted grandpa paid for his action with a year's probation, courtesy of the local magistrate.

When I think of priests, I always picture men like Father Leo and "St. Chocolatus," not the warped and twisted image of the Catholic clergy projected by the media. Perhaps the answer to this anti-Catholic viewpoint lies in a deeper, more insidious myth that the Protestant world holds dear: that marriage to a good and understanding woman can prevent this social ill by channeling sexual desire and frustration in a more positive way.

It is a fact that many Catholics want to see their priests have the freedom to marry. And Catholic men, such as my husband, have had to choose between the Church and familial life with a wife and children, depriving the faithful of new priests and the ability to rid themselves of bad apples more easily. But to say that marriage can "cure" or "prevent" pedophilia is a foolish notion. Pedophilia is not a married versus celibate problem, neither is it truly a gay versus straight problem. It is a human dilemma that is present in every segment of society and has no specific racial, religious, ethnic or cultural origin.

Marriage as a safeguard against sexual perversion is only as strong as the married individual's commitment to God and his/her spouse. Let us not forget that married spouses often indulge in adulterous affairs or visit prostitutes, bringing home sexually transmitted diseases to their families. Then, there is the dark specter of incest that almost always begins in childhood when a child's love and trust is strongest towards a parent. If marriage were such a cure, incest would be a rare, no freak, occurrence. While I have no personal knowledge of an abusive priest and his victim(s), I have at least four acquaintances that were victims of incest: two were molested by their fathers and two by their grandfathers.

What about Christian singles? Unmarried Christians should live celibate lives because sexual acts committed without benefit of marriage are fornication, a serious sin. If we assume that marriage is some great preventative measure, then shouldn't singles get the same scrutiny that priests get? Other than vocation, the only difference between a celibate priest and a celibate Christian single is the potential for marriage. So, those members of the Christian community who never marry should receive the exact same treatment as do Catholic priests, no matter what denomination they hail from.

Society continues to jail predators who outwardly exemplify all that is good and noble to Protestants. Many are family men, with prosperous careers, beautiful houses, wives, and children. And yes, some who fall from grace are ministers. I believe that

Protestants want to believe that pedophilia within a body of believers is mostly a Catholic problem, but truth is that it is widespread.

The following information was first published in ***The Christian Science Monitor*** (a non-Catholic source) in an article by Mark Clayton, one of its staff writers. His article centered on findings by Christian Ministry Resources (CMR), which is a tax and legal advice publisher that serves a multi-denominational contingent of more than 75,000 congregations and 1,000 denominational social agencies throughout the US. In a series of studies dating back to 1993, each covering 1,000 churches across every denomination, CMR found that the number of reported cases of sexual abuse averaged around 70 cases per week. However, out of the 350,000 churches in the US, only 19,500 are actually Catholic (5.57%). In reality, Protestants have more cases of sexual abuse as opposed to Catholics. James Cobble, executive director of CMR, who oversees the survey, said, ***"The Catholics have gotten all the attention from the media, but this problem is even greater with the Protestant churches simply because of their far larger numbers."***

But surprisingly, the clergy, in general, were not the chief offenders. ***Of the reported incidents, the highest percentage (42 percent) offenders were actually unpaid volunteers working within church communities. Only 25 percent were the clergy and paid staff members together. Another 25 percent of sex offenders were (believe it or not) children preying upon other children.***

As for the issue of settling out of court and "hush money," it may be interesting to note that ***21 percent (according to CMR's 2000 survey)*** of the cases of reported sexual misconduct in churches ended with out of court settlements. Part of an out of court settlement is the use of non-disclosure clauses, in which the plaintiff agrees to refrain from discussing specific details of a case. It is a standard procedure in the legal world. (Clayton, reprinted ***Catholic News & Herald,*** 4/19)

And I believe that the majority of independent churches have greater reason to hide offenses through non-disclosure clauses than do larger, organized churches. Independent groups do not have access to outside funding from a larger organization and must directly rely upon the financial resources of their congregations. A scandal of any kind can cause members to withdraw their monetary support, which is an independent church's lifeblood. If the contribution well runs dry, the doors can close. Furthermore, since there is no hierarchy to report to, it is easier to hide "hush money," because of the lack of external controls.

The majority of churches in America have had to institute such precautions as background checks and fingerprinting to discern any prior violent or sexual offenses of potential caregivers. Some have even issued photo IDs to insure that the proper people are in restricted areas with children. Nurseries usually stipulate that only female staff members are allowed to change diapers, and that bathrooms are inspected for any unauthorized adult before children are allowed in. And the "one-on-one" dynamic between children and adults is frowned upon as a precaution against possible future incidents of abuse. Multiple caregivers are also a means of preventing false accusations against clergy and staff. Not only do these measures significantly reduce the possibility of abuse, but control the cost and availability of liability insurance.

Even so, this form of abuse cannot completely be eradicated. My parents had high standards concerning my care as a child, electing to place me with my grandmother or older church matriarchs of impeccable reputations. Still, reading those formerly mentioned sex abuse statistics touched on an ugly childhood memory of my own, one that I did not tell my parents until well after my thirtieth birthday.

When I was nine, an older teenager attending my church repeatedly molested me. After school, I would take the bus to a church lady's home to be cared for until my parents could collect me. She was a good caregiver who was well respected at church. As such, other matriarchs would often visit and chat about church affairs. Among them, was one woman who brought her son, a boy in his middle teens. Oily and oozing with charm, he would often insist on baby-sitting me in an adjacent room with the door closed. But his view of baby-sitting was vastly different from mine.

After a few of these episodes, I began to conclude that what he was doing to me was wrong and made a concerted effort never to allow us to be alone again. I deliberately took my baths at the time that he and his mom would arrive, always locking the bathroom door before turning the water on and staying as long as I could in there, without arousing suspicion. Then, I would come out, sit, and play near the warmth of her wood stove, rather than go into the colder part of the house with Him. It was a practical solution that worked well, much to my abuser's disappointment and my delight.

But the result of this molestation was an intense fascination with sex. I would peruse magazines such as **Penthouse** and **Playboy**, and then draw what I saw. My teachers were the first to notice my behavior and wanted a conference with my parents as soon as possible. Being both terrified and embarrassed at the time, I managed to convince them that this was normal childhood curiosity, and that no foul play was involved.

As a preteen, I continued my fascination into the exploring phase. I wanted to know everything about sex, and books were not enough. But I saw boys as dangerous, predatory, and aggressive. Girls were a much safer alternative. As is common with this age group, I, like so many other preteens, began to experiment within my small circle of girlfriends. They, too, were struggling to make sense of their bodies and budding sexual identities. Many of these incidents would be considered very innocent by today's standards, featuring the lightest touches and the occasional kiss.

Oddly enough, it was a Catholic priest who introduced me to healthy sexuality. No, it wasn't an affair; it was a book. I remember stumbling across Father Andrew Greeley's *The Magic Cup,* a version of the Irish Arthurian myths with the High King Cormac McDermot and his lovely Brigid. Unlike the cooler English version, the Irish myth ends in a happy marriage. Andrew taught me that men could be the sexual partners they were supposed to be, loving and gentle on one hand, but ferocious protectors when needed. (I also became aware of the Celtic culture and grew to admire the passion and spirit of the Celts, something that continues to this day.)

Slowly my attention drifted back to boys. By the time my thirteenth birthday arrived, I had developed a massive crush on Carlton, a good-looking dish of a boy who also went to my childhood church. This adoration was strictly from afar and never reached any fruition, but it was certainly fun to fantasize.

Though I was able to work through my confusion and establish a healthy sexual identity, the experience of being molested did have a lasting effect. When it first occurred, I felt lots of guilt and shame, believing that somehow I had been the cause of the abuse. And it was at this time that I began overeating and gaining weight. I now feel that I took comfort in food and that food acted as a kind of armor against sexual predators. My young mind probably reasoned that if I made myself ugly enough, no one would be interested in victimizing me again. Besides, I thought the most victims were small people; and offenders are less likely to attack someone who outweighs them. I still deal with my weight today, along with the rejection and cruelty suffered at the hands of classmates and well-meaning family members due to being obese.

I am lucky because I was able to have some closure when other abuse victims never see it. During my late teens, this boy, now a man, came to me, apologized for what he had done, and asked my forgiveness. It's amazing what forgiveness can do for the person giving it. Because of his humility, his identity will remain a secret, known only by close family members.

This life experience taught me that sexual predators come in all shapes, sizes, and forms and that no church or denomination is immune to this evil. Churches, in general, are atmospheres of implicit trust coupled with spiritual authority. Whereas an abuser may gravitate toward a position such as a coach, teacher, counselor, or scout master, a post such as a minister or priest is particularly attractive as it manipulates a victim, twisting and coloring both the religious and secular worlds with each act of abuse.

Marriage is not some magic bullet against sexual perversion. The number of married predators in our inmate population proves that. The best defense against pedophilia lies in educating a child that anyone can be a pedophile, even those whom we trust. And parents should carefully watch those who interact with their children and the dynamics of each relationship.

The Petrine Doctrine

Since the earliest days of the Reformation, there has always been a dispute between Protestants and Catholics concerning the roots of the Catholic Church. Catholicism has always maintained that it was founded on none other than Peter who is considered the first Pope, and that the current Pope is the spiritual descendent of Peter through Apostolic Succession. Catholic doctrine teaches the Peter was the "Prince of the Apostles." The word "prince" comes from the Latin word, *princeps*, which means *"first, chief, originator."* (Wilson 96) While the Apostles were basically equals, they still needed a leader or spokesman, and Christ chose Peter for the position. Protestants have always endorsed total equality among the Apostles and the belief that there is no Apostolic Succession.

But which side is correct? To answer this question, we have to look closely at the scriptures. I have observed that many believers have little practical knowledge regarding the history and surrounding culture of the scriptures. What's worse is seeing that defect passed on in various books, pamphlets and the efforts of well-meaning ministers. To really understand the Bible, we must know about whom, when, and why parts were written as well as the social/ political climate they were written in. While we may easily grasp the fundamental ideas, we tend to miss the subtle nuances and important meanings without careful attention.

Even before the Roman Emperor Diocletian formalized it, the Roman Empire was divided west and east. The language of commerce and diplomacy for the western part was largely written in Latin while the eastern portion recognized Greek as its primary tongue. As stated before, this is largely due to the influence of Alexander the Great who propagated the Greek language, arts and culture as he conquered various parts of the Middle East. When the Romans took control, they allowed Greek to remain the official language. So, the New Testament was written in Greek in order to reach as many people as possible in the vicinity.

But, non-Grecian areas kept their own individual dialects in their daily affairs. In Israel, there were two primary languages. Hebrew was the sacred language of the priests, reserved strictly for worshipping God in local synagogues and in the Temple. Aramaic, a linguistic cousin of Hebrew, was the common tongue. This is much like the use of Latin and Italian in Italy. Latin dealt with sacred texts and prayers while Italian was used on an everyday basis. In reality, most Jews conducted their business with Rome using Greek; spoke Aramaic in the marketplace, and Hebrew in the Temple.

Some might argue about the valid use of Aramaic as the common tongue, but according to ***The History of Ancient Israel***, by Michael Grant, from the time of Ezra, Aramaic, a northwest Semitic tongue, replaced Hebrew as the common tongue of the people. It was also the preferred language of official Persian documents. Examples of Aramaic can be found in the original text of the Book of Ezra. Aramaic is still spoken today in some villages near Damascus. (Grant 191)

Jesus was a "man of the people," ministering to mostly the working class of Jews. While he spoke Hebrew, this would have been limited to reading and discussing the scriptures in local synagogues or at the Temple. Christ never cared for politics or business ventures, so he would have had little use for Greek. Our Savior more than likely spoke the language of the common man- Aramaic.

Like most languages, Greek and Aramaic are not always compatible with one another. For example, Matthew writes, *"And I say also unto thee, that thou art Peter, and upon this rock, I will build my church; and the gates of hell shall not prevail against it."(Matthew 16:18, KJV)*

When translating the Aramaic word ***Cephas*** to Greek, Matthew chose two words: ***Petros*** for the proper name and ***petra*** for the rock. Because ***petra*** is a feminine noun, it could not be used for a proper male name. Many languages class their words as feminine or masculine, and adjectives and names must agree with the sex of the original word. The closest masculine word to ***petra*** was ***Petros***, which means "small rock or pebble." This is the famous "***Petros/petra***" argument against the primacy of Peter.

But the Petros/petra theory is what many classical debaters would call a "straw man" or something with no real substance. As stated before, there is evidence that Christ spoke Aramaic. Look at His statement to Peter in the Gospel of John,

> *One of the two which heard John speak, and followed him, was Andrew, Simon Peter's brother. He first findeth his own brother Simon, and saith unto him, "We have found the Messias", which is, being interpreted the Christ.*
>
> *And he brought him to Jesus. And when Jesus beheld him, he said, "Thou art Simon the Son of Jona: Thou shalt be called Cephas", which is by interpretation, a stone. (John 1:40-42, KJV)*

If Christ did not speak Aramaic, then why call Peter Cephas. ***Cephas*** comes from the Aramaic word, ***kepha***. Until the time period of the New Testament, ***kepha*** was always used as a common noun. It meant, "large stone outcropping," "bedrock," "foundation stone," "cornerstone,"- or "BIG SLAB O' ROCK!" Logic says that it makes more sense to build the church on a large stone outcropping rather than a small pebble. It is interesting to note after Jesus uses the word "Cephas" in a naming fashion, it becomes a proper name. Other Aramaic words in the Gospels include ***talitha qumi*** and the most famous of all- ***abba***. (Laux 10) Remember that Jesus called God, the Father, ***Abba***. This supports the position that our Savior spoke Aramaic in His normal, everyday activities.

It is also interesting to note that Jesus' commission to Peter has a precursor in the Old Testament, in the Book of Isaiah:

> *And it shall come to pass in that day, that I will call my servant Eliakim the son of Hilkiah: And I will clothe him with thy robe, and strengthen him with thy girdle, and I will commit thy government into his hand: and he shall be a father to the inhabitants of Jerusalem, and the house of Judah.*
>
> *And the key of the house of David will I lay upon his shoulder; so he shall open, and none shall shut; and he shall shut; and none shall open. And I will fasten him as a nail in a sure place; and he shall be for a glorious throne to his father's house, the offering and the issue…(Isaiah 22:20-24, KJV)*

Now, let's examine the words that Jesus spoke to Peter, when He declared: *"And I will give unto thee the keys of kingdom of heaven: and whatsoever thou shalt bind on earth shall be bound in heaven: and whatsoever thou shalt loose on earth shall be loosed in heaven." (Matthew 16:19, KJV)*

When we compare these two passages, it becomes clear that Peter was separated from the other Disciples and given special authority, and while Protestants love to claim that Christ is speaking to all His Disciples denoting an equal footing, grammar rules undermine this argument. The word "thee" is very important. It denotes second person singular status and is not a plural pronoun. In Southern lingo, Christ isn't saying "y'all." Christ speaks ONLY to Peter when saying this statement.

We should also remember that giving an individual "keys" to any building or gate bestows the power and authority to allow or deny entry within that building or gate. In effect, Peter was given the power of allowing or denying entrance to heaven itself. As stated earlier, the power to loose and bind means the ability to declare what is and is not a sin. Remember Christ's words from *the Book of John 20:23, KJV: "Whose soever sins ye remit, they are remitted unto them; and whose soever sins ye retain, they are retained."* To retain means to hold. Holding implies the act of binding.

But why single Peter out of the rest of the Disciples in the first place? What set him apart from the others? For that answer, let's look at the Gospel of Matthew, chapter 16, verses 15-17. *"He saith unto them, "But whom say ye that I am?" And Simon Peter answered and said, 'Thou art the Christ, the Son of the Living God.' And Jesus answered and said unto him, 'Blessed art thou, Simon Bar-Jona: For flesh and blood hath not revealed it unto thee, but my Father which is in heaven.'"*

So, we see that it is Peter's confession that leads to this honor of being earthly shepherd to the whole flock. Jesus knows whom to choose because God the Father has revealed it to Peter- and only Peter. And just before His ascension, Jesus does place Peter in charge of the body of believers, the flock:

> *He saith unto him again the second time, "Simon, son of Jonas, lovest thou me?"*
> *He saith unto him, "Yea, Lord; thou knowest that I love thee."*
> *He saith unto him, "Feed my sheep."*
> *He saith unto him the third time, "Simon, son of Jonas, lovest thou me?"*
> *Peter was grieved because he said unto him the third time, "Lovest thou me?" And he said unto him, "Lord, thou knowest all things; thou knowest that I love thee."*
> *Jesus saith unto him, "Feed my sheep." (John 21:15-17, KJV)*

First of all, the preceding passage illustrates a three-fold acclamation by Peter. This is important because it occurs after the crucifixion. Peter had previously denied Christ three times. Now, he declares his devotion for the Son of God three times, thereby reclaiming his leadership of the Apostles and the rest of God's flock. The word "lambs" refers to the ordinary followers and lay ministers, the most tender and weak of Christ's followers. The sheep are the Apostles themselves and will later be: deacons, priests, bishops and cardinals. (Morrow 109) Again, our Savior addresses Peter using the second person singular, "thou," which stresses that only Peter has authority over Christ's flock on earth. Who but the shepherd has dominion and authority over a flock of sheep?

Another interesting observation that anyone will make when reading the New Testament is the fact that from the time Peter becomes a Disciple until his death, his name is constantly listed first- even to the extent of mentioning only that name. (Judas Iscariot's name is always last, if listed at all.) Even Matthew refers to Peter as the "first Apostle" when he lists the various Disciples in Matthew 10:2-4, KJV. But Peter was neither the first to join nor the oldest, those honors belong to Andrew. If not by order or age, then Peter can only be the first in authority.

I doubt that many Protestants are truly aware of the large amount of evidence pointing to the primacy of Peter. I certainly wasn't until I began to research the Bible myself. Yes, we have the words of Christ and the way Peter is listed and described in the New Testament, but the most astounding proof lies in his actions after Christ leaves for heaven. The Book of Acts demonstrates Peter's leadership as opposed to the other Apostles.

Peter Uses His Christ Given Authority

Peter preaches the first sermon and admits the first Jewish and Gentile converts at Pentecost:

> *And how hear we every man in our own tongue, wherein we were born: Parthians and Medes, and Elamites, and the dwellers in Mesopotamia, and in Judea, and Cappodocia, in Pontus, and Asia, Phrygia, and Pamphylia, in Egypt and in the parts of Libya about Cyrene, and strangers of Rome, Jews, and proselytes, Cretes and Arabians, we do hear them speak in our tongues the wonderful works of God?" And they were all amazed, and in doubt, saying one to another, "What meaneth this?"*
>
> *But Peter standing up with the eleven, lifted up his voice, and said unto them, "Ye men of Judaea, and all ye that dwell in Jerusalem, be this known unto you and hearken my words." (Acts 2:8-14, KJV)*
>
> *...Then Peter said unto them, "Repent and be baptized all of you in the name Jesus Christ for the remissions of sins, and ye shall receive the Holy Ghost. For the promise is unto you, and your children, and to all that are afar off, even as many as the Lord God shall call."*
>
> *And with many other words did he testify and exhort, saying, "Save yourselves from this untoward generation."*
>
> *Then they that gladly received his word were baptized: and the same day there were added unto them about three thousand souls. (Acts 2:38-41, KJV)*

Peter is the first Disciple to perform a miracle after the Ascension:

> *And a certain man lame from his mother's womb was carried, whom they laid daily at the gate of the temple which is called Beautiful, to ask alms of them that entered the temple. Who seeing Peter and John about to go into the temple asked an alms.*
>
> *And Peter, fastening his eyes upon him with John, said, "Look on us."*
>
> *And he gave heed unto them, expecting to receive something of them. Then Peter, "Silver and gold have I none; but such as I have give I thee: In the name of Jesus Christ of Nazareth, rise up and walk." And he took him by the right hand and lifted him up: and immediately his feet and ancle bones received strength. (Acts 3:2-7, KJV)*

Peter metes out the first punishment:

> *But a certain man named Ananias, with Sapphira his wife, sold a possession, and kept back part of the price, his wife also being privy to it, and brought a certain part, and laid it at the Apostles' feet.*
>
> *But Peter said, "Ananias, why hath Satan filled thine heart to lie to the Holy Ghost, and to keep back part of the price of the land? While it remained, was it not thine own? And after it was sold, was it not in thine own power? Why hast thou conceived this thing in thine heart? Thou hast not lied unto men, but unto God."*

And Ananias hearing these words, fell down and gave up the ghost; and great fear came on all of them that heard these things. And the young men arose, wound him up, and carried him out, and buried him.

And it was about the space of three hours after, when his wife, not knowing what was done, came in. And Peter answered unto her, "Tell me whether ye sold the land for so much?"

And she said, "Yea for so much."

Then Peter said unto her, "How is it that ye have agreed together to tempt the Spirit of the Lord? Behold the feet of them which hath buried thy husband are at the door, and shall carry thee out."

Then fell she down straightway at his feet, and yielded up the ghost: and the young men came in, and found her dead, and, carrying her forth, buried her by her husband. (Acts 5:1-10, KJV)

Peter expels the heretic Simon Magus:

And when Simon saw that through laying on the Apostles' hands, the Holy Ghost was given, he offered them money, saying, "Give me also this power, that on whomsoever I lay hands, he may receive the Holy Ghost."

But Peter said unto him, "Thy money perish with thee, because thou hast thought that the gift of God may be purchased with money." (Acts 8:18-20, KJV)

Peter is the first to visit the churches:

Then had the churches rest throughout Judaea and Galilee and Samaria, and were edified; and walking in the fear of the Lord, and in the comfort of the Holy Ghost, were multiplied. And it came to pass, as Peter passed throughout all quarters, he came down also to the saints which dwelt at Lydda. (Acts 9:31-32, KJV)

Peter is the final authority in settling disputes:

But there rose up certain of the sect of Pharisees which believed, saying that it was needful to circumcise them, and to command them to keep the law of Moses. And the Apostles and elders came together for to consider this matter.

And when there had been much disputing, Peter rose up, and said unto them, "Men and brethren, ye know that a good while ago God made choice among us, that the Gentiles by my mouth should hear the word of the Gospel, and believe. And God, which knoweth all hearts, bare them witness, giving them the Holy Ghost, even as he did unto us. And put no difference between us and them, purifying their hearts by faith.

"Now therefore why tempt God, to put a yoke upon the neck of the Disciples, which neither our fathers nor we were able to bear. But we believe that through the grace of the Lord Jesus Christ we shall be saved, even as they."

Then the multitude kept silence, and gave audience to Barnabas and Paul, declaring what miracles and wonders God had wrought among the Gentiles by them. (Acts 15:5-12, KJV)

And when the Sanhedrin questions the Apostles, Peter is the first to answer them:

> *And it came to pass on the morrow, that their rulers, and elders and scribes, and Annas the high priest, and Caiphas, and John, and Alexander, and as many as were of the kindred of the high priest, were gathered together at Jerusalem. And when they had set them in the midst, they asked, "By what power, or by what name, have ye done this?"*
>
> *Then Peter, filled with the Holy Ghost, said unto them, "Ye rulers of the people and elders of Israel, if we this day be examined of the good deed done to the impotent man, by what means he is made whole. Be it known unto you all, and you all the people of Israel, that by the name of Jesus Christ of Nazareth, whom ye crucified, whom God raised from the dead, even by him doth this man stand here before you whole.*
>
> *"This is the stone which was set at nought of you builders, which is become the head of the corner. Neither is there salvation in any other: for there is none other name under heaven given among men, whereby we must be saved." (Acts 4:5-12, KJV)*

The primacy of Peter has been a bone of contention since the earliest days of the Protestant Reformation because it conflicts with the existence of any other church except the Catholic Church. And while people have tried to justify the position of total equality among the Disciples by using the scriptures, they tend to shy away from passages like those that I have just shared with you. The Petrine Doctrine is easily proven by the preponderance of biblical evidence at our disposal.

The Church's Infallibility

A hundred and fifty years ago in America, many people who considered themselves "good upstanding Christians" thought it perfectly okay to own another human being. Women and children had little legal protection, and were considered the "property" of the men in their families.

Fifty years ago, the idea of "separate but equal" prevailed in politics. The races, particularly Negroes and Caucasians, could be legally separated, providing each group had their own public restrooms, sectional seating, schools, colleges, etc. Women, although able to vote, suffered civil repression in many career fields and many had no identity of their own save as extensions of their husbands. During these times in history, churches often reflected the social views of their time.

Today, it's hard to believe that someone would approve of slavery or the mistreatment of women and children, but many churches once turned a blind eye or even went so far as to endorse these things in a religious context. But as time went by, society's views of these issues began to differ, and Christian churches began to reflect those different attitudes. It wasn't God who changed, but Christianity's understanding of God that changed. We finally became sensitive to the fact that our relationship with our fellow human beings is a direct reflection of our relationship with God. And although we have yet to completely win the war on these social fronts, we can look back and see the difference.

I suppose that this relates to the issue of infallibility, which is a unique trait of Catholicism, as Protestant churches do not embrace infallibility. When the Catholic Church infallibly defines something, it becomes doctrine for all Catholics to follow. A declaration of infallibility does not imply that some new doctrine is being created, but that the Church is now formally acknowledging or clarifying an aspect of faith understood from the very beginning.

This conflicts with some Catholic bashers who believe that our leadership "changes its mind" frequently and therefore has no right to believe itself infallible. Witness the big controversy around infants who die unbaptized. In ancient times, Catholicism taught that the unbaptized went to limbo as opposed to heaven. Then, Vatican II declared that the Church entrusted their fate to the mercy of God. For our critics, this was their proof that we "changed our minds."

But what exactly is "limbo?" Early theologians didn't know exactly where to put these souls in the ordered state of the universe. They didn't deserve to go to hell. And as they had no venial sins to purge away, purgatory was also out. But these children were born with original sin, and no sin of any kind can enter Heaven. So, Catholic scholars believed that unbaptized infants went to a place of "natural happiness" called limbo. According to Webster's Encyclopedia of Dictionaries, the term "limbo" comes from the Latin word ***limbus***, meaning *"the edge."* (219)

While modern Catholicism still doesn't know what happens to these little ones after death, it no longer tries to place them in the amorphous place called limbo. Instead, Catholicism leaves these unbaptized children in God's hands. And the Church lovingly gives them full funerary rites. Did God change or did the Church's understanding of God change?

Just as individuals grow in Christ, so does the Church. What does not grow and flourish will stagnate and die. This is a universal axiom that transcends all religions and cultures. While many outsiders see her as stubbornly clinging to the Middle Ages, Holy Mother Church does, in fact, change and adapt, learning more about her Creator through divine Revelation.

The Catechism of the Catholic Church writes:

The supreme degree of participation in the authority of Christ is ensured by the charism of infallibility. This infallibility extends as far as does the deposit of divine Revelation; it also extends to all those elements of doctrine, including morals, without which the saving truths of the faith cannot be preserved, explained, or observed. (492)

In other words, the sphere of infallibility covers all aspects of Catholic religious life, governing the Magisterium, which lays down and enforces canon law, the leaders who shepherd the flock, the laity who aid them, and the daily affairs of all believers. The Catholic Church is infallible because she, through the Pope and his bishops, is the representative of Christ on earth and speaks with His voice. The power to teach with Christ's authority has been embraced by the Disciples and their spiritual descendents from the very beginning. In his first letter to the church at Thessalonica, the Apostle Paul declares, *"For this cause also thank we God without ceasing, because when you received the word of God which ye heard of us, ye received it not as the word of men, but as it is in truth, the word of God, which effectually worketh also in you that believe". (I Thessalonians 2:13, KJV)*

Other churches and denominations patently deny any specific church or leadership's ability to teach and speak for Christ on earth. Unfortunately, the very Bible that they live by does not endorse this belief. So, how does a teaching become infallible? Here are the steps:

1) The Pope convenes a General (or Ecumenical) Council, consisting of all the bishops and all those others who have the authority to vote, thus representing the entire teaching body of the Church. Among those present will be bishops, cardinals, abbots, and the leaders of certain religious orders.

In AD 50, the very first General Council was held in Jerusalem. Even then, the decrees were not considered as coming from men, but from God: "For it seemed good to the Holy Ghost, and to us, to lay upon you no greater burden than these necessary things:" (Acts 15:2, KJV)

2) The Pope or his legate presides over the General Council. A representative number of those entitled to vote must be present. Once the Pope confirms the decrees, they are binding on all Catholics, and there is no appeal.

3) It is not necessary to have a unanimous vote. A majority vote is all that is required.

4) Outside of a General Council, if there is a unanimous teaching from all of the world's bishops, it is considered an infallible teaching. If it were not so, the Church would be in error, which Christ declared **impossible. (Morrow 147)**

Here are all the other ecumenical councils; the first seven are also accepted by the Eastern Orthodox, Anglican, and Anglo-Catholic Churches:

Nicea I- 325 - Declared Arianism a heresy, laid foundation for the Nicene Creed, Pope St. Sylvester I

Constantinople I- 381 - Formalized the Nicene Creed, which is technically called Constantinopolitan-Nicene Creed, condemned Macedonius, who denied the Divinity of the Holy Ghost, Pope St. Damasus I

Ephesus- 432 - Condemned Nestorianism, declared Mary as Mother of God, condemned Pelagius, Pope St. Celestine I

Chalcedon- 451 - Condemned Monophysitism, Pope St. Leo I (the Great)
Constantinople II- 553 - Confirmed actions of the preceding councils, condemned Origen as well as certain writings of Theodoret, or Theodore, Bishop of Mopsuestia and Ibas, Bishop of Edessa, Pope Vigilius

Constantinople III- 680-681 - Condemned Sergius, Pyrrhus, Paul, Macarius and all Monothelists, defined the two wills of Christ, the Divine and the human, Pope St. Agatho

Nicea II- 787 - Restored the use of icons in churches, Pope Adrian I

Constantinople IV- 869-870 - Last Eastern council, condemned Photius as a false patriarch, condemned the acts of the irregular council called by Photius against Pope Nicholas and the legitimate Patriarch of Constantinople, Ignatius, Pope Adrian II

Lateran I (Rome)- 1123 - Instituted celibacy for the priesthood, discussed the recovery of the Holy Land from non-Christians, and abolished investiture with ring and crosier of lay princes to church offices, Pope Callistus II

Lateran II- 1139 - Condemned the errors of Arnold of Brescia, Pope Innocent II

Albi- 1176 - Condemned Albigensianism and Waldensianism, Pope Alexander III

Lateran III- 1179 - Continued condemnation of Albigensianism and Waldensianism, and issued various moral reforms in the Church, Pope Alexander III

Lateran IV- 1215 - Condemned the Trinitarian errors of Abbot Joachim, issued the Firmiter credimus (an enlarged creed) against Albigenses, published 70 reformatory decrees and marked the height of the Church's influence and papal power, Pope Innocent III

Lyons I- 1245 - Excommunicated and deposed Emperor Frederick II and commissioned a new crusade against the Seracens and Mongols, Pope Innocent IV

Lyons II-1274 - Effected a temporary union with the Greek Orthodox Church, laid down rules for papal elections, discussed ways to free Palestine from the Turks, Pope Blessed Gregory X

Vienne (France)-1311-1312 - Addressed various crimes and errors of the Knights Templars, the Fraticelli, the Beghards, and the Beguines. Commissioned a new crusade, more clerical reforms, and learning Oriental languages in universities. Pope Clement V

Constance- 1414-1418 - Held during the great Schism of the West with the hope of ending the divisions within the Church. Pope Gregory XI & Pope Martin V

Basle-Ferrara-Florence- 1431-1445 - Another brief reunion with the Greek Orthodox Church, dealt with addressing heresy, Church reform and peace within the Christian world. Pope Eugene IV

Lateran V- 1512-1517 - Disciplinary decrees for the Church, planned another crusade, but abandoned the idea after the Protestant Reformation began in Germany. Pope Julius II & Pope Leo X

Trent- 1545-1563 - Addressed corruption in the Church, instituted reform to religious life of its members, attempted to differentiate Catholicism from Protestantism, and established seminaries to more properly train priests in the faith, Pope Paul III, Pope Julius III, Pope Marcellus II, Pope Paul IV, and Pope Pius IV.

Vatican I- 1869-1870 - Declared papal infallibility and the teaching authority of the Papacy, Pope Pius IX & Pope Leo XIII

Vatican II- 1962-1965 - Gave the laity a greater role in liturgical life and gave bishops more authority over their flocks. Its most important document was The Constitution on the Church, Pope John XXIII & Pope Paul VI

Special Note: Information on the Councils is blended together from Anatolios & Brown, pages 39-53, Morrow, page 142, and Knight, pages 4-8.

Papal Infallibility

One of the big problems within the Protestant community is its steadfast refusal to accept authority from one leader. This problem has been the source of constant splits and divisions, which continue to wound the Body of Christ today. Catholicism recognizes the importance of spiritual rulership in the office of Pope.

While Americans are quick to criticize and blame their president and current congress, the truth is that America's infrastructure would collapse without her government to rule and guide her. The same could be said for Rome. The Catholic Church is a vast enterprise that could not run without a supreme leader and a governing hierarchy. Jesus knew that when He founded the Christian Church on Peter and made him the Chief Shepherd. (Matthew 16:19 & John 21:15-17, KJV. Please refer back to the previous chapter on the Petrine Doctrine.)

Protestants point out the excesses and spiritual faults of certain ruling pontiffs, particularly in the Middle Ages. However, they fail to separate the men from the office of Pope. Yes, there have Catholics who were undeserving of the honor of being Pope, such as the infamous Borgia Popes, but the Papacy is above the machinations and deviance of any one man or succession of men. The fact that it has survived should attest to its divine origin.

The infallibility of the Papacy lies in the realm of faith and morals and in disciplining the universal Church. This power extends to all parishes, clergymen, layministers, general membership, etc. (Morrow 124) In his book, My Catholic Faith, the Most Reverend Louis LaRavoire Morrow, a Bishop of Krishnagar, says, *"the Pope is the teacher of all Christians"* and *"chief shepherd of the shepherds and their flocks."* (124)

Encyclicals and Papal Bulls, pastoral letters concerning the Church's teaching on spiritual matters, are expressions of the ordinary papal magisterium. Papal Infallibility does not extend outside the sphere of faith and morality. Books written by various popes are privately published, as they can err just as the writings of any other Catholic teacher. (Morrow 147)

While a comment made by the Pope carries great weight and should be carefully considered by all Catholics, "speaking infallibly" is rare and has its own set of rules and regulations.

> *1) The subject must answer a question in the realm of faith and morals. The Pope will not speak infallibly about other issues unless they directly countermand revealed truth.*
>
> *2) He must speak ex-cathedra or from the throne of Peter, as the Vicar of Christ, to all Catholics throughout the world.*
>
> *3) The Pope must formalize his intent to speak infallibly by using words such as, "We Proclaim..." or "We define..." (Morrow 147)*

So, you see, there are specific conditions for infallibility for both the Church and the Papacy. Opinions stated in Catholic theological writings or in various speeches should be given the respect they deserve, but are not considered infallible because those requirements have not been met.

Apostolic Succession

Another controversy with accompanies the Petrine Doctrine is the belief in Apostolic Succession. This doctrine allows the passing of authority from the Apostles to their successors into the modern age. Protestants tend to believe that this spiritual lineage is not valid. This is incorrect. The Bible sets up a precedent in the book of Acts that allows other called people to take the reins of leadership should a position need to be filled.

> *(Peter said) "For it is written in the book of Psalms, 'Let his habitation be desolate and let no man dwell therein: and his bishoprick let another take' Wherefore of these men who have accompanied with us all the time that the Lord Jesus went in and out among us, Beginning from the baptism of John unto the same day that he was taken up from us, must one be ordained to be a witness with us of his resurrection." And they appointed two, Joseph called Barsabas, who was surnamed Justus, and Matthias.*
>
> *And they prayed, and said, "Thou, Lord, which knowest the hearts of all men, shew whether of these two thou hast chosen, that he may take part of this ministry and Apostleship, from which Judas by transgression fell, that he might go to his own place."*
>
> *And they gave forth their lots; and the lot fell upon Matthias; and he was numbered with the eleven Apostles. (Acts 1:20-26, KJV)*

Here we have the Apostles choosing a successor to Judas Iscariot's position will have his authority. (Webster's Encyclopedia of Dictionaries defines the word ***bishoprick*** as ***"the jurisdiction and charge of a bishop."***) (646) This event sets the pattern of Apostolic Succession that has continued in an unbroken line to this day. Each time a position is vacated, another individual is chosen to continue the Church's work. Popes, in particular, are usually chosen from the College of Cardinals.

All churches have some form of Apostolic Succession (legalities aside), whether they wish to admit it or not. Consider, without Apostolic Succession, ***no*** position could be filled once vacated. Churches would have no ministers, no deacons, no nothing!

Learning the 2 P's of Prayer

When we analyze American culture, it becomes apparent that our society runs at almost "break-neck" velocity. And the Internet and the Information Age have only enhanced this speed. We have little patience for concepts that cannot be summed up in a sound byte or a catchy slogan.

For example, politicians are expected to explain their platforms in just a few sentences though they may involve extremely complex issues that demand more words than what the press is willing to accept. When this isn't possible, we often confuse indecision with the need for accuracy and total exploration of an issue.

In many ways, this craving for brevity is present in our religious viewpoints. In the Protestant world, Christians often define words according to popular wisdom and not according to their classical definitions. An excellent example of this tendency lies in the word "pray." Common Protestant wisdom says that the word "pray" means to address a deity, whether it is the Christian God or a pagan deity. However, this definition is really incomplete.

It might interest the reader that this word comes from the Latin term *precari,* and means to *"ask earnestly, to entreat, to petition."* It is only in the third and fourth definitions where the word "God" is mentioned. (Webster's 288) Furthermore, synonyms used for the word pray are often *"beg, beseech, entreat, implore, solicit, supplicate, adjure, invoke, or crave."* (Webster's 489) When we examine its etymology, it becomes clear that there is a secular definition for this word, something that the Protestant world largely ignores. Though it may offend many ears to hear this, this secular form of pray has been used and can be traced through classical works of literature.

William Shakespeare used it in its contracted form, *prithee,* which means, *"pray thee"* or in common terms, *"ask you."* Though often associated with "high-browed" entertainment, Shakespeare catered mostly to the common folk of his day. His works are literally brimming with sexual intrigue and violence, hardly what one might call deeply spiritual or Christian. Shakespeare did not use the word *prithee* in its sacred form.

As a Southerner, I have often heard someone ask, "And where have you been, pray tell?" This query was always aimed at another human being and not God. In modern words, the question means, "And where have you been? Please tell me." This is a clear example of the word pray in its secular form.

Unlike Protestantism, Catholicism embraces the complete definition for the words "pray" and "prayer." We know the difference between addressing Mary and the saints in heaven and communing with God and the Holy Trinity. When we pray to the Blessed Mother and other saints, we entreat them for their prayers on our behalf, and when we address the Trinity, we communicate directly with God.

I remember trying to explain this idea to a proselytizer who declared, "*Those people are dead. They can't help us.*"

To which, my reply was, "*Dead on earth, but alive in Christ.*"

If we, as Christians, are to believe in eternal life, then we must embrace the idea that death is but a door to another existence outside the confines of our mortal shell. If we still live on, we must also communicate in some way. Catholics believe that the family of God is a spiritual continuum, that although we cannot see the spiritual and heavenly realms, they are still joined to us, nonetheless. So, asking the saints for their prayers in Heaven is no different that asking an earthly congregation for their prayers. The only difference is that the saints are in God's immediate presence and are no longer concerned with ordinary earthly affairs. They worship and pray to God constantly. So, why not ask for their prayers?

Protestants want to believe that Catholics give the same type of respect and reverence to the saints as we do God. This is a very wrong assumption based on ignorance. In no way do our prayers to the saints place them on a level equal to the Trinity. While some human beings have become excellent Christian examples, no saint can ever attain "godhood."

The Litany of the Saints

There are times when Catholics ask a favorite saint for his/her prayers, particularly if there is a specific cause or need involved. I like telling folks *"If it's underwater-basket weaving, there's probably a saint somewhere who can help out."* Catholicism has patron saints for all kinds of professions, special needs or objectives, even countries. It's wonderful to know that we can ask these holy men and women for their help when we need it. But there are special occasions, such as Confirmation, when Catholics call down the prayers of the entire heavenly host, specifically mentioning patron saints. This is known as the Litany of the Saints, where both Heaven and earth are joined in prayer for the benefit of those being spiritually anointed. This plea often ends with *"...all you holy men and women, pray for us."*

Other words that Catholics use that can be synonymous with the word "pray" are "intercede" and "mediate." Whenever we pray for others, we are involving ourselves in their affairs. This is very much like what a mediator may do in the secular world. Mediators place themselves between two different sides in a conflict. What do the parties do when there is a labor disagreement and a strike ensues? They often call in a mediator to help to resolve the problem. How many times have Christians said words like, *"Lord, forgive him!"* or *"May God forgive him!"* These are sentences, which convey a plea for mercy for someone, though we are not personally involved.

If one intercedes, one also intervenes. An excellent example of an intercessor is a lawyer who represents someone's interests in the courtroom. He defends and argues on behalf of his client. While Christ is the ultimate intercessor, we as Christians, also intercede for our fellow men, asking for God's grace and mercy on them. Let's not forget that we are always encouraged to pray for the sick and dying, for safe trips when individuals travel, even for special blessings on upcoming services and events. If we couldn't truly make a difference, then why bother?

So, we see that Catholicism embraces both the secular and sacred definitions of the words "pray," "mediate," and "intercede" while the Protestant world tends to over-generalize these terms. This, combined with the heightened need for brevity, has distorted the image of the Catholic Church, making it appear idolatrous to the unschooled. But when we explore the meanings of these words, as they are classically defined, we soon learn that this image is, indeed, false and misleading.

Many churches ask their congregations to pray for specific members. "Brother Jones is traveling this week and asks your prayers for his safe journey." Or "Sister Meyers is having surgery this coming Wednesday. She would like everyone to pray for her swift recovery." How much more effective are the prayers of those who are *already* in heaven? The Book of Revelation says:

> *And when He had opened the seventh seal, there was silence in Heaven about the space of half an hour. And I saw the seven angels which stood before God; and to them were given seven trumpets. And another angel came and stood at the altar, having a golden censer; and there was given unto him much incense, that he should offer it with the prayers of all saints upon the golden altar which was*

before the throne. And the smoke of the incense with came with the prayers of the saints, ascended up before God out of the angel's hand. (Revelation 8:1-4, KJV)

We must remember that the word "pray" does not mean "to praise." Pray means "to ask, beg, beseech, and supplicate." But why ask anything? After all, they are in heaven, in paradise with no worry. The only reason why they would pray would be to beg for God's love and mercy towards those on earth who need it.

The Veneration of the Saints

In comparing Catholicism to another country, we understand that it has its own head of state, ruling body, and legislative branch. We have explored its linguistic differences from that of the outside Christian world. Now, let's have a look at its cultural differences.

Every country that I've ever heard of has its leaders and military heroes. Americans visit the Lincoln Memorial or the Washington Monument. There are the Vietnam and the World War II Memorials, which remember those who have died for our country. And almost every city or town has some kind of military statue, honoring someone who has served America with distinction. And how many times have prayers been said at the foot of these revered places? Did those praying before the statue of Lincoln actually worship him? When we salute the flag, do we worship its fibers? No, of course we don't. These people, places and things are icons for the principles, values, and virtues that Americans cherish the most.

Now, let's look at the Catholic Church. It has almost two millennia of spiritual leaders and heroes. We lay flowers at their tombs and remember them in song. Their statues, stained-glass images, and paintings remind us that we too can be leaders and heroes when we let God have total control over our lives. (Morrow 201)

Protestants have real trouble when they see a Catholic kneel and pray in front of a statue or image. The minute that they witness such a display, their minds scream, "idol worship." And to the unschooled, it certainly looks that way. But when Catholics kneel and pray at the foot of these things, they do not worship them but see them as tangible reminders of everything that is good and honorable about Christianity. The saints are there to inspire us with their exemplary faith and to help us with daily obstacles by praying for God's favor and grace on our behalf. But no saint, no matter how beloved, can displace any member of the Triune Godhead. (Morrow 201)

Relics

What is a relic? Relics are the remains of saints or objects that are personally tied to the saints or to our Lord Jesus Christ. Christians in every denomination treat their sanctuaries with the greatest respect and reverence. But the ultimate temple or sanctuary is not made of wood or mortar, but flesh and blood. Verified saints were the temples of the Holy Spirit and the conduits for His grace.

And any saint's relics can still be a medium for miracles. God still uses them as vehicles of His glory and grace. Sounds odd, doesn't it? Well, we know that when ordinary things are soaked and saturated with certain chemicals or elements, those agents leave traces that can never be completely removed. The power of God makes any earthly agent pale in its ability to saturate. Remember that when a saint lived, that person glowed and radiated with the presence of God. It is certainly not a great leap of faith to believe that some of that "residual energy" is still there and can reach out to do the miraculous (if God wishes it.) Does the Bible speak of human remains healing individuals? As a matter of fact, it does:

> *And Elisha died, and they buried him. And the bands of the Moabites invaded the land at the coming in of the year. And it came to pass, as they were burying a man, that, behold, they spied a band of men; and they cast the man into the sepulcher of Elisha: and when the man was let down, and touched the bones of Elisha, he revived, and stood up on his feet. (II Kings 13:20-21, KJV)*

Another healing incident occurred involving the Apostle Paul's handkerchiefs and aprons*: "And God wrought special miracles by the hands of Paul: so that from his body were brought unto the sick handkerchiefs or aprons, and the diseases departed from them, and the evil spirits went out of them." (Acts 19:11-12, KJV)*

Even Peter's shadow healed people:

> *Insomuch that they brought forth the sick into the streets, and laid them on beds and couches, that at the least the shadow of Peter passing by might overshadow some of them. There came also a multitude out of the cities round about unto Jerusalem, bringing sick folks, and them which were vexed with unclean spirits: and they were healed every one. (Acts 5:15-16, KJV)*

While these passages might sound too fantastic to believe, we must remember that simple things have radiated with the God's power in the Bible and human contact with that power has resulted in all sorts of miraculous events. Remember Naaman, who dipped himself in the Jordan River and was healed of leprosy. How about the story of the woman being healed after touching the hem of Christ's robe? Did the river and the robe have intrinsic healing properties? Or did they function as mediums for the power of God? (Morrow 201)

Sacred Images

Just as each family keeps cherished photographs in a family album, so Catholicism cherishes the images of Jesus and His saints. We show images respect and do not worship them. When a Catholic kneels and prays before an image, that individual honors what the image represents in the realm of faith. No one should believe that pictures can, in and of themselves, hear and answer prayer. But Catholics do believe that certain images, particularly icons, have also acted as conduits for God's power and grace. (Icons are sacred paintings, traditionally used in Eastern Catholic Churches, which communicate the message of the Gospel.) (Catechism 882) So, is there actual biblical evidence supporting this belief? Believe it or not, yes there is. Let's look at the Book of Numbers:

> *And the Lord sent fiery serpents among the people, and they bit the people; and much people of Israel died. Therefore the people came to Moses and said, "We have sinned for we have spoken against the Lord, and against thee; pray to the Lord, that he take away the serpents from us."*
>
> *And Moses prayed for the people. And the Lord said unto Moses, "Make thee a fiery serpent, and set it upon a pole: and it shall come to pass, that every one that is bitten when he looketh upon it, shall live."*
>
> *And Moses made a serpent of brass, and put it upon a pole, and it came to pass, that if a serpent had bitten any man, when he beheld the serpent of brass, he lived. (Numbers 21:6-9, KJV)*

Yes, indeed, it is possible for God to perform miraculous works through common conduits, and the Bible says so. Even though this event occurred in the Old Testament, can we as humans limit God to the past and say that He cannot do the same miracles today?

But while there is always the possibility for miracles, most Catholics understand that images inspire the faithful, instruct them on faith, and to keep them focused on their devotion to God during prayer and other Christian pursuits. (Morrow 201) But is there scriptural proof that God approves of beautiful paintings and sculpture? Protestants often hint that Catholics are idolatrous because of the way we adorn our places of worship. They forget that God not only approves of such things but also has commissioned their creation on specific occasions. Witness the explicit details that God gives Moses for the sculptures on the top of the Ark of the Covenant:

> *And thou shalt make two cherubim of gold, of beaten work shalt thou make them, in the two ends of the Mercy Seat. And make one cherub on the one end, and the other cherub on the other end: even of the Mercy Seat shall ye make the cherubim on the two ends thereof. And the cherubim shall stretch forth their wings on high, covering the Mercy Seat with their wings, and their faces shall look one to another; toward the Mercy Seat shall the faces of the cherubim be. And thou shalt put the Mercy Seat above upon the Ark; and in the Ark thou shalt put the testimony that I shall give thee. And there I will meet with thee, and I will commune with thee from above the Mercy Seat, from between the two cherubim which are upon the Ark of the testimony, of all things which I give thee in commandment unto the Children of Israel. (Exodus 25:18-22, KJV)*

Now, let's see how Solomon's Temple was constructed:

> *And the word of the Lord came to Solomon, saying, "Concerning this house which thou art in building, if thou wilt walk in my statutes, and execute my judgments, and keep all my commandments to walk in them; then will I perform my word with thee, which I spake unto David thy father: and I will dwell among the children of Israel, and I will not forsake my people Israel."*
> *... And within the oracle he (Solomon) made two cherubim of olive tree, each ten cubits high. And five cubits was the one wing of the cherub, and five cubits the other wing of the cherub: from the uttermost part of the one wing to the uttermost part of the other were ten cubits. And the other cherub was ten cubits: both the cherubim were of one measure and one size. The height of the one cherub was ten cubits and so was it of the other cherub. And he set the cherubim within the inner house: and they stretched forth the wings of the cherubim, so that the wing of the one touched the one wall, and the wing of the other cherub touched the other wall; and their wings touched one another in the midst of the house.*
> *And he overlaid the cherubim with gold. And he carved all the walls of the house round about with carved figures of cherubim and palm trees and open flowers, within and without. (I Kings 6:11-13, 23-29, KJV)*

So, we see that God loves artwork when it is done for His glory to further His heavenly kingdom. Nothing captures the wandering mind like touching and experiencing the pain and triumphs of a saint or gazing upon the shape, color, and form of a picture.

Sacramentals

What does it mean to bless? The act of blessing calls down the Holy Spirit upon both people and things. When an object is blessed it becomes a sacramental. The most common sacramental is water blended with salt, which acts as a conduit in the making of other sacramentals. Holy Water is prepared when the priest blesses salt, then the water itself, and prays particular prayers as he puts the two together. Water symbolizes the purity of the soul while salt stands for prudence. When combined, they symbolize purity and immortality.

The following is the ***Blessing and Invocation of God over the Holy Water:***

Father,
You give us Grace through sacramental signs,
which tell us of the wonders of Your unseen power.
In baptism we use Your gift of water,
 which You have made a rich symbol of the grace
 You give in this sacrament
At the very dawn of creation Your Spirit breathed on the waters, making them a wellspring of all holiness.
The waters of the great flood You made a sign of the waters of baptism that make an end of sin and a new beginning of goodness.
Through the waters of the Red Sea
 You led Israel out of slavery to be an image of God's holy people,
 Set free from sin by baptism.
In the waters of the Jordan
 Your Son was baptized by John and anointed with the Spirit.
Your Son willed that water and blood should flow from His side
As He hung upon the cross.
After His resurrection He told His Disciples: "Go out and teach all nations, baptizing them in the name of the Father, and of the Son, and of the Holy Spirit."

Father,
Look now with love upon Your Church
And unseal for it the fountain of baptism.
By the power of the Holy Spirit give this water
The grace of Your Son, so that in the sacrament of baptism
All those whom You have created in Your likeness may be cleansed From sin and rise to a new birth of innocence by water and the Holy Spirit.

The celebrant touches the water with his right hand and continues:

We ask you, Father, with Your Son
To send the Holy Spirit upon the waters of this font.
 May all who are buried with Christ in the death of baptism
Rise also with Him to newness of life.
We ask this through Christ our Lord. Amen (Rites IA, 399-400)

This liquid is kept in little bowls or ***fonts***, which sit in stands or are directly attached to the wall next to the main inner entrance in churches. Catholics use Holy Water to bless themselves as they enter and leave the Church. We dip our fingers in the water, and make the sign of the cross. Catholic homes also have fonts, so that family members can bless themselves on a daily basis. Catholicism teaches that we should do this as often as possible. Remember when I mentioned indulgences in the earlier chapter about Penance? An indulgence removes the stain of sin after it has been forgiven, so that the individual does not have to pay for it in purgatory. Did you know that blessing oneself with Holy Water carries an indulgence of seven years, each time it is done?

Does the Bible support this practice? Well, yes it does. Remember that Jesus used things in the Gospels to bear witness to the power of God. What about the water, which was turned into wine at the wedding feast of Cana, the loaves and fishes that fed the multitude, even the mud, used in healing the blind man? These things became vehicles for Christ's miracles.

Jesus gave the Church the power to call down the presence of the Holy Spirit. Peter used this power when he called down the Holy Spirit upon Ananias and Sapphira who were struck dead for their sin.

> *But a certain man named Ananias, with Sapphira his wife, sold a possession, and kept back part of the price, his wife also being privy to it, and brought a certain part, and laid it at the Apostles' feet.*
>
> *But Peter said, "Ananias, why hath Satan filled thine heart to lie to the Holy Ghost, and to keep back part of the price of the land? Whiles it remained, was it not thine own? And after it was sold, was it not in thine own power? Why hast thou conceived this thing in thine heart? Thou hast not lied unto men, but unto God."*
>
> *And Ananias hearing these words, fell down and gave up the ghost; and great fear came on all of them that heard these things. And the young men arose, wound him up, and carried him out, and buried him. And it was about the space of three hours after, when his wife, not knowing what was done, came in. And Peter answered unto her, "Tell me whether ye sold the land for so much?"*
>
> *And she said, "Yea for so much."*
>
> *Then Peter said unto her, "How is it that ye have agreed together to tempt the Spirit of the Lord? Behold the feet of them which hath buried thy husband are at the door, and shall carry thee out."*
>
> *Then fell she down straightway at his feet, and yielded up the ghost: and the young men came in, and found her dead, and, carrying her forth, buried her by her husband. (Acts 5:1-10, KJV)*

So, we see that the power of the Holy Spirit may be called down upon common everyday things, such as the water/salt mixture that we call Holy Water. Holy Water is used in blessing all sorts of objects such as statues, rosaries, crucifixes, religious medals, and scapulars. Scapulars are pictures of Jesus, Mary, or a saint, often made of cloth, plastic, or ceramic clay that are suspended by a cord of some sort. It is a great tradition within Catholicism to bless and sprinkle these objects with Holy Water to set them aside as belonging to and serving God. Homes, crops, and vehicles have also been blessed. One of the most unusual blessings I have ever witnessed involved a clerical blessing upon some vats of beer in a brewery. I couldn't help but giggle when the priest said something like, **"Lord, make it good beer..."**

The principal use of a sacramental is to remind us of our commitment to Christ, and by doing so, help us to avoid sinful behavior. Protestants also have crosses, Christian jewelry and catch phrases that accomplish the same objective. The famous ***"WWJD"*** or ***"What Would Jesus Do?"*** slogan is a gentle, but strong aid to preventing sinful behavior by calling the believer away from temptation. (Morrow 385) The big difference between the sacramentals of the Catholic realm and their Protestant cousins is the lack of a spiritual blessing upon such objects. However, it is not uncommon for a Protestant minister to bless objects while rejecting the idea of sacramentals as a whole. This I find more than a little amusing.

The big myth about sacramentals is that Catholics supposedly view them like religious versions of a "lucky rabbit's foot or horseshoe," believing that these items can prevent bodily injury, disease, or help the wearer win the local lottery jackpot. This is nothing short of superstition. (Morrow 384) The only power that any sacramental has lies in the heart of the believer and in the power of God. Can God act through a sacramental? Absolutely. God can use anything that He wishes to accomplish the miraculous. But sacramentals have no intrinsic power of their own. If a miracle occurs, it is God using whatever medium He chooses to accomplish it. (Morrow 385)

The Origin and Creation of Saints

Since we began learning about how Catholics pray and the Communion of the Saints in an earlier chapter, let us continue with explaining the institution that we know as sainthood. Protestant theologians have taken a simple idea and twisted it to provide a false and misleading view of idolatry within the Catholic Church. When we hear the words pray, intercession, intervention, and mediation, it is natural to jump to the wrong conclusion.

But, upon examining each word's proper definition, it becomes clear that this premise is incorrect. According to the dictionary, they mean: to ask, plead for, get involved, and facilitate communication on someone else's behalf. Using these words when addressing a saint does not imply that the saint is equal to the Trinity. It is opposing theologians who have fostered the idea that these words can only be used when speaking to and describing the Christian Godhead, mostly due to a simple lack of knowledge or willful denial of fact. Saints can never be on the same spiritual level as God, Christ or the Holy Spirit. However, a saint is as close to spiritual perfection as any ordinary Christian can get.

We all have individuals who have inspired us with their faith. We see them as great examples of what God can do with human beings. Maybe it's that sweet old lady who never uttered a mean word or the generous man who devotes himself to church, family and community. Ordinary individuals can go to heaven and be counted among the heavenly throng of holy men and women we know as saints. But to be a canonized saint of the Catholic Church, the individual must be more than a good, sound believer.

In the beginning, during the Roman persecution of Christians, it was simple to determine who was a saint. They were those who laid down their lives for their faith. Early believers would gather up their remains and lovingly entomb them. A martyr was called a ***hagioi*** or ***"holy one."*** Martyrs' tombs became the site of early Christian worship and were later transformed into chapels, cathedrals, and even large basilicas.

When the Edict of Milan was passed and the Roman Emperor Constantine decriminalized Christianity, it became harder to determine who was and wasn't a recognized saint. And so, a new classification of saint was created for those who did not die for their faith, confessors. Confessors were not those who performed the Sacrament of Confession, but those who "confessed" their Christianity in every aspect of their lives, thus showing what is known as "heroic virtue" or an exceptional amount of faith, hope, love, prudence, justice, perseverance and temperance.

As the Church began to blossom and grow, the process of determining sainthood became reminiscent of the courtroom process where we had petitioners, procurators, and promoters of the faith. Of these three, promoters had the famous title "the Devil's Advocate." No, he wasn't in league with Satan, but had the job of making sure that the evidence brought forward was genuine, making sure that the person discussed was indeed a saint. This method was first introduced in 993 when Pope John XV approved the canonization of Bishop Ulrich of Augsburg.

In the 1700s, Pope Benedict XIV wrote five volumes on the processes of beatification and canonization, which served as the cornerstone for the declaring holy men and women as saints. 1917 saw this work become part of Canon (Church) Law. Finally, the process developed from the adversarial drama of a court trial to its present research process format under Vatican II and was later finished under Pope John Paul II, in 1983. The current method is more efficient, streamlined. Because of these changes, Pope John Paul II has been able to beatify and canonize more people than any other Pope was.

Steps to Sainthood

1) People within a specific community, order, or organization began to wonder if a deceased person was a saint. Again, that individual must have shown "heroic virtue." Being a good person is not enough.

2) There must be support for the person's cause at the local level. The individual must be publicly acclaimed. This goes back to the very beginning of Christianity, no public acclaim, no saint.

3) Those who know the individual, band together, possibly making a private pilgrimage to his/her grave. They often begin asking that person to pray for them, believing that the deceased is now in the direct presence of God. There are also prayers to heaven that the Church may indeed canonize that person.

4) Miraculous deeds or intercessions that the person is connected with can be very helpful in acquiring grass roots support. But these events must be carefully investigated and recorded. These events also serve to bring more supporters into the group.

5) The core group behind this canonization effort meets and prays in homes and at the grave, but not church. This is called a private devotion. (Remember people can be devoted to each other and not take away from the ultimate devotion given to God.)

6) The core group will then want to keep and catalog everything that this potential saint used or owned because, if declared a saint, these items will be considered relics.

7) The group then gets the local bishop to lend support to the idea which actually begins the formal process.

8) When the bishop's help is enlisted, then the job of the core group is largely done, except in the realm of financing the formal procedure of declaring an individual a saint. While it is true that no one may buy a canonization, it is equally true that extensive research into that person's history must be done. The case must be prepared for presentation to the Vatican. Unfortunately, like any endeavor, funds must be raised on the grass roots level to do this, so the core group is largely responsible for raising the money.

9) The postulator will gather the information and see that it is properly prepared before sending it to Rome. This documentation is then presented to the Congregation for the Causes of Saints and is the basis for the positio or case file for the potential saint.

10) The body of the deceased will be exhumed and examined for signs of incorruptibility. This is called the body translation. Signs of decay are not necessarily cause for concern. The main reason for this exhumation is to place the body in an area more accessible by pilgrims who wish to visit the remains.

11) After extensive examination of the evidence presented, the Congregation for the Causes of Saints will present its opinion to its head, or prefect, and membership, and they will decide on whether to present the case to the pope.

12) The first title conferred on an individual is Servant of God when the cause is opened, then the title "Venerable" is bestowed when it is determined that the person led a life of great virtue.

    The last steps of the process are largely based on the will of God. In order to be beatified and canonized, a deceased individual must have one verifiable miracle attesting to their presence in heaven for each classification for a total of two miracles. (In earlier times, two miracles were needed for each classification for a total of four miracles. As always, martyrs do not need an association with miracles to be Blessed or canonized.)

    A miracle is an event that cannot be scientifically explained. As most of these events involve healing, a group of Roman physicians, the Consulta Medica, investigates in order to search for natural causes for the event. They will not declare an event "miraculous," but find that science has no rational explanation for what took place.

13) When an individual is beatified, he or she is given a particular place on the local Church's calendar and public devotion or respect may be given in the Church. Finally, the pope will decide whether to beatify or canonize an individual. This usually occurs at St. Peter's Basilica in Rome, however, the Pope may elect to hold the ceremony elsewhere.

Canonization sounds extremely cold and formal, even political, but remember that the Catholic Church is very large and it takes great organization to accomplish anything in something so vast. The process is very drawn out and often stalls and is never completed. Many people remain Servants of God or Venerable or Blessed without the final honor of the title "Saint." But these people along with a multitude of believers that bears no number, still have a feast day. November 1rst is the day when we remember all the saints in heaven; we know it as All Saints Day.

<u>Special Note:</u> *All of the information that I have given regarding the formal declaration of saints comes from the in-depth article, "Making Saints" by Bill Dodds in the November 2000 issue of the Columbia magazine, vol. LXXX, no. 11, pp 16-19.*

For those of you who are interested, Mother Teresa's was beatified on October 19, 2003 and is now formally known as the Blessed Mother Teresa. According to the January 10, 2003 issue of *The Catholic News and Herald*, the Vatican formally acknowledged the first miracle due to her heavenly intervention and prayers on December 20, 2002. Over a dozen physicians were consulted in both Rome and India concerning the spontaneous healing of an Indian woman, named Monika Besra. In August 1998, Ms. Besra, originally diagnosed with tubular meningitis and tuberculosis, developed what appeared to be a large ovarian cyst. This was discovered during an ultrasound. The attending physicians ordered exploratory surgery, but only after her condition could be stabilized under the constant care and help of the sisters who ran the Missionaries of Charity Navajivan Home in Patiram, India.

During a memorial Mass for Mother Teresa on September 5th, 1998, special petitions were given for her prayers on Besra's behalf. Then, a miraculous medal that had been touched to Mother's body was placed on Monika's abdomen and kept there. After Besra fell asleep, the sisters left her for the evening. In the early morning hours, the woman awoke to find that the cyst had completely disappeared.

Doctors interviewed concerning Besra's condition said that tubular meningitis could cause swellings that, treated with drugs, can gradually disappear. Others stated that the cyst might have burst; however, there were no signs of illness or rupture. While some physicians hinted that Besra might not have been aware of the gradual disappearance of the cyst, they also stated that medical science would have no explanation for the sudden disappearance of such a thing.

This miracle is only one of 800 graces and favors believed to be bestowed by God as a result of Mother Teresa's help in heaven. (1 & 14) She will only need one more verifiable miracle attributed to her aid to be canonized by the Church.

Laying the Oldest Myth to Rest

The cable channel TNT (Turner Network Television) presented the miniseries, ***The Mists of Avalon.*** Since I have always been fond of the Arthurian legends, I had my husband tape it while I was at work. First let me say that this production was well done; the cast, costumes, scenery, acting, and cinematography were all first rate.

But there were things that bothered me. The movie, which was from the viewpoint of a priestess of the Mother Goddess who trained on Avalon, looked at the older religion as mostly good and without attempting to explain how dark it could be. There was absolutely no mention of human sacrifice, which was a palpable part of the Celtic religion. When the crops failed or great calamity struck, many Celts willingly went to their deaths to appease the gods. (Castle Ghosts of Ireland) Knowing all of this in advance, I was repulsed when the priestess connected the Mother Goddess to the Virgin Mary at various times and at the end of the movie. I was sure that many Protestants watching this show said a silent "Amen." After all, Hollywood was only documenting the truth about Catholicism. Or were they?

Yes, Celtic Christians did make Mary their "May Queen." Catholics still crown her statues with flowers and ask for her prayers on their behalf; but this reminds us all of the removal of a bloody ritual. The May Queen was often sacrificed if things did not go well for the Fall harvest. When the Celtic world became Christianized, we were freed from this barbaric ritual and now remember God's handmaiden, who brought the Son of Man into this world. It is fitting that we honor her as the ultimate example of virtue and beauty. But there's a difference between seeing Mary as God's most beloved human creation and seeing her as some sort of goddess. (While Jesus was fully human, He was never created but forever existed before and after His earthly life.)

Mariolatry does exist, but it was and still is the province of neo-Christians that convert from paganism. Even today, pagan converts have problems letting go of the older religion that they were raised in. Having been reared around a pantheon of gods and goddesses, it's hard for these individuals to get their heads around God as one being who takes care of all of creation. And as non-Christians, they probably worshipped goddesses who begot this or that god. Because it is easy to place Mary in the same category, it becomes common for pagans to try to blend Christianity with other faiths.

Case in point, my dad's cousin, Margot, was a Baptist missionary. Upon coming home from working in a small African country, she remarked how local natives would sacrifice a chicken on Saturday night to the old deities, and then attend morning services at the Baptist church without being ruffled. But the Catholic Church takes a very dim view toward those who persist in the practice of Mariolatry.

Nevertheless, Protestants nurture the idea of Mariolatry and Catholics often confuse and muddle the role of Mary, furthering an idolatrous picture of the Church. I often feel that certain prayers to Mary that seem fine to the average Catholic are, in fact, ammunition for the other side. In order to understand them, we have to look at the language used from a technical point of view, not from popular tradition. In the Protestant world, certain terms and phrases are only used when addressing the Trinity, but in Catholicism, there is a generic use. An example of this is the word "prayer" itself which I discussed at length in the previous chapter. In Protestantism, prayer is reserved for the Trinity alone, while Catholicism recognizes both the sacred and secular forms of the word "pray."

Having been labeled as a Mary worshipper, I can tell you that that difficult and ugly accusation makes my skin crawl. Let me say once and for all, "***I DO NOT WORSHIP MARY!!!***" And I know of no Catholics who do such a thing. Once, I was speaking to a local minister trying to convince him that the Pope did not endorse the worship of Mary. At first I was frustrated, but then I gave him a little challenge.

"Find me a Papal Encyclical or Bull that says so, and then we'll sit down together and analyze the Pope's words in their proper context."

He looked at me, and answered, *"I can't do that."*

I replied back, *"Then I can't believe you."*

You see, many reporters and writers often take the Pope's words and declarations out of context, fueling the division between Protestants and their Catholic brothers and sisters. Anything can be warped and twisted in the press. I wanted the Pope's exact words. The minister had only to go to the Vatican's website on the Internet. But he refused that simple request.

Then, there are countless ex-Catholics that swear that we do worship Mary. This is particularly hurtful, but I have to question how well they were taught their catechism. Any properly trained Catholic will disagree with that declaration. I also wonder if they truly paid attention in class because prayers to Mary usually end with a plea for her prayers on another person's behalf. When we address Jesus, the Holy Spirit, or God, the Father, we do not ask them for their prayers on our behalf. That would make no sense at all.

I also see many ex-Catholics as spiritually blinded by some painful incident(s) to the point of losing objectivity. Disenfranchised from the local Catholic community, they channel their resentment into demonizing Catholicism, in general, failing to realize that the true fault lay with an individual and not the Church itself. Any perceived fault Catholicism might have is quickly adopted, whether true or not. In the end, they spread a dark poison in the Protestant community that can sicken the spirit of all good Catholics everywhere, adding more credibility to centuries of half-truths, innuendo, and pure ignorance.

My husband is Marian, having the utmost respect and affection for Our Lady, but I have never heard or seen him place Mary as an equal to the Trinity. I think he's sees Mary in every woman or child, and that has led to a deep love and appreciation of the female sex. Would that every man see the Blessed Virgin in his friends and relatives, the percentages of criminal and social ills would be drastically reduced. And if we saw Christ in every man or boy, the world, as we know it, would be a Utopia- a beautiful place where poverty, crime and cruelty would have no foothold.

Mary **IS** a beloved figure in the Church. She is revered as not only the ultimate wife and mother, but the ultimate Christian as well. Why her and not the Apostles? Her veneration is above them because she was totally submissive to God's plan for her life. Judas betrayed. Peter denied. Thomas doubted. Even John the Beloved jockeyed for the top position in heaven at Christ's side. Mary was never willful or proud, hot tempered or impetuous. She embodied all the nobility and serenity of the ideal follower of Christ in the midst of the religious and political storm that was Roman oppressed Israel at that time.

Martin Luther agreed that Mary is the ultimate follower of Christ for he wrote, *"Mary is the highest woman and the noblest gem in Christianity after Christ... She is nobility, wisdom, and holiness personified. We can never honor her enough." (Christmas sermon*, 1531)

Biblical Titles of Mary

Mary has many titles and one of the most controversial is ***Mater Dei*** or Mother of God. Most Protestants feel that we are placing Mary on the same level (or even above) as the Trinity, insinuating that she is above God. This is a very wrong assumption. Since Jesus IS God, as evidenced in the section on the Holy Trinity, and Mary IS the mother of Christ, she is, by definition, the Mother of God. This is NOT merely Catholic word play. We read in the Gospel of Luke, *"And it came to pass, that, when Elizabeth heard the Salutation of Mary, the babe leaped in her womb; and Elizabeth was filled with the Holy Ghost: And she spake with a loud voice, and said, "Blessed art thou among women, and blessed is the fruit of thy womb. And whence is this to me that the mother of my Lord should come to me?" (Luke 1:41-43)*

Elizabeth called Mary "The mother of my Lord", in other words, "The Mother of God." Some theologians have seen her title as ***Mater Redemptoris*** and have assumed that we call her "Mother Redeemer" or "Redeeming Mother." And for those who do not truly know their Latin, it certainly appears so. But any Latin scholar will tell you that the "-is" ending on redemptoris is the genitive, or possessive form, meaning "redeemer's" as belonging to the Redeemer. Christ is our Redeemer, and His mother was Mary.

Mary's title of Queen of Heaven is often considered heretical; and again, some writers and ministers say that Catholics consider her some sort of goddess. Renaissance painters weren't very helpful in clarifying this title as many of them envisioned lots of cute little cherubs placing a crown on her head.

But the scripture passage that gives her the title, ***Regina Caeli***, is a fierce one and very biblical indeed. It comes from John's vision in the book of Revelation:

And there appeared a great wonder in heaven; a woman clothed with the sun, and the moon under her feet, and upon her head a crown of twelve stars. And she being with child cried, travailing in birth, and pained to be delivered.

And there appeared another wonder in heaven; and behold a great red dragon, having seven heads and ten horns, and seven crowns upon his heads. And his tail drew the third part of the stars of heaven, and did cast them to the earth: and the dragon stood before the woman which was ready to be delivered, for to devour her child as soon as it was born. And she brought forth a man child, who was to rule all nations with a rod of iron: and her child was caught up unto God, and to His throne. (Revelation 12:1-5, KJV)

First of all, we have a woman wearing a crown of twelve stars. According to classical literature standards, we must consider her as having a royal status. Only royalty may wear crowns. More than likely, she is a queen as a princess would wear a tiara. She is clothed in the sun and standing on the moon, literally attired in and around heavenly bodies. The woman gives birth to a child destined to rule the nations with an iron rod. This child can only be Jesus, and we have a good idea who His mother was. While the queen will go on to symbolize the Church when she flees into the desert, in the previous passage, she can *only* be Mary. The Church never gave birth to Christ. It was Christ who founded the Church.

There's also a small detail that many prophecy buffs do not notice. This child is going to rule with a rod of iron. First of all, iron was the principal metal of Rome and the Roman military. While the heyday of the ancient Greeks was the Bronze Age, Rome heralded the Iron Age. Iron symbolized stability and fidelity. Even Roman wedding rings were made from iron.

The child wields a rod, not a scepter. This is very important. Rods were given to Roman generals when they took possession of an area. Roman statuary depicts famous generals holding rods as a symbol of political power and clout. Some Protestants love to call the Catholic Church the "whore of Babylon," but given the importance of an iron rod in Rome and its usage in this passage, is it not entirely possible that the Catholic Church will be Christ's instrument on earth instead?

As mentioned earlier, I have heard of the unsavory comparison of Mary to Babylonian goddesses as a possible link to the New Age religion due to her title as "Queen of Heaven." This presumption demonstrates an ignorance of classical literature. If we look at all types of mythology, we soon realize that it is the male gods who dominate the sky. With very few exceptions, goddesses have always governed the earth, fertility, the home, handicrafts, music, the arts, war, even the moon, but not the sky itself. The sky is male territory. Witness the likes of Zeus, Jupiter, and Odin. The Babylonian god of the sky, **Anu**, was male also. (Ward & Kuntz 22)

We need to remember that with the exception of a ruling queen and her consort, few queens have had actual political power except through their own personal influence. Mary's post as Queen of Heaven or **Regina Caeli** is likened to the post of the Queen Mother in England. Any power or influence that she enjoys comes from her special place in Christ's heart who is the King of the Universe. And just as with the English people and their Queen Mum, Catholics have a tremendous affection for Mary, who is our Queen Mum.

Did you know that, in the days of ancient Israel, the Queen Mother's throne always sat next to that of her son, the reigning monarch? In fact, the post of Queen Mother (or **Gebirah**, in Aramaic) to the King of Israel was extremely important as she was the official representative of the people and was considered "their mother." While the king could be sought out without her help, the Queen Mother often mediated and petitioned on behalf of the people. (Valentim, Mary 1) This is illustrated in the First Book of Kings:

And Adonijah the son of Haggith came to Bathsheba the mother of Solomon. And she said, "Comest thou peaceably?"

And he said, "Peaceably."

He said, "Moreover, I have somewhat to say unto thee."

And she said, "Say on."

And he said, "Thou knowest that the kingdom was mine, and that all Israel set their faces on me, that I should reign: howbeit the kingdom is turned about, and is become my brother's: for it was his from the Lord. And now I ask one petition of thee, deny me not."

And she said unto him, "Say on."

And he said, "Speak, I pray thee, unto Solomon the king, (for he will not say thee nay,) that he give me Abishag the Shunammite to wife."

And Bathsheba said, "Well; I will speak for thee unto the king."

Bathsheba therefore went unto King Solomon, to speak unto him for Adonijah. And the King rose up to meet her, and bowed himself unto her, and sat down on his throne, and caused a seat to be set for the king's mother; and she sat on his right hand. Then she said, "I desire one small petition of thee; I pray thee, say me not nay."

And the king said unto her, "Ask on, my mother: for I will not say thee nay."

And she said, "Let Abishag, the Shunammite be given to Adonijah thy brother to wife." (I Kings 2:13-21, KJV)

Now, let's move forward to the wedding feast at Cana where Mary's influence with Jesus is illustrated:

And the third day there was a marriage in Cana of Galilee; and the mother of Jesus was there: And both Jesus was called, and His Disciples, to the marriage. And when they wanted wine, the mother of Jesus saith unto Him, "They have no wine."

Jesus saith unto her, "Woman, what have I to do with thee? Mine hour is not yet come."

His mother saith unto the servants, "Whatsoever He saith unto you, do it."

And there were set there six water pots of stone, after the manner of the purifying of the Jews, containing two or three firkins apiece. Jesus saith unto them, "Fill the water pots with water." And they filled them up to the brim. And He saith unto them, "Draw out now, and bear unto the governor of the feast."

And they bare it. When the ruler of the feast had tasted the water that was made wine, and knew not whence it was: (but the servants which drew the water knew;) the governor of the feast called the bridegroom, and saith unto him, "Every man at the beginning doth set forth good wine; and when men have well drunk then that which is worse: but thou hast kept the good wine until now." (John 2:1-10, KJV)

Here, we see Mary ask for Jesus' help, and He objects. He's not ready to work miracles. Yet, Mary persists in her belief, and Jesus relents. The correlation between both passages is clear. As Bathsheba begged a favor from Solomon, who was an earthly king, Mary entreats help from Jesus at the wedding feast of Cana. And just as Adonijah asked for help from Bathsheba, Catholics often ask for Mary's help in their daily problems, believing that a prayer by the Virgin on someone's behalf has a strong effect. Mary is known as a mediatrix, a mediator between God and His followers. (***This is not to say that we cannot approach God on our own, but The Virgin is there as the spiritual advocate of the people.***)

Remember what I said about mediation in my chapter on prayer. **While Christ is our *Chief Intercessor* (no one disputes or argues with this in Catholicism) we all, in effect, mediate and intercede when we pray on someone else's behalf.** If the prayers of a saint take away or diminish His authority, then no human may pray for any other human, even on earth. That flies in the face of Holy Scripture that tells us to pray for one another unceasingly. The saints are in heaven, not on extended vacation. The Virgin constantly prays with and for us in heaven. Now, that we understand that there are two types of prayer, it becomes easier to grasp the most famous Mary prayer of them all. The "Hail Mary" is composed mostly of scripture:

Hail Mary, full of grace.
The Lord is with thee.
Blessed art thou among women.
(And the angel came in unto her, and said, 'Hail, thou that art highly favoured, the Lord is with thee: blessed art thou among women. (Luke 1: 28, KJV))

And blessed is the fruit of thy womb, Jesus.
(And she (Elizabeth) spake out with a loud voice and said, 'Blessed art thou among women and blessed is the fruit of thy womb.' (Luke 1:42, KJV))

Holy Mary,
(For he hath regarded the low estate of His handmaiden: for, behold, from henceforth all generation shall call me blessed. (Luke 1:48, KJV)

Mother of God,
(In the beginning was the Word, and the Word was with God, and the Word was God... And the Word was made flesh, and dwelt among us, (and we beheld His glory, the glory as the only begotten of the Father,) full of grace and truth. (John 1:1,14, KJV))

Pray for us sinners, now,
And at the hour of our death

The Rosary

The most famous "Marian meditation" is the rosary. Rosaries are fashioned with links and small and large beads. There are usually five sets of ten beads (called decades) in a circle with a small "tail" of beads, ending in a crucifix. This device resembles a Y necklace, but it is not really appropriate to wear these beads as jewelry. The beads represent prayers and can be followed when the eyes are closed, by touch.

The origin of the Rosary lies in monastic prayer. Monks would recite great numbers of certain prayers, counting as they prayed. The standard rosary comes from the Dominicans, founded by St. Dominic. They would recite all 150 Psalms every week. Because this was a difficult task to master, the Dominicans created the standard Rosary for the average layman as a common form of prayer. (Martin, home.earthlink.net, 1/2003)

The Dominican Rosary is centered on 20 sacred mysteries within the lives of Jesus and Mary. As the individual prays each decade, there is focus on a separate mystery.

They are as follows:

> **A) The Joyful Mysteries surrounding Christmas/Christ's Early Life**
> *(Mondays, Saturdays, except during Lent, and Sundays from First Sunday of Advent until Lent)*
> **1- The Annunciation**
> **2- The Visitation of Mary to Elizabeth**
> **3- The Birth of Christ**
> **4- The Presentation of the Lord in the Temple**
> **5- Mary and Joseph finding our Lord in the Temple**
>
> **B) The Luminous Mysteries- (recently added by Pope John Paul II in 2002)**
> *(Thursdays, except during Lent)*
> **1 - The Baptism of Christ in the Jordan River**
> **2 - The miracle at the wedding feast at Cana**
> **3 - Christ's proclamation of the Kingdom of God and call to conversion**
> **4 - The Transfiguration**
> **5- The Institution of Holy Eucharist as a sacramental expression of the Paschal Mystery**

C) The Sorrowful Mysteries of Easter *(Tuesdays, Fridays, and every day during Lent)*
1-The Agony in the Garden
2-The Scourging at the Pillar
3-The Crowning with Thorns
4-The Carrying of the Cross
5-The Crucifixion and Death of our Lord
D) The Glorious Mysteries *(Wednesdays, except during Lent, and Sundays from Easter until Advent)*
1-The Resurrection
2-The Ascension
3-The Descent of the Holy Spirit
4-The Assumption of Mary
5-The Coronation of our Blessed Mother

While concentrating on each of these events, we entreat Mary to pray with us with ten Hail Marys, and then both heaven and earth join together in the Lord's Prayer. It is traditional to meditate on different groups of mysteries throughout the week. However, some people concentrate on the whole twenty at one time. The prayers are not set in stone. Many people pray for family and friends with each decade. Others design their own prayers to God using this format. They might not say a lot of Hail Marys as much as they will personally lift special needs and people in prayer to God Himself.

The Dominican Rosary is not the only rosary Catholics use. In fact, rosaries are not always Marian. Some are devoted to **Christ's Holy Wounds, His Sacred Face, His Sacred Heart, Holy Eucharist (Communion),** and **The Holy Trinity**. Then, there is the **Chaplet of Divine Mercy**, a shortened rosary, which is devoted to pleading for the Father's universal mercy against a sinful world.

The Rosary is simply a tool of meditation and prayer. It is not crucial to being a Catholic or a Christian. Some Catholics use it regularly while others do not. Protestants criticize Catholics for having formulated prayers, saying that these ruin the spontaneity and genuine nature of prayer. However, there are times the mind fails to focus, when the cares of the world seem to overwhelm us. Instances of great worry or tragedy make it hard to pray "original prayers" because our thoughts are so jumbled and confused. Meditations such as the Rosary help us to strip the influence of the world away, so that we can truly focus on what's important. They act as a kind of mental cleanser.

Marian Doctrines within Catholicism

We know that God hates sin and cannot tolerate its stain in heaven. Yet, Mary, this young village girl, bore the Incarnate God within her body for nine months. This involves knowing God in the most intimate way. It's one thing to let the spirit of God reign in our hearts and minds, but to experience God as a mother does when she carries a child is almost unimaginable. Remember, Jesus was God Incarnate not from His birth, but from His conception. Listen to the words of John: *"In the beginning was the Word, and the Word was with God, and the Word was God. The same was in the beginning with God. All things were made by Him; and without Him was not anything made. In Him was life; and the life was the light of men." (John 1:1-4, KJV)*

I remember my father once said that Mary was just a vessel. Yes, but what a vessel! Logically speaking, given all that we know about God, Mary had to have been an extraordinary person. From a scientific perspective, Jesus' genetic information had to come from only her. (His Father was not Joseph.) God chose Mary's DNA to decide how Jesus' would look and appear to people: His eye and skin colors, the texture of His hair, His bone structure. Everything that humans are is written down on a cellular level- God's computer program for the creation of all living things. Over time, Catholic theologians postulated that she was conceived and brought into this world without the stain of original sin in preparation for the time when she would carry the Son of God. This was done with the grace and help of the Holy Spirit so that Mary would have no spot or blemish- the purest daughter of Judah. It only stands to reason that God would want only the best physical home for his beloved Son. Mary's conception was cleanly wrought for the best reasons and inspired by the purest motives- an **Immaculate Conception.** According to Pope Pius IX, *"The Most Blessed Virgin Mary was, from the first moment of her conception, by a singular grace and privilege of Almighty God and by virtue of the merits of Jesus Christ, Savior of the human race, preserved immune from all stain of sin." (Catechism 124)*

Our Catechism continues with:

The "Splendor of an Entirely Unique Holiness" by which Mary is "enriched from the first instant of her conception" **comes wholly from Christ: she is "redeemed, in a more exalted fashion, by reason of the merits of her Son."**
The Father blessed Mary more than any other created person "in Christ with every spiritual blessing in the heavenly places" and chose her "in Christ before the foundation of the world, to be holy and blameless before Him in love." (124)

Martin Luther also endorsed the Immaculate Conception during his "Sermon on the Day of the Conception of the Mother of God," in 1527. He said: *It is a sweet and pious belief that the infusion of Mary's soul was effected without original sin; so that in the very infusion of her soul she was also purified from original sin and adorned with God's gifts, receiving a pure soul infused by God. Thus from the first moment she began to live she was free from all sin.*

Catholicism views Mary as the Perpetual Virgin while Protestants have entertained the notion that she had other children besides Jesus, citing references to Jesus' "brothers and sisters." The problem with that assumption is that when Jesus was crucified, he gave Mary over to John the Beloved. *"When Jesus therefore saw His mother, and the Disciple standing by, whom He loved, He saith unto His mother, 'Woman behold thy son!' Then saith He to the Disciple, 'Behold thy mother!' and from that hour that Disciple took her unto his own home." (John 19:26-27, KJV)*

Jesus uses an ancient ritual that is reserved for the last surviving child of a widow. In Jewish culture, it was up to the family to take care of the elderly. When a widow's last child died, she was forced to beg in the streets. If, however, the last child gave their mother into the care of another person in a public ceremony, the woman would become, for all intents and purposes, a part of that family, and would be cared for. In order for Jesus to use this ritual, he would have to be the only surviving child. Had Jesus had a living sibling, Mary would have simply moved in with that child and their family. Otherwise, that public ritual would have been a grave insult because Jesus would be saying that any surviving siblings were unfit to care for Mary.

We also need to remember that these "brothers and sisters" had been rude to Jesus, telling Him to work his miracles elsewhere. Jesus was a "first born" male child. If these had been His biological siblings, they would not have dared to do this. Under Mosaic Code, being disrespectful of the eldest son was tantamount to being disrespectful of the father of the family, which was punishable by death. One did not sass one's father or eldest brother without dire consequences.

Catholic tradition has always taught that Joseph was an old man when he married Mary and more than likely had children from another union. In those days, there was no such term as "step-brother" or "half-sister." A step or half sibling would've simply been known as a brother or sister. Jesus is always referred to as the son of Mary; no one else has the distinction of being referred to as her child. Furthermore, it should also be noted that the words that are translated as "brother" and "sister" could also be translated as "kins man" and "kins woman," terms for relations such as cousins. This is illustrated in the Second Book of Kings, Chapter 10, verses 13-14, KJV:

Jehu met with the brethren of Ahaziah king of Judah, and said, "Who are ye?"
And they answered, "We are the brethren of Ahaziah; and we go down to salute the children of the king and the children of the queen.
And he said, "Take them alive. And they took them alive and slew them at the pit of the shearing house, even two and forty men; neither left he any of them.

Now, I've heard of large families in my time, but forty-two children from a single set of parents?! (That's if there were no women born from the union.) My deepest sympathies go with their poor mother. The mind boggles at the wear and tear that forty-two pregnancies and successful births took. Of course, it is almost certainly a bunch of cousins with different parents that this passage is referring to. Even in the age of large families, forty-two children from one set of parents would be unthinkable. That many children would be rare, even in the case of multiple wives and multiple births.

Our names for the complex interrelations of family members are, relatively speaking, new. Consider that Jesus is called "Son of David." They aren't saying that Jesus was the actual son of David; just that David was His ancestor. Also bear in mind that the title "first born" does not necessarily mean that there were other children. The title merely means that this is the first child that the woman has, regardless of whether or not she has any others.

Both Martin Luther and Ulrich Zwingli endorsed Mary's perpetual virginity. In the work, "***Corpus Reformatorium***," Zwingli says, *"I firmly believe that Mary, according to the words of the gospel as a pure Virgin brought forth for us the Son of God and in childbirth and after childbirth forever remained a pure, intact Virgin."* (1:424)

Luther wrote, *"He, Christ, our Savior, was the real and natural fruit of Mary's womb...This was without the cooperation of a man, and she remained a virgin after that."* ("*Sermons on John,*" Chapters 1-4, 1537-39)

The ***Assumption of Mary*** is another controversial doctrine embraced by the Catholic Church. The idea is simply that God would not have allowed her body to decay and wither upon death. Instead, she was assumed up into heaven completely intact upon the moment of her death. Why would they have this belief?

Well, we have absolutely no reference to her death and/or burial. The Bible mentions the deaths and burial places of other famous Jewish matriarchs, but not the mother of the Incarnate Word. Mary is the most important matriarch in the Bible, Old or New Testament included. It has also been the practice of the Church to start and found parish churches using some holy object or relic of Christ or the saints. We have no death relics belonging to Mary.

Biblical scholars agree that a few people have been assumed in the Old Testament; so, there is a precedent for taking truly holy people bodily into heaven without a death occurring. Here is a passage of such an event:

And it came to pass, when they were gone over, that Elijah said unto Elisha, "Ask what I shall do for thee, before I be taken away from thee."

And Elisha said, "I pray thee, let a double portion of thy spirit be upon me."

And he said, "Thou hast asked a hard thing: nevertheless, if thou see me when I am taken from thee, it shall be so unto thee; but if not, it shall not be so."

And it came to pass, as they still went on, and talked, that, behold, there appeared a chariot of fire, and horses of fire, and parted them both asunder; and Elijah went up by a whirlwind into heaven. (2 Kings 2:9-11, KJV)

If Elijah was assumed, how much more deserving of such a fate is the mother who brought our Lord and Redeemer into this world? While there is no absolute proof that the Assumption took place, nothing has ruled the possibility of this event out either. Unless archeologists unearth Mary's occupied tomb, the Assumption will remain Catholic doctrine.

The Immaculate Conception, Perpetual Virginity, and Assumption of Mary are dogmas, which are central teachings to Catholicism, based on logic derived from the scriptures. Now you may wonder, "What sort of logic?" For that answer, let us turn back to a previously discussed passage. *"Then said Mary unto the angel, "How shall this be, seeing I know not a man?" And the angel answered and said unto her, "The Holy Ghost shall come upon thee, and the power of the Highest shall overshadow thee: therefore also that holy thing which shall be born of thee shall be called the Son of God." (Luke 1:34-35, KJV)*

This passage has led mainline Christian theologians to conclude that Jesus was conceived by the Holy Spirit (and rightfully so). However, few Protestant theologians are prepared to explore the exact implications of this act. Though Christ's conception was non-sexual, leaving Mary's virginity intact, the fact remains that conceiving a child conveys the intimacy of marriage. Children are the fruition of marriage, and no child may be conceived without some act of consummation. In fact, a marriage is not truly valid if consummation does not occur. So, logically speaking, the act of conception made Mary the earthly spouse of the Holy Spirit. While Joseph was indeed her husband, the union was never sexual.

The previous passage speaks of the Virgin being "overshadowed" by God. To "overshadow" meant to "spread one's cloak or wing" over a woman in Jewish culture, implying a marital relationship. Under Mosaic code, betrothal automatically meant marriage. The Hebrew term for "betrothed" is **kiddush** from **kadash**, meaning **"holy or consecrated."** According to the **Oral Law of Kiddushin,** *"the husband prohibits his wife to the whole world like an object which is dedicated to the sanctuary."* (Opisso 1)

Because Mary became pregnant while betrothed to Joseph, he, being honorable before God, would have nothing to do with her afterward. Joseph could've have chosen to have Mary publicly shamed and executed, but decided to put her away privately. (Re: Matthew 1:14, KJV) But an angel comes in a dream to tell him that Joseph that he has nothing to fear in taking Mary for his wife. The child within her is conceived of the Holy Spirit and will save His people from their sins. (Re: Matthew 1:20-21, KJV) However, the angel never says to "go in unto" or "come together" with Mary, two common biblical phrases that mean to "enter into a sexual relationship." The original term for "wife" in this passage was ***paralambano gunaika,*** which ***infers a non-sexual relationship.*** (Opisso 1)

Here's another tidbit to consider: Joseph is believed to have been a very devout man by both Catholics and Protestants. According to the Jewish faith, the High Priest, a yearly post, would abstain from sexual activity with his wife to be as pure as humanly possible in order to go into the Holy of Holies and commune with God on the Day of Atonement on behalf of the Jewish people. Could we expect any less of Joseph than the High Priest, knowing that he had the Incarnate Word made flesh, physically residing in his home? This duty would not be for just a year; it would never end. Joseph is still standing in the direct presence of Jesus. Put yourself in Joseph's shoes for a moment and use a little common sense: you're just a poor carpenter, and God has chosen you to be the protector of His Son. Would you even dare to peek around the corner when that child's mother was bathing or dressing herself? If I had been Joseph, I would've been afraid to even approach her sleeping quarters. She would've been completely off limits.

Remember that every Jew knew that God's presence was in the Holy of Holies; for Joseph, the place where Mary and Jesus, the child, slept would have been considered a new Holy of Holies. To add to this idea, the old Ark of the Covenant housed the word of God, etched in stone tablets. Mary would have been the new Ark because she housed the Word of God made manifest, not just words in stone.

Now, I want to restate that this does not make Mary a goddess or an equal to the Trinity, but it does support the dogmas of Immaculate Conception, Perpetual Virginity, and the Assumption. To have participated in the conception of Christ implied the need for unparalleled purity. The Immaculate Conception prepared Mary for such an honor. And Joseph could never physically claim the "bride of the Holy Spirit" as his own. Any action of that sort would have been the worst adulterous offense. Finally, if truly holy people, who were born with original sin, can be assumed into heaven, then what of the person who never knew original sin and was spiritually fit enough to be the Mother of God Incarnate?

Mary and the Church

The Virgin is also seen as a messenger to the Church. Over the past two millennia, there has been thousands of reported Marian apparitions throughout history- some laughable, others shown to be genuine. For example, in Fatima, Portugal, Mary appeared before some children and told them that the war (WWI) that Europe was involved in would end soon. However, she also warned the Church that it must draw closer to God or another evil would emerge and cause great suffering. World War I did end, but the 1930's saw Hitler come to power, and millions died in the Second World War.

The last ten years have witnessed an explosion of Marian apparitions. Many believe that she is sending a strong message to Roman Catholics to come back to their faith, or there will be dire consequences. Recently, Pope John Paul II told Catholics that Catholicism would see a new "springtime" providing that we are "docile" to the workings of the Holy Spirit. On the other hand, if Catholics do not rededicate themselves to God, Mary's warning of disaster may be waiting in the wings. (Faith 9/18/99)

I believe that Protestants have trouble with the human aspect of Christ. While they identify with the idea of Christ as a babe or as the risen sacrifice for sin, they do not see Christ as truly part of humanity. Put simply, non-Catholics tend to see Christ as God and do not truly accept that he knew and understood all the drives, emotions, desires and even hormones of a man but was without sin.

There is also an innate need for some Christian men to diminish any honor given to a woman in the Bible- including Our Blessed Mother. Part of it is the religious conflict between the sexes, while another is the instinctual fear of being too close to the pagan Mother Earth religions. It is easier to separate Jesus from His human aspect when we seek to diminish the Virgin's rightful place of honor. If we refute Christ's humanity, then we reduce the magnitude of His sacrifice on the cross and devalue Salvation itself. And diminishing the Virgin is also insulting to her Son for she is inextricably linked with Him. Even today, a favorite way to demean someone is to attack that person's mother.

Mary is considered by many theologians to be the "Second Eve." Whereas the original Eve was blamed for letting sin enter the world, Mary brought the cure to sin; she is the vindication of all women. Our Blessed Mother is also the fulcrum upon which the Bible swings- the human doorway through which the Prince of Peace entered the world. Everything before her is the Old Testament; everything after her is the New Testament. Before Mary, we have the human King David in the earthly Jerusalem. After Mary, we have the God King Jesus in the heavenly Jerusalem.

We should remember that God thought it necessary to bring His Son into the world as we all came- born of a woman. Jesus did not arrive in a doctor's bag; a celestial stork did not deliver Him. There has never been nor will there ever be another Mary. She occupies a unique place of honor in Heaven and in the heart of her beloved Son that no other Christian could ever hope to fill. It would be illogical, unnatural and improper for Christians to think otherwise.

Part III
Inside the Catholic Faith

We enter Your Holy Temple,
And raise our voices,
A blended people-
Many colors from many lands,
Rich and poor,
Male and female,
United in Christian Love,
Sealed with Divine Grace,
And ransomed by Sacred Blood,
-The Author

Protestant faiths often contend that they are friendlier and open to new people. But I have found that Catholicism is generally more accepting of the average individual than its Protestant neighbors. One of the first things that I noticed when I began attending my parish was that Catholicism welcomes the poor and wealthy alike. While the Church expects its lectors, cantors, Eucharistic Ministers, etc. to look nice when in front of the congregation, the dress code for members of the congregation is somewhat relaxed. There are a wide variety of styles of clothing, from business suits and elegant dresses to the latest teen fashions boasting tee shirts and over-sized pants. The main emphasis is on a modest, tasteful appearance without obsessing on the length of a haircut or the use of makeup and jewelry. We are more involved with inner change and following Christ's example and less interested in grading one another.

This is one of the greatest "turn-offs" in Protestantism today. I have frequently heard individuals say that they would not feel welcome as part of the congregation in most churches because they have few suitable outfits to wear. Though having much to offer in the way of time and talent, people have grown tired of being scrutinized and rejected. And it is a fact that some Protestant churches will not let members participate in their services if they do not meet exaggerated standards of dress. These disenfranchised members often refuse to come back, and leave Christianity all together, looking for acceptance elsewhere.

For example, Corey, one of my good Baptist friends, related how his buddy, Craig, was not able to be an usher or youth minister because he had no suits to wear on Sunday. The best that his wardrobe boasted was polo shirts and khakis. Though Craig looked clean-cut and had excellent rapport with the kids, it was not enough for some of the "pillars of the church." So, in their infinite wisdom, the church elders opted for a married couple who lacked integrity in dealing with their own problematic children. Who cared that they were not truly qualified for their post, just as long as they looked fashionable.

I can identify with people who lack the funding and time to look as though they came out of a fashion catalog on Sunday morning. Once, my mother was a little shocked and surprised when she noted that I had just come from Mass wearing a sweater and colored jeans. Money has never been abundant, and both my husband and I have mostly casual clothes in our closet. And time is always a factor, especially for Sunday morning. I work on weekends, closing after eleven or midnight. It is not unusual to finally see my bed at one or two in the morning. So, when I rise at eight o'clock, the last thing I have time for is excessive primping or rifling through hangers, looking for that perfect outfit.

There may be thirty minutes to eat and dress before it's off to church. It's important to look good, but everything is much simpler and streamlined.

During the week, it is common to see parishioners dressed in jogging suits and shorts at morning Mass. Some stop off before going to work or to the gym for their morning workouts. Michael has memories of attending Mass at the Co-Cathedral of St. Thomas Moore in Tallahassee, which is situated just across the street from Florida State University. College students would often go to Mass before their weekend trip to the Gulf of Mexico or on the way back. While Mike would be dressed in a suit and tie, these others would wander in with slicked back hair and tank tops.

I once even heard of John and Jean Gunn attending a Christmas Mass in the Philippines where one guy came down for Eucharist dressed in a red pair of long johns. As he knelt down to receive it everyone noticed that a button was missing, exposing a small triangle of brown skin. Did anyone pull him aside later? No, the consensus was that this was probably his best outfit. After all, only the best would do for Christmas.

Following the Great Commission

Catholic witnessing is much warmer and more personal than Protestantism. Yes, I know that common wisdom dictates that Catholics do not witness to others, but that is not an accurate statement. Upon becoming a child of Rome, I learned a different way to witness my Christian faith. Catholicism demands that one's life is not compartmentalized. Reflecting the virtue of social justice in society speaks volumes. We minister to the poor, imprisoned, sick, and dying- seeing Christ in the unloved and unwanted. Good Catholics vote for those who uphold the sanctity of life and proper stewardship of the earth and its treasures and protest loudly when we see injustice and prejudice.

I find the use of tracts offensive and believe that they undermine and sabotage the Great Commission. Why? Because tracts are cold and judgmental. They patronize and make assumptions about the reader and the condition of his/her soul. Bringing Christ to the people does not consist of handing them pamphlets or shoving a piece of paper under their windshield wipers in parking lots. This is a lazy man's way to witness.

For Catholics, witnessing is an intimate sharing of our hearts and humanity. Faith is often discussed on a personal basis. This really became apparent to me when I participated in the Rite of Christian Initiation for Adults as a sponsor. My godchildren would often come over for meals and holiday activities. And during their sampling of the delicious smells and tastes of my kitchen, we would often sit and talk about the Bible and Christian life. Then, there have been countless times when I have talked frankly with many teens at work, always trying to steer them down the Christian path.

Each time we inspire others to follow Christ, we fulfill the Great Commission. A loving heart, a kind spirit, and a sense of humor are infinitely more useful than a piece of paper. True Christian faith is not born out of fear, but out of falling in love with Jesus and seeking to do His will out of that love. Beating someone over the head with the Bible never truly works. In fact, it usually drives away those who need God the most.

When I think of witnessing in its most positive and effective way I remember Mother Teresa of Calcutta. This tiny, fragile woman glowed with the Holy Spirit, and everywhere that she went she inspired a deep desire to follow Christ. Mother Teresa did not hand out pamphlets and tracts; she gave herself as a living sacrifice to God before the world.

While Catholicism does produce informative pamphlets, they often defend tenets of the faith itself. The closest thing to a tract in the Catholic world is a prayer card that makes no judgments about the reader at all. Prayer cards are gentle reminders that Jesus is patiently waiting for the return of His lost and errant lambs. And unlike the tract, they call all readers to a continuing life of conversion.

Religious Inbreeding

My husband, Michael, once had a good friend in college who owned a cocker spaniel named "Sebastian Magnus Norton, IV" (the name has been changed to protect the dog). His elegant name denoted a long distinguished pedigree. Sebastian was a purebred, blue-blooded hound with a silky, curly mane and dramatic doe-like eyes for which spaniels are so famous. Given his "good breeding," this animal should have epitomized the essence of the finest canine. But ole Sebastian had a serious problem. He was as dumb as a brick.

In fact, his stupidity is legendary. Michael remembers the hapless creature running into coffee tables, backing up, and doing it again. Friends of the owner would come over and play games like "find the snack" where cheese balls were thrown about the room, and Sebastian would go about catching and eating them. At times, Michael would palm the snack and pretend to throw it. Sebastian never got wise to this practice, still electing to the search the room for a cheese curl that wasn't there. Michael would finally show the snack to the dog, which would reject the notion that this was the original cheese curl. Sebastian wouldn't even eat it. Most of the time, Michael would have to drop the snack in a corner so that it could be "found."

In contrast, Mike also had a dog named "Maggie." Maggie was a mutt, a mix of German shepherd and pit-bull terrier. She was known for her loyalty and quick-wittedness. Unlike Sebastian, Maggie never ran into tables and caught on to Michael's tricks with cheese curls after a few times. Once wise to it all, the dog would calmly wait, watching my husband's hand as if to say, *"I know what you're up to, now hand it over."*

This story, though anecdotal, has a powerful message when you look closely. What distinguished Sebastian from Maggie? Sebastian was the product of a limited genetic pool while Maggie reaped the benefits from a "mixed" parentage. The problem with purebred animals or people is the genetic abnormalities that accompany selective breeding.

I don't understand racial purists of any kind. The reality is that there are precious few humans with "pure bloodlines." Genealogy has always been a pet subject of mine, and like so many Americans, my own family history is a tapestry of nationalities and races. I'm a blend of German, English, Irish, Scottish, and Native American, with hints of Spanish or Mediterranean blood. (One grandmother was famous for her dark eyes, black hair, and olive skin.) And, my husband's family history combines German, Norse, and Scottish with Jewish blood. Any children that we have will have a vast genetic pool at their disposal- both biologically and socially, being the products of six nationalities and three races.

The truth is that the farther you trace your family tree, the more likely that you'll find another race or nationality you weren't expecting or planning for. While it is enlightening, it is usually unnerving as well, serving an ample dose of humility to the proud purist who finds him/herself not as pure as previously thought.

Racism & Christianity

There are two main schools of thought in Christianity regarding the creation of the universe; some believe in the literal translation of the book of Genesis while others tend to believe in an evolution that was brought about and directed by God. No matter which idea is adopted, every Christian should believe that God is the Creator of the universe and every living thing in it. So, if we believe that God created the world, we must also, by logic, understand that God set up governing ideas and principles regarding the running of such a vast enterprise. God, the Father, is a being of order, not chaos.

Now let's look at nature. The world we live in is rich in variety. There are myriads of plants, animals, and microscopic life forms that live around us. Many subspecies are capable of breeding and producing viable offspring. Imagine what the world would look like if there were only one kind of flower, or bird, or insect, etc. Nature stresses genetic diversity in order to ensure the survival of all living things. Any species that has a limited genetic pool runs the risk of dying out. For example, the cheetah, famed for its speed and grace, is endangered not only because of poachers but because it has a limited gene pool. This has caused decreased numbers of these large cats to the point of conservationists artificially inseminating females in the wild using the sperm from captive cheetahs in zoos in an effort to save the species.

Just as with nature, there is great diversity in humanity. We have all manner of skin tones from the palest beige to the darkest brown. Human hair varies in color from glorious reds and blondes to smoldering browns and blacks and softer grays. Our eyes can be blue or green, brown, gray or even violet. We can be short, tall, large or small. These characteristics illustrate the vast genetic pool at humanity's disposal and the almost endless combinations humans come in. Given what we know about Homo sapiens, it becomes clear that God loves variety. So, why do we, as a species, disrespect God by hating and mistreating one another on the basis of how we look? How can we love God and hate His handiwork? The answer is simply that we can't and still love God. Scripture bears this out. John writes: *"If a man say, "I love God," and hateth his brother, he is a liar; for he that loveth not his brother whom he hath seen, how can he love God whom he hath not seen. And this commandment have we from Him, that he who loveth God love his brother also." (1 John 4:20-21, KJV)*

Jesus, Himself, declares, *"...Thou shalt love the Lord thy God with all thy heart, and with all thy soul, and with all thy mind. This is the first and great commandment. And the second is like unto it, thou shalt love thy neighbor as thyself. On these two commandments hang all the Law and the prophets." (Matthew 22:37-40, KJV)*

Racism has no geographical home. It is an ugly shadow in society, existing in every level or class, in every race or subculture. No one is immune to racism or racist views. For many of us, our race monster is a yapping French poodle in the corner of our psyche; others have a rabid Rottweiler that dominates their whole being. The key to reducing the size of one's monster is remembering that when we label, mistreat, and hate on the basis of race, we are offending God. A true child of God seeks only to please him.

Furthermore, Christian churches should strive to be more representative of the worldwide body of Christ in their communities. It's hard to mistreat someone you worship with as an equal. Of all the churches that I have known, the Catholic Church is the most racially and culturally integrated. It is a great joy to sing and pray with people of every race and nationality. I also believe that it is also the closest to what heaven will be like. I doubt very seriously that God segregates His people in paradise. Instead, I imagine heaven to be a wondrous place in which we will sit and talk with the prophets, ancient kings, Apostles, martyrs, saints, and the lost heroes of the body of Christ. We'll get to meet the "rest of the family."

Another spiritual problem that some Christians have is harsh feelings against the Jew. This is true of both Protestant and Catholic theologians. (The Catholic theologian

St. Alphonsus Liguori was responsible for anti-Semitic writings.) But while Catholicism continues to spiritually grow in this arena, some Protestant theologians are lagging behind. Many even go so far as to assert that Jesus was not Jewish. But those who back this position are forgetting the obvious fact that Jesus is descended from King David. He was circumcised and taught in various synagogues. And the Sanhedrin, Israel's religious ruling body, would not have considered Christ a threat if he were not Jewish. After all, no one would have listened to an unclean infidel. And they would have had no power to have him arrested.

The Christian is greatly indebted to the Jew. The scriptures were written by Jewish authors, and God's greatest gift to man was revealed in the person we know as Y'shua Hamashiach, a product of the Jewish nation. Now, some people blame the Jew for Christ's death, but without death, Christ would've never paid for humanity's sins. Judaism is like a tree. Christ was its flower after centuries of spiritual preparation. But in order for there to be the fruit that we call Christianity, the flower had to die. Yes, the Jews rejected Jesus, but He begged forgiveness from God on their behalf during the Crucifixion. If Jesus loved His people that much, can Christians do anything else but follow His example?

Bless the Jew and extend the hand of friendship, and God will bless you in your life. Remember that God told Abraham that he would bless those who blessed and curse those who cursed Abraham and his descendants. At no time does Jesus revoke this promise. It is interesting to note that history has shown that those who have persecuted Jews have paid an enormous price for their folly. The most memorable persecution in recent history was by the Germans in World War II, which has left Germany with a lasting shame that clouds their many achievements today.

God loves every human being, no matter the race, ethnicity, or nationality. Just as diversity is important in nature, it is also important within the body of Christ. Salvation is not the province of a few people who are the right color. When we do not appreciate other races and nationalities as part of our Christian family, we limit our growth in faith and become spiritually inbred.

The "Chicken Little" Syndrome

Most children are afraid of the dark or monsters under the bed, but my most frightful nightmare as a child was waking up late at night and wandering through an empty house. My parents and siblings would be missing and the air would be deafened with the silence of final and forever separation. Everyone would be gone, and they hadn't just left the house, but the planet. My family and all the saints that I knew and loved would be caught up to be with Christ, and I would be left behind. The "rapture" had come, and I would have to struggle through the "Great Tribulation."

I'm sure that many fundamentalists have had such fears realized in dreams and visions of the future. I recall many fiery sermons about the end of the world, and the usual speculation that people did concerning how current events fit into biblical prophecy. Studying the Book of Revelation was and still is a passion among Christians. But this passion has been known backfire on many occasions.

For example, at the turn of the century, one group of followers had been told the Christ would come back on a particular date, at a particular time. The members sold all that they owned including their homes, dressed in white robes and gathered at the top of a mountain. When the appointed time came and went, many of them were disillusioned and had problems with their faith afterward. Other groups of Christians have changed their proclamations when the "dates and times" didn't work out.

But the late twentieth century saw the rise of many doomsday cults who locked their followers away from society and exacted a terrible price in human life. Have we forgotten the likes of Jim Jones, David Koresh, and Heaven's Gate? This is the dark side of prophecy, when obsession leads to paranoia.

Remember the much-touted Y2K computer bug? Most of us stored extra water and supplies like batteries, but some crackpots and crazies were turning their homes into military bunkers complete with guns and ammunition. And some Christian sects were thoroughly convinced that the Apocalypse would occur at the stroke of midnight. You can imagine the kind of spiritual crisis these people suffered when everything didn't happen as planned. One church leader in Africa even murdered his followers when they began to doubt him.

Do Catholics believe in the Second Coming of Christ? Of course, however, they tend to shy away from those who've "cracked the biblical code or deciphered a special verse" that reveals secret knowledge. Catholicism has been around for two millennia. (Most American churches consider themselves old if they were founded around the Revolutionary War.) And because Catholics have seen their share of prophecy buffs and "false alarms," they tend to be more skeptical of the current books and theories on the end times.

Instead, the emphasis is placed on living a life of faith and devotion to Christ and handling daily challenges. This is wise because these prophecy experts, no matter how smart or well-read, fly in the face of scripture. Let's look at the words from the Gospel of Mark: *"Heaven and earth shall pass away: but my words shall not pass away. But of that day and that hour knoweth no man, no, not the angels which are in Heaven, neither the Son, but the Father." (Mark 13:31-32, KJV)*

No one can know when Jesus returns, not even Christ Himself. Only God the creator is privy to such knowledge, and He's not telling. We should never pretend to know the mind of God, the Father. Christians should walk, no run, away from people who traffic in fear. Just before His Ascension, Jesus warns the faithful about trying to discern the exact time and historical conditions of His return and the creation of the new Heaven and earth:

When they therefore were come together, they asked of Him, saying, "Lord, wilt thou at this time restore again the kingdom of Israel?"
And he said unto them, "It is not for you to know the times or the seasons, which the Father hath put in His own power. But ye shall receive power, after that the Holy Ghost is come upon you: and ye shall be witnesses unto me both in Jerusalem, and in all Judea, and in Samaria, and unto the uttermost part of the earth." (Acts 1:6-8, KJV)

If the previous passage isn't enough to make prophecy buffs think twice, then they should consider the words of Peter:

We have a more sure word of prophecy; whereunto ye do well that ye take heed, as unto a light that shineth in a dark place, until the day dawn, and the daystar arise in your hearts: knowing this first that no prophecy of the scripture is of any private interpretation. For the prophecy came not in old time by the will of man: but holy men of God spake as they were moved by the Holy Ghost.

But there were false prophets also among the people, even as there shall be false teachers among you, who privily shall bring in damnable heresies, even denying the Lord that bought them, and bring upon themselves swift destruction. And many shall follow their pernicious ways; by reason of whom the way of truth shall be evil spoken of. And through covetousness shall they with feigned words make merchandise of you: whose judgment now of a long time lingereth not, and their damnation slumbereth not. (II Peter 1:19-2:3, KJV)

Volumes about the "end times," no matter how well thought out and cleverly written, are, at best, educated guesses about a secret that no man is meant to truly know. Many prophecy buffs are also forgetting that John was forbidden to write certain end time "surprises" down. The scriptures say,

And I saw another mighty angel come down from heaven, clothed with a cloud: and a rainbow was upon his head, and his face was as it were the sun, and his feet as pillars of fire: and he had in his hand a little book open: and he sat his right foot upon the sea, and his left foot on the earth, and cried with a loud voice, as when a lion roareth: and when he had cried, seven thunders uttered their voices.

And when the seven thunders had uttered their voices, I was about to write: and I heard a voice from heaven saying unto me, "Seal up those things which the seven thunders uttered, and WRITE THEM NOT." (Revelation 10:1-4, KJV)

John isn't even allowed to divulge this information, so how could anyone possibly be sure of anything when it comes to end-of-the-world-biblical prophecy. Remember that seven crucial things are left completely out of the scriptures, by God's command. If I was going to make a homemade chocolate cake, and I removed chocolate, sugar, flour, butter, eggs, shortening and leavening, would I have a chocolate cake? Would I have anything even resembling a cake? If one element out of place can change the whole picture, then what of seven elements?

So, we see that attempts to unlock biblical secrets and cast judgments about the future contradict the very scripture that these ministers and authors prize so highly. Prophecies of any kind are always murky and highly symbolic, and biblical prophecies are often manipulated and shaped to further less than honorable agendas that ultimately divide the Body of Christ. Belief in the Rapture comes from a misinterpretation of I Thessalonians 4 and I Corinthians 15, which speak of living believers being "caught up" to be with Christ when He returns. I Thessalonians 4:16-17, KJV reads, *"For the Lord Himself shall descend from heaven with a shout, with the voice of the archangel, and with the trump of God: and the dead in Christ shall rise first: then we which are alive and remain shall be caught up together with them in the clouds to meet the Lord in the air: and so shall we ever be with the Lord."*

And I Corinthians 15:51-52, KJV states, *"Behold, I shew you a mystery; we shall not all sleep, but we shall be changed, in a moment, in a twinkling of an eye, at last trump: for the trumpet shall sound, and the dead shall be raised incorruptible, and we shall all be changed."*

Notice that Paul is speaking only of the Second Coming. There is no mention of to the Great Tribulation or an initial seizing of believers before the Second Coming takes place. This will be with the blast of a trumpet, hardly what someone might call quiet. It might interest the reader that belief in the Rapture is relatively new (just two hundred years old) and a tenet originally adopted by groups such as the 7th Day Adventists and Jehovah Witnesses (Matthews, Rapture.) Evangelical theologians would later follow their example. Nowadays, the Rapture is widely accepted by Protestantism as a whole.

The idea of being "left behind" comes from a misinterpretation of Luke 17:34-36, KJV, when Jesus tells His Disciples, *"I tell you, in that night, there shall be two men in one bed; the one shall be taken and the other left. Two women shall be grinding together; the one shall be taken, and the other left. Two men shall be in the field; the one shall be taken and the other left."*

Many theologians stop there, declaring this passage as proof of the "Rapture" or believers being initially "caught up" to be with Christ so that they are protected against the coming terror of the Great Tribulation. But they forget to finish the passage. It continues, *"And they answered and said unto Him, 'Where Lord?' And He said unto them, 'Wheresoever the body is, thither will the eagles be gathered together.'(Luke 17:37, KJV)*

We should note that the Greek word for **taken** means **"taken to destruction."** The last lines of this passage speak of being taken to the place where the body (not the soul) is and the eagles gather. Many birds, including eagles, are also carrion eaters, picking at dead flesh with their sharp beaks and devouring that which other creatures will not touch. In the Gospel of Matthew, Jesus compares those who are "taken" to those who were lost in the flood where only those who were left were actually saved.

> *But as the days of Noah were, so shall also the coming of the Son of man be. For as in the days that were before the flood they were eating and drinking, marrying and giving in marriage, until the day that Noe entered into the ark, and knew not until the flood came, and took them all away; so shall also the coming of the Son of man be. Then shall two be in the field; the one shall be taken, and the other left. Two women shall be grinding at the mill; the one shall be taken, and the other left. Watch therefore: for ye know not what hour your Lord doth come. (Matthew 24:37-42, KJV)*

Given the comparison to those who were lost in the flood to those taken, no literalist can interpret Christ's words as a trip to paradise. Jesus then warns us at the end of this passage, saying,

> *But know this, that if the goodman of the house had known in what watch the thief would come, he would have watched, and would not have suffered his house to be broken up. Therefore be ye also ready: for in such an hour as ye think not the Son of man cometh.*

> *Who then is a faithful and wise servant, whom his lord hath made ruler over his household, to give them meat in due season? Blessed is that servant, whom his lord when he cometh shall find so doing. Verily I say unto you, That he shall make*

him ruler over all his goods. But and if that evil servant shall say in his heart, "My lord delayeth his coming"; and shall begin to smite his fellowservants, and to eat and drink with the drunken; the lord of that servant shall come in a day when he looketh not for him, and in an hour that he is not aware of, and shall cut him asunder, and appoint him his portion with the hypocrites: there shall be weeping and gnashing of teeth. (Matthew 24:43-5,1, KJV)

It might interest the reader that even **Tim LaHaye**, author of the celebrated **Left Behind** books, had to admit that *"no one passage of Scripture teaches the two aspects of His Second Coming separated by the Tribulation." Furthermore, "no passage teaches a post-Tribulation or mid-Tribulation rapture, either."(Madrid 79, originally quoted from Rapture Under Attack, 75)*

Actually, the belief that believers would be removed in the Rapture conflicts with the words of Christ, who prayed that we would remain. He spoke to the Father, saying these words:

While I was with them in the world, I kept them in thy name: those that thou gavest me I have kept and none of them is lost, but the son of perdition; that the scripture might be fulfilled. And now come I to thee; and these things I speak in the world, that they might have my joy fulfilled in themselves. I have given them thy word; and the world hath hated them, because they are not of the world, even as I am not of the world. I pray not that thou shouldest take them out of the world, but thou shouldest keep them from the evil (John 17:12-15, KJV)

How can we have the Rapture when the Final Judgment involves separating the sheep from the goats, those loyal to Christ from those who reject Him? Matthew 25: 32-33 says, *"And before Him shall be gathered all nations: and He shall separate them one from another, as a shepherd divideth his sheep from the goats: and He shall set the sheep on His right hand, but the goats on the left."*

Revelation 20:11-15 reiterates that we shall all be present before the white throne:

And I saw a great white throne, and Him that sat on it, from whose face the earth and the heaven fled away; and there was found no place for them. And I saw the dead, small and great, stand before God; and the books were opened: and another book was opened, which is the book of life: and the dead were judged out of those things which were written in the books, according to their works.
And the sea gave up the dead which were in it; and death and hell delivered up the dead which were in them: and they were judged every man according to their works. And death and hell were cast into the lake of fire. This is the second death. And whosoever was not found written in the book of life was cast into the lake of fire.

If the Rapture theory is true, then the faithful sheep will have already been separated from the goats in this momentous event. This is why Catholicism does not espouse the Rapture. Instead we believe what the scriptures endorse: one return of Jesus Christ, one resurrection of the body, and one general judgment of the living and the dead. **The Rapture Theory is actually saying that Christ did come and will come to earth three** times: once 2,000 years ago, then to secretly retrieve the faithful, and finally, to judge the living and the dead and begin His earthly reign.

This may be hard for **Left Behind** readers to accept, but the **Left Behind** series smacks of a little known brand of heresy called **Pelagianism** due to the fact that the characters in the books seem to be working to redeem themselves. Pelagianism contended that grace depended on human initiative, not God's initiative. These books offer an ugly portrayal of God as well as denying the need for baptism- a spiritual command from Christ Himself. Salvation is described in the children's **Left Behind** series as a "deal" or "transaction," the product of saying a verbal formula of words. Catholicism embraces salvation as an ongoing process beginning with the sacraments of initiation and continuing throughout one's lifetime. (*Catholic News & Herald, 4/23/04*)

Finally, while La Haye and his contemporaries may have honorable intentions and never see themselves as altering the Book of Revelation, the realism that they bring to readers retains the effect of adding or subtracting from John's original visions. The Book of Revelation expressly forbids this, declaring,

> *For I testify unto every man that heareth the words of the prophecy of this book, if any man shall add unto these things, God shall add unto him the plagues that are written in the book: and if any man shall take away from the words of the book of this prophecy, God shall take away his part out of the Book of Life, and out of the Holy City, and from the things that are written in this book. (Revelation 22:18-19, KJV)*

Damnation is attached to altering this book! Trying to fit biblical elements to world events and adding conjecture here and there is playing a dangerous game with Almighty God, one in which a person's soul is in jeopardy. The wise man leaves the Book of Revelation alone and avoids making pronouncements of any kind.

Catholicism stresses the importance of having our "spiritual bags packed" and living each day as if it were our last. And being Christians, we should always spread the belief in Christ to those who are spiritually dead. If we do our part for Christ, He will keep us safe and deliver us from our enemies. We needn't fear the coming of our Lord, but wait in "joyful hope." Be watchful? Of course, but we should also never be hostages to predictions and speculation. Scare tactics do not work. Instead, we need to focus on living the life that God expects us to live. A good Christian example is the greatest means to witness and bring the lost to Christ.

Special Note: In this section, we will be exploring various elements of Catholic Liturgy as well as highlights of the liturgical year, particularly the fall and winter holidays and Easter. So, all scripture readings will be taken from the <u>Catholic Bible</u>. This is to maintain the integrity of my sources and to help you see the similarity between the Protestant and Catholic Bibles.

<u>Liturgical Life</u>

For those unacquainted with the term, the word *liturgy* is defined as a "public work" or service conducted for the benefit of God's people. A liturgical year is a cyclic period of time that Christians celebrate events in Jesus' life, from His birth through the Resurrection as well as honor biblical and historical saints of the Church. This creates a basic rhythm of prayer and worship within the lives of believers. (Catechism 886)

<u>Catholic Symbolism</u>

One of the most misunderstood aspects of Catholicism dwells in the use of statuary, paintings and symbols. Popular Protestant wisdom would suggest that Catholics "worship idols" when we show reverence for images of any kind. But that is untrue. We do not worship statues, but we revere the beliefs and concepts illustrated in statuary, paintings, and symbols. In the past, art was commissioned to transport the viewer back in time, and by doing so, give a reality or clarity to some great moment in the Bible. Catholic paintings and statuary often tell Bible stories or document the heroism of the saints. Why do this?

Well, most people seem blissfully unaware that most of humanity could not read or write until the later half of the nineteenth century. In fact, literacy did not start to become widespread until the rise of factories and the responding growth of urban life in cities such as New York and Chicago. These places became industrial magnets with people abandoning the family farm for the financial prospects, culture, and convenience that city life offered. And somewhere along the way, a greater emphasis was placed on education as a means of personal advancement.

But before literacy began to flower, precious few individuals could read or write, beyond the most elementary level, if at all. Education was the realm of the rich. If you wanted to learn and poverty was an issue, you might be able to land a rich sponsor who had a share in your future. You could also enter an ecclesiastical institution such as a Catholic monastery or abbey as a novice, and the Church would educate you in return for a life dedicated to the priesthood or laity, as a nun or a monk. Public education for all people was largely nonexistent.

So, how did folks learn in a non-literate world? They learned visually, through the use of pictures and symbols. The general public even conducted mundane affairs outside by symbols. Needed to see the boot maker or cobbler? Then, you might look for a boot or shoe over his door. Maybe there were legal problems, and a lawyer was called for. The emblem for the law was a set of scales, often used as an advertisement to gain new clients. And if you had the courage to look for a doctor, you would search for that telltale snake and staff moniker called the *caduceus*, which bespoke the office of a healer.

Catholic symbolism still pervades religious artwork today. Jesus has many symbols within the Catholic world, the most prolific of which is the cross in all its variations. The **Chi Rho** is actually a Greek abbreviation of the word "Christ", using the Greek letters "X" and "P" and is often seen with the Alpha and Omega symbols. IHS, IHC, IC and XC are not English but actually Greek letters, standing for Jesus or Jesus Christ. Other popular symbols include the ***fish, the "Good Shepherd,"*** and the ***cross on an orb***. Most

Christian churches and denominations have borrowed these symbols from Catholicism, and one can find them almost anywhere. (Morrow 411)

But there are other, lesser-known symbols, which the untrained eye may not associate with Christ. There is the ***five-pointed star***, ***the mother pelican feeding her young with her blood***, and ***the unicorn***. Though some Christian scholars malign the unicorn as a symbol of the New Age, this mythical beast is actually an ancient Christ symbol. According to mythology, only the pure of heart may see this gentle creature. The prefix "uni-" means "one," and there is but one Savior, Jesus Christ. It's also curious to note that the unicorn is linked with virginal women, for only they may touch it. Only the pure of heart may see God. Jesus was born of a virgin, and she was the first to experience His love.

But my favorite symbol of Christ is that of a ***lamb with a cross***, often seen ***with a victory banner or sitting on a book with seven seals.*** This is called the ***Agnus Dei*** or, translated from Latin, the ***"Lamb of God."*** Another variation of this symbol has ***the lamb pierced with a cross with seven drops of blood from the wound, each drop representing one of the seven sacraments***. (Morrow 411)

The use of ***triangles***, ***triangles interwoven with circles***, and ***interlocking circles*** are common affectations for the Triune Godhead or the Trinity. The Holy Spirit is often depicted as a dove (as with Jesus' Baptism) or as various fiery emblems. Consequently, the gifts of the Holy Spirit are represented in sevens: ***seven doves, seven flames, a seven-pointed star***, even ***a seven-branched candlestick holder***. (Morrow 410-411)

God, the Father is often symbolized by a ***hand, extending beyond bright, billowing clouds, a six-pointed "Creator's star" and the eye within an equilateral triangle, also known as the "all-seeing eye."*** (Morrow 411) The "all-seeing eye" is another emblem, which has been maligned by well meaning, but ignorant, Christian authors as symbolic of New Age.

The Church, in general, is associated with images of ***Noah's ark***, ***the Ark of the Covenant***, ***a woman trampling the dragon***, ***a crowned-woman***, and ***a bride with a chalice and a book***. Christ's Bride is also seen as ***a house on a rock*** and ***a city on a hill***. (Morrow 411)

Her servants also have their own symbols. For example, we often associate the use of ***animals*** around the figure of St. Francis of Assisi, who nursed injured and sick animals back to health. If you examine older paintings, Peter is depicted as carrying ***a set of keys***, which harks back to the scriptures and references the "keys to the Kingdom of Heaven," which Christ gives him in the Gospel of Matthew.

Their own particular emblems identify the four Gospel writers as well. Since Matthew begins his Gospel by documenting Christ's human lineage, he is represented by ***a winged-man***. Mark's Gospel starts with John the Baptist, who lived with wild animals in the desert, so Mark's emblem is that of a ***winged-lion***. Luke's moniker is a ***winged-ox*** because oxen were the sacrificial animals of the Judaic priesthood and his Gospel originates in the Temple with the priest Zachary, who became the father of John the Baptist. And finally, John the Beloved's emblem is ***an eagle*** as his Gospel goes from Heaven to Earth and back again. These symbols are not always winged, but can be seen in their simplest forms. (Morrow 411)

The Virgin Mary's flowers are the ***lily*** or ***fleur-de-lis*** and ***the rose***, in varying forms. Her rose, whether white or pink, is seen ***without thorns***. Other Marian emblems are ***a crescent moon, a crown of stars, a star, a flowering almond, a closed gate***, or ***a sealed book***. (Morrow 411) Her monogram design allows for the shape of each letter in her name.

So, artwork within Catholic sanctuaries was used to teach and inspire the faithful, while symbolism identified various people in paintings and sculpture. But symbolism also marks and enforces the traditions of the Church with the use of colored vestments and banners. *Green*, the most commonly used color, marks what is known as "ordinary time." This is the time between specific celebrations or feasts. *Purple* is the color for Advent and Lent, Ember Days (days reserved or honoring the priesthood and clerical vocations), Vigils, and Rogation Days (specific petition days). *Red* is used for the Easter Passion, Pentecost, and the Feasts of the Apostles or Martyrs. And white is the color used for Christmas, Easter, Our Lady, the Angels, Confessors, and Virgins. (Morrow 298) Other colors associated with Mary are *blue* and *rose*.

Although **black** and **purple** are traditionally the colors for funerals, the American Catholic clergy now uses *white* because the Church looks upon these instances hopeful in the promise of eternal life. (Rite A 935)

Catholicism and the Fall and Winter Holidays

Symbolism supports the Christian traditions that keep us in step with yearly events and life itself. They call us back to our Christian journey and help us to renew our relationship with God when we wander too far away. For me, this calling begins and is most keenly felt in fall, my favorite season. The air is crisp and charged with electricity. Trees are resplendent with scarlet, bronze, gold and orange leaves, some of which are actually a mix of blazing color as if air- brushed by a celestial hand. This beauty is set against an azure sky and the rich green and gold of fertile hills and mountains.

Fall is the time to begin a new school year or college term. It brims with the added excitement of football games and parades. Numerous street festivals beckon to our visitors with their crafts and music. It's not unusual for a city to block whole streets and avenues off from normal travel in order to secure space for booths and tables. Amid the homemade and hand painted, one can smell and taste the treats of the season. Pumpkin and apple pies charm the nose with their spicy scents while cakes and cookies offer an aromatic whiff of chocolate as you pass each table. And, of course, there is the expected smoke from barbecue fires and grills.

Spring and summer have sent us away to other places. Having traveled far in our thoughts and pursuits, we hear an invitation to return to hearth, heritage and family ties, especially our faith. The senses bring us home to the comfort we knew as children, and we are invited to renew our Christian faith.

Halloween

Pop culture has contributed to a renaissance of the pagan celebration of Samhain. We forget that Halloween, as a Christian holiday, is taken from All Hallow's Eve, which begins a day of celebrating the heroism and devotion of the holy men and women that Christianity sees as its saints. This day is called the Feast of All Saints. As a reflection of this, Catholic Churches often encourage children to dress up as their favorite saints and participate in parish-sponsored events in response to the perversion of All Hallow's Eve by Hollywood and the media.

While many conservatives may wince at these words, Halloween, as it is celebrated in pop culture, offers Christians the sobering truth that Lucifer is alive and well in our world. We are reminded that there are powers and principalities that would like nothing better than the corruption and ultimate destruction of God's people. And this holiday also reiterates the fact that most of us have truly pagan roots and have little, if any, Jewish blood. We are products of the Great Commission and God's continuing harvest of souls. Halloween reminds us that we are no longer bound to pagan gods and goddesses, but part of God's family, a holy nation, ransomed by the blood of the Lamb.

The Feast of All Souls follows the Feast of All Saints, which is also extremely important in the Catholic calendar. We remember our beloved dead at Mass, holding them up to God in prayer and begging His mercy upon them as they continue their path to Heaven. We believe that the power of Holy Eucharist brings down heavenly mercies, which speed souls on their way to paradise.

I've heard many Protestants condemn Catholicism for this practice, contending that we believe that we can "pray" someone into Heaven. That is an ugly distortion of a good and holy act. While we do believe that fervent prayer can make a difference, it is God's love and forgiveness that ultimately opens Heaven's gates to those weary pilgrims. Our prayers simply appeal to God's generous nature.

Thanksgiving

> *Come, sit at the table,*
> *That the Lord has set before His people.*
> *Eat honeyed grain and roasting meat.*
> *Fill your goblets with wine and milk.*
> *Celebrate the glorious Harvest,*
> *And sing of the Father's Love.*
> *-The Author*

Americans often feel that Thanksgiving is an American holiday, but this idea is not entirely true. Thanksgiving's roots originate from the pagan harvest celebrations in the Celtic world. Ancient man's life was centered on the growing and maintaining of grain, produce, and animal husbandry. A healthy food supply was a mark of wealth for any country. Insects, blight, and disease would run rampant, devastating whole communities, leaving starvation and death in their wake. So, ancient men appealed to "the gods" for their protection that they might be spared and prosper.

As Christianity began to spread throughout Europe, appealing to a pantheon of deities was slowly replaced with petitions to God, the Father for His blessing on the land and a fruitful harvest. This was usually done on special feast days called Rogation Days. The fulfillment of the petitions offered on those Rogation Days was a celebration in the fall, the time of harvesting crops and preparing for winter.

Most people are unaware that "thanksgiving" celebrations have been around since man began opting for an agrarian lifestyle, instead of the hunting/gathering culture of prehistoric man. The American holiday known as "Thanksgiving" is simply the continuation of this extremely old tradition.

Christmas

Every since I could remember, Christmas has been my favorite holiday. When I undertook my Catholic conversion, it added a dimension to the holiday that I never knew existed. I began to understand where all the beautiful customs and practices came from.

First of all, the very name "Christmas" is a contraction of "Christ's Mass." Mass is a Catholic term referring to a church service where Eucharist is celebrated. It comes from the Latin terms ***missa est*** which means "you are sent" as Christians are sent out into the world to bring it to Christ. This was originally a pronunciation made by the priest at the completion of worship.

There is historical data that suggests that Christ was more than likely born in late spring, early summer. One does not "watch flocks by night" in the winter as it is extremely cold. Most animals are corralled and sheltered at that time. One prophecy tells us that the Messiah would be born "between the lion's paws." Astronomers have noted that a star known as **Regulus** went super nova around the birth of Christ, and it was located in the constellation of Leo (between what would have been seen as the lion's paws). Leo is a summer constellation. So, why do Christians celebrate Christmas in the winter?

Because, the pagan world had a holiday called the "Winter Solstice." It was the rebirth of the sun. It was Catholic theologians who decided to adopt this time of year as a time to introduce those who worshipped the sun to "the Son of God," who had defeated sin, death and the devil. Early pagans feared when darkness fell easily on the earth and the sun left the sky early in the evening, but were restored in their hope with the Winter Solstice, which marked the sun's return. When the sun came back, it brought hope with it, and the greatest hope that the Christian has lies in Jesus. Over time, Christ's Mass or Christmas overshadowed the Winter Solstice, which became a astronomical date on the calendar. Christ became our source of hope, not the celestial body we know as the sun.

Most Christians enjoy hanging greenery in windows, over doors, around banisters, etc. But holly, mistletoe, and ivy are remnants of the Nine Sacred plants in the Celtic religion. Catholics took these plants and used their evergreen quality to represent Christ who gave us eternal life. (Perry 1) While Protestants have criticized the Catholic Church for these practices saying that we have adopted pagan practices and subverted Christianity, most are not ready to give up the Christmas holidays as we know them to be. We should always remember that Christianity grew as a result of these practices. In a strange way, Catholicism evangelized much of the western world using these tactics.

Christmas is also a season of light. Modern man loves strings of twinkling electrical bulbs, but has yet to replace the warmth of the fireplace and candles. Candles possess a special significance in Catholicism. They represent both the soul and the presence of the Holy Spirit. Catholics also have prayer candles, which are lit to symbolize a prayer on someone's behalf. It is believed that while the light burns, the prayer is continuously heard in heaven.

The advent wreath is a grouping of four candles, traditionally three *purple* candles and one *rose* colored one. However, they can vary in colors, so long as there are three darker candles with one pale one. This wreath is a way of counting each week (marked by lighting a candle on four successive Sundays) until the coming of Christ as a babe at Christmas. The first Sunday of Advent is especially significant as it begins the Catholic liturgical year.

The nativity or crèche, which depicts the story of the birth of Christ, is actually the creation of St. Francis of Assisi who founded the Franciscan order of monks, a Catholic saint. This was his way of teaching the Christmas story to those who could not read.

Many of the greatest Christmas hymns are in fact Catholic in origin. Beside typical hymns like "*Ave Maria*," and "*Panis Angelicus*," many favorites such as "***O Come All Ye Faithful***," "***O Come, O Come Emmanuel***," and "***Silent Night***" were also penned by Catholics. Let us not forget "***The Magnificat***," which was Mary's response to the angel Gabriel. Versions of this work are often found in Protestant cantatas. Even the word *cantata*, comes from the Latinate *missa cantata* or "a sung Mass." Do some research on your own. If a hymn was written before the 1500s, it is a Catholic hymn. The Protestant Reformation did not happen before 1500. Was it translated from Latin? Chances are that it is Catholic. Does it have French roots? Remember that France has always been a prominent Catholic country. Many of these old hymns have a lyrical quality to them. One of silliest myths that I have heard is the notion that Catholics don't have good music. Pure nonsense, I assure you. Even secular Christmas songs have Catholic roots. "***Deck the Halls***" refers to hanging holly (a sacred Celtic plant) and the Yule log, which comes from the celebration of the Winter Solstice. This song shows evidence of the early Christians modifying pagan ideas and practices in their evangelization of Europe.

"***The Twelve Days of Christmas***" is particularly Catholic in its creation. In the days when being a Catholic in England could get you killed, this song was a code for Catholic children to learn their catechism. The phrase "my true love" actually refers to God the Father. The "partridge" is the personification of Christ. Mother partridges would often sacrifice themselves for their young by luring predators away from their nests while feigning injury.

Here is what the other things meant:

2 Turtle Doves- The Old and New Testaments
3 French Hens- Faith, Hope, and Charity-the Theological Virtues
4 Calling Birds- The Four Gospels/Evangelists
5 Golden Rings- The first five books of the Old Testament,
which gives the history of man's fall from grace also known
as the "Pentateuch"
6 Geese A-Laying- The six days of Creation
7 Swans a-Swimming- The seven Gifts of the Holy Spirit and/or the seven Sacraments
8 Maids A-Milking- The eight Beatitudes
9 Ladies Dancing- The nine Fruits of the Holy Spirit
10 Lords A-Leaping- The Ten Commandments
11 Pipers Piping- The eleven Faithful Apostles
12 Drummers Drumming- The twelve points of doctrine in the Apostles Creed.
(Stockert 8)

How many Protestants grew up singing this song, never realizing that they were singing something specifically designed to teach Catholicism? The irony of it all is astounding. It is also ironic that Protestants still love the old Renaissance style angels in their elegant glory. In fact, most depictions of these celestial beings are inspired from Renaissance artwork, and the artist mainly responsible for these beautiful representations, particularly cherubs, is Raphael. Raphael, like Michelangelo, De Vinci, and Donatello, was a Catholic whose work was commissioned by Rome. Without the patronage of the Vatican, much of the greatest artwork ever created would not have been possible.

Religious writers have badmouthed Santa Claus, but even his roots come from the Christian world. Forget the elves and reindeer and remember that the jolly old fat man was fashioned on the Catholic saint, St. Nicholas, who was actually a bishop in Myra, Turkey. (The figurines showing a kneeling Santa before the Christ Child hark back to the bishop who devoted his life to Jesus.) St. Nicholas personified the virtue of Christian charity, not the greed we see so evident in department stores.

Speaking of shopping, I generally do not spend much time in stores buying gifts for family and friends. We have ten siblings with spouses, nineteen nephews and nieces, and two sets of parents on our Christmas list. Because of the sheer size of this bunch, I get very creative around Christmas. I love to give handmade gifts such as homemade chocolates and Christmas tapes filled with rare and beautiful music that most people never hear. One year, I gave each family an ancient prayer from Ireland, which had been printed with Celtic artwork on parchment paper and framed in gold. I have always believed that people like the thought of a gift that was specifically made for them.

But the greatest beauty of Christmas is revealed on Christmas Eve, at midnight. I do not understand the concept of not going to church on Christmas. For the Catholic, this day is considered a Holy Day of Obligation. There is a type of expectation, which permeates the air on Christmas Eve. My husband and I observe an Old World styled Christmas. Christmas Eve begins with a late and leisurely supper with our godchildren and close friends around 8 to 9pm. (This past year, we served chicken roasted in honey, butter and soy sauce, sautéed vegetables in garlic and olive oil, buttered corn, Irish potatoes in cream sauce, crescent rolls and red velvet cake- all by candlelight.) After the meal, we dress in our best clothes and go to church.

By now, it is 10:45. We come early to find a good seat as the sanctuary will fill up soon. The church is dimly lit with three candle globes in each of the ten stain-glass windows. There is a large cedar tree in the corner with its tiny white lights, decorations, and Moravian star at the top. Red and white poinsettias adorn the altar and the tabernacle. There are so many plants that they nestle our large nativity scene like a small forest. The walls, painted ivory and dotted with the Stations of the Cross, hang with fresh evergreen wreaths and scarlet bows. Some parishioners take this time to quietly greet friends while others slip away in their thoughts and prayers. Around 11pm, the choir begins its concert with many traditional favorites and a few contemporary pieces. When midnight strikes, the bells ring in over the silent congregation, which has amassed to three to four hundred people. It is "standing room only" for some unless the ushers ferret out a place to put them. Advent or the waiting period for Christ is over, and he comes once again like he did two millennia ago, as a child.

Beautiful music fills the air, the processional begins. In walk a group of priests and acolytes as well as our resident deacon, dressed in robes of white and gold, the color of incorruptible joy. The scriptures and psalms enthrall us, and we are called to meet with God in the "Miracle of the Mass"- Holy Communion. Father reminds us never to lose sight of the man on the cross when we gaze at the child in the manger. This is the first service of Christmas. It marks the beginning of a time of happiness for the faithful and sanctifies the rest of the festivities of the following morning. After church, we bid our friends sweet dreams and a Merry Christmas. Upon reaching home, we open our presents, then drift away in contented sleep. Michael and I usually rise around 10 or 11 in the morning, just in time for lunch at my mother's home.

Most Protestants see Christmas as one day, but Catholics should see Christmas as the inauguration of an eight-day celebration (called an *octave*) which includes specific feasts honoring **The Holy Family and Mary**, **Mother of God**. January is the month that we celebrate the **Epiphany of the Lord** (the arrival of the Wise Men) and well as **His Baptism**. And one of the great things about being a Catholic is that no matter where you go, you can still attend church services. There are few places where Catholics don't have a sanctuary to worship in. Even if you're in a foreign country, you can whip out your own missal and follow the service. (**Missals** are books made of prayers, scripture, and songs. They are universal in translation and go by set cycles.)

No matter how some people may try to downplay it, the reality is that Christmas is, in fact, very Catholic. The closer we look at history and western culture, the more apparent this revelation becomes. At the heart of this holiday are the Mass and God's Holy Banquet that we call communion or Eucharist. Without Christ, Christmas becomes another excuse to spend too much money, eat too much food, and wrangle with our relatives.

Reflections on Lent

When you hear the term **Mardi Gras**, what do you think of? I'll wager your thoughts deal with parades, excessive alcohol, and sexual promiscuity. After all, we're so familiar with the pictures and clips of New Orleans, as well as the exploits attempted and achieved during Carnival in the Caribbean and in South America. It is easy to let the excessiveness of the holiday cloud its true meaning much like the materialism of Christmas. But why have a celebration at all?

Well, the day after Mardi Gras is Ash Wednesday, which begins the season of Lent, a time of penance, prayer, fasting and abstinence in preparation for Easter. Mardi Gras originates from the days when there were few ways to preserve food for extended periods of time, and no refrigeration. To rid a house of sweets, meats, and other goodies, the family has a grand feast to avoid any spoilage or wasting of foods that would interfere with spiritual pursuits. Mardi Gras or Fat Tuesday was the last day for feasting before Lent.

Although many believers scoff at the idea of fasting and abstinence, it's interesting to know that almost every religion emphasizes self-denial as a way to draw closer to God. For the Muslim, there is Ramadan. The Jew has Yom Kippur and Passover. And the Christians remember the forty days that Jesus spent in the desert, before beginning His ministry. The term **Lent** actually comes from the Old English word, **lentcten**, meaning "*spring.*"*(*Webster's 216)

We relive Christ's final days as a human, walking beside Him, witnessing His temptations, hearing Him speak and warn His Disciples of what's coming. There is somber feel to our sanctuary as if permeated by an air of terrible excitement. The church walls and altar are hung and covered in **purple** cloth, the color of royalty, penance and remembrance. We place rocks and sand at the front of altar as symbols of the spiritual desert that we have entered.

Devout Catholics understand that Lent is a period of personal reflection and spiritual purification. Many Christians still avoid eating meat on certain days and over-celebrating as whole. It is traditional to give up something you particularly like during Lent. Common things are sweets (in general), chocolate, caffeine, junk food, and activities such as dining out or going to the movies. Others devote themselves to public service, going out of their way to perform random acts of kindness. The idea is sacrifice, and we make an extra effort to be living sacrifices for God. This practice helps us to become more attuned to the gravity of Christ's suffering on the cross. However, even though Lent, by its nature, is a somber time, our self-denial should always be done with joyful, happy hearts.

> *Moreover when ye fast, be not, as the hypocrites, of a sad countenance: for they disfigure their faces, that they may appear unto men to fast. Verily I say unto you, they have their reward.*
>
> *But thou, when thou fasteth, anoint thine head, and wash thy face; that thou appear not to fast, but unto thy Father which is in secret: and thy Father which seeth in secret, shall reward thee openly. Lay not up for yourselves treasures upon Earth, where moth and rust doth corrupt, and where thieves break through and steal.*

But lay up for yourselves treasures in Heaven, where neither moth nor rust doth corrupt, and thieves do not break through nor steal. (Matthew 6:16-20, KJV)

My personal memories of Mardi Gras do not include the type of drunkenness and debauchery that is often associated with the holiday by the media. Michael and I are largely temperate creatures, reserving wine and cocktails for rare occasions. Instead, we usually entertain friends and family. Strains of big band, swing, jazz, and blues drift between animated conversations and the occasional burst of laughter. Maybe, someone will pull out traditional games to entertain the troops, supplanting the use of videos and electronic diversions with the likes of chess and Monopoly.

As with most Southern American homes, much of the guest activity creeps into the kitchen. The aroma of roasting meat and veggies draws more than a little attention from those who visit. Our celebration ends on a sweet note as we fix "fast-nachts," which are German-styled doughnuts. The words mean "the night before the fast," and have been long-associated with the Mardi Gras feast. Dough is fried in oil or fat, then rolled in powdered sugar and cinnamon and served hot with fresh coffee, tea, and milk.

This is the way devout Christians celebrate Mardi Gras. And after an evening of music, socializing, games and delicious food, we fall asleep with new memories of good times. Morning comes early. Wednesday bids us to rise up, sleepily dress, and make our way to church. Ash Wednesday Mass reminds us of our mortality and the need for a strong relationship with God. We do not sing the Gloria and the Alleluia during Lenten Masses because of their solemn nature.

The name "Ash Wednesday" comes from the fact that the priest will mark each of the congregation with the ashes of palm branches used on the previous Palm Sunday. These sacred remnants are mixed with consecrated oil, and then used to make the sign of the cross on each forehead. We hear the priest declare: **"Remember man, that thou art dust, and unto dust, thou shalt return."**

This serious declaration calls to mind our sinful nature and human frailty. But the mark is often a great conversation piece for the uninformed public, who almost always assume that it's a smudge. As most believers do not wash the mark away, but let it "wear" off, someone will invariably suggest a trip to the bathroom to fix the "problem." This is a perfect chance to explain the meaning of that "smudge," and share one's faith.

Protestant Christians often misunderstand the meaning and origin of Mardi Gras, believing it to be some pagan practice incorporated into the Catholic calendar. They witness the drunken, lusty behavior of revelers and often try to say that Catholicism blesses and endorses such acts. But they forget that humans will use any excuse to free themselves from society's mores and taboos. But Mardi Gras has a honorable origin, which rejects this image. The devout Catholic takes this day to celebrate before entering the spiritual desert called Lent. Each makes this spiritual sacrifice as Christ commands us, with a jubilant heart and a willing, contrite spirit.

Special Note: Let me remind the reader again that since I'm using actual readings from Catholic liturgical sources, the scriptural readings will come from the Catholic Bible to keep the integrity of my work and to show similarities between the King James Version and the Catholic scriptures

Palm Sunday

It is a lovely spring day as we stand on the steps and around the small courtyard in front of our church. The surrounding flowerbeds are emblazoned with a myriad of colored blossoms. The sky is a deep azure blue and the clouds have run away to reveal only the beauty of sunlight. The wrought iron railing in front of the oak doors is fashioned with palm branches and crimson ribbon.

Father is with us, dressed in scarlet robes and holding dozens of palm branchlets, which have been consecrated with sacred water. Our deacon speaks:

The Lord be with you!
And with your spirit!
A reading from the holy Gospel according to Luke.
Glory to you, O Lord!

Jesus went ahead with His ascent to Jerusalem. As he approached Bethphage and Bethany on the mount called Olivet, he sent two of the Disciples with these instructions: "Go into the village straight ahead of you. Upon entering it you will find an ass tied there which no one has yet ridden. Untie it and lead it back. If anyone should ask you, 'Why are you untying the beast?' say, 'The Master has need of it.'"

They departed on their errand and found things just as He had said. And as they untied the ass, its owners said to them, "Why are you doing that?"

They explained that the Master needed it.

Then they led the animal to Jesus, and laying their cloaks on it, helped Him mount. They spread their cloaks on the roadway as he moved along; and on His approach to the descent from Mount Olivet, the entire crowd of Disciples began to rejoice and praise God loudly for the display of power they had seen, saying: "Blessed be He who comes as king in the name of the Lord! Peace in heaven and glory in the highest."

Some of the Pharisees in the crowd said to him, "Teacher, rebuke your Disciples."

He replied, "'If they were to keep silence, I tell you the very stones would cry out!" (Luke 19:28-40)

The Gospel of the Lord
Praise to you, Lord Jesus Christ

We then enter our sanctuary, carrying our blessed branches, singing our entrance hymn of praise:

Laudate, laudate Dominum
Omnes gentes, laudate Dominum.
(Praise the Lord, all you peoples)
(Gather 525)

Text: Psalm 117, *Praise the Lord, all you peoples;* Taizé Community, 1980
Tune: Jacques Berthier, 1923-1994
© 1980, Les Presses de Taizé, GIA Publications, Inc., agent

As we do this, we see baskets, prepared for each confirmation candidate, which have been placed in front of the altar. Our Paschal baskets are different than their fluffier cousins, which are given to children. While the average gift may contain chocolate treats and stuffed bunnies, these baskets contain special gifts that will be an aid to Holy Week. They are assembled and presented by each sponsor to his/her corresponding candidate.

It is common to place a small bottle of wine, a loaf of bread, a cross or crucifix, prayer books, rosaries, spices, and blessed oil along with personal gifts such as musical tapes and CDs. These are wrapped in purple tissue paper and tied with white or purple curling ribbon. Having been a godparent twice, I always make it a point to add little touches such as ribbon and fresh flowers with my gifts. The first basket that I made was a creation of rough-hewn grapevines, festooned with white, wired chiffon ribbon and had a potted tulip as its centerpiece. My godson received an air cactus (a plant known for easy care and maintenance). His basket was decorated with ribbon, also made of purple paper. Each gift is marked for a specific day in the week, so that the coming Easter holidays are enriched with tangible reminders of their spiritual importance.

Though we witness Jesus' triumphant entry on Palm Sunday, we are also mindful of His coming sacrifice. We understand that many of the very people who rejoice and welcome Him will reject our Lord in the end. And so we relive His betrayal and death when we read and participate in the passion of our Lord as written in the Gospel of Matthew.

This is why Palm Sunday is also known as Passion Sunday. Many Protestants embrace passion plays as a method to illustrate the gravity of Easter, but few are truly aware that this is also a Catholic tradition which dates back before the year AD 1000. Today there will be no sets or costumes. Instead the congregation, designated readers and the priest will read different pieces of scripture, weaving them into the story of Good Friday.

Palm Sunday sets the tone for the Triduum, a three-day festival, celebrating the "Passover" of our Lord. The Triduum starts on Holy Thursday and continues through Holy Saturday evening, which actually begins Easter. Catholicism follows the Judaic practice of beginning a day on the previous evening. This early celebration is called a vigil. Though lasting for three days, the Triduum is actually one Mass, punctuated by "open" periods dedicated to prayer, fasting, and penance.

The Triduum

Holy Thursday

During Holy Week, I will often be away from work from Tuesday through Sunday as my religious and familial responsibilities take center stage. Other Christians that I know seem to take exception to this, claiming that I am merely following a man-made set of holidays. But they are wrong, of course. Easter is closely tied to Passover, even if the days do not coincide. Holy Week was instituted by Christ, being the last week of Jesus' human life. It began as he rode into the city of Jerusalem and ended with His triumphant Resurrection. There is an interesting correlation to the six days of creation from the Book of Genesis to these events. Christ rode in and rose on the first day of the week, which is the "day of light" in Genesis and died on the six day of the week, which is "day of man" in the creation story. Every event of this journey is marked and celebrated by Catholics.

The truth is that other Christians are more involved with buying a new outfit, hunting Easter eggs and hanging up bunny rabbits at this time than remembering the passion of our Lord. I find that offensive. New clothes, eggs, and rabbits are perfectly fine as they remind us of new life and rebirth, but we cannot have these things without Jesus. He is at the heart of it all.

Because I will be sharing the Catholic Triduum with my audience, I will also provide some of our actual readings from the Catholic Bible. This will illustrate how closely the Catholic scriptures resemble their Protestant counterparts. But because of the sheer volume of scriptures, I cannot use them all. So, I will touch on the highlights of this religious festival, which begins with the Feast of the Last Supper on Holy Thursday evening.

Our first reading takes us back to the book of Exodus, Chapter 12:1-8 and 11-14, to the story of Passover. We remember the very first Passover when God's angel of death passed over the land of Egypt and struck down each of the Egyptian firstborns. The Israelites were spared when they took the blood of a lamb without blemish and marked the doorposts and lintels on each home. The blood identified people inside as the children of God. Passover continues to be the holiest time of the year for Jews. But the Christian remembers how Christ became our Passover or Paschal Lamb. It is His blood, which marks the homes of all believers, so that we may never die, but receive everlasting life. And so, we celebrate the inauguration of Holy Eucharist and the spiritual transformation of bread and wine into the body, soul, and divinity of Christ.

The Washing of Feet

Holy Thursday Mass also calls us to serve one another. This is illustrated during the Last Supper when Christ washes each Disciple's feet.

> *Before the feast of Passover, Jesus realized that the hour had come for Him to pass from this world to the Father. He loved His own in this world, and would show His love for them to the end.*
>
> *The devil had already induced Judas, son of Simon Iscariot, to hand Jesus over; and so, during the supper, Jesus- fully aware that He had come from God and was going to God, took off His cloak. He picked up a towel and tied it around Himself. Then He poured water into a basin and began to wash His Disciple's feet and dry them with the towel He had around Him. Thus, He came to Simon Peter, who said to Him, "Lord, are you going to wash my feet?"*

>Jesus answered, "You may not realize now what I am doing, but later you will understand."
>
>Peter replied, "You shall never wash my feet!"
>
>"If I do not wash you," Jesus answered, "you will have no share in my heritage."
>
>"Lord," Simon Peter said unto Him, "then not only my feet, but my hands and head as well."
>
>Jesus told him, "The man who has bathed has no need to wash [except for his feet]; he is entirely cleansed, just as you are; though not all." (The reason He said, "Not all are washed clean," was that He knew His betrayer.)
>
>After He had washed their feet, He put His cloak back on and reclined at the table once more. He said to them: "Do you understand what I just did for you? You address me as 'Teacher' and 'Lord,' and fittingly enough for that is what I am. But if I washed your feet- I who am your teacher and Lord- then you must wash each other's feet. What I just did was to give you an example: as I have done, so you must do. (John 13: 1-15)

Foot washing was a sign of hospitality and the domain of household servants who sought to refresh their master's guests by removing the dirt and grime from a day's journey on unpaved, dusty streets. Now, here is God Incarnate, acting in the role of a servant, exemplifying His love for His own. So, following the example set down by Jesus, a group of men will come and sit down in front of the congregation. Then the attending priest will wash their feet as the people sing and worship God. While we witness the washing of feet during Mass, we recall Jesus' words, *"I give you a new commandment: love one another; as I have loved you, you also must love one another." (John 13:34, Jerusalem Bible)*

>*While he was at supper on the night before he died for us,*
>*He took bread in His hands, and gave you thanks and praise.*
>*He broke the bread, gave it to His Disciples, and said:*
>*Take this, all of you, and eat it:*
>*This is my body, which will be given up for you.*
>*At the end of the meal, he took the cup.*
>*Again he praised you for your goodness,*
>*Gave the cup to His Disciples and said:*
>*Take this, all of you, and drink from it:*
>*This is the cup of my blood,*
>*The blood of the new and everlasting covenant,*
>*It will be shed for you and for all so that sins may be forgiven.*
>*Do this in memory of me.*
>*(Cristo 48)*

On Holy Thursday evening, the celebrant will consecrate enough of the bread to last through Good Friday. After Communion, the priest takes the Blessed Sacrament and carefully wraps it in a vestment called a **humeral veil.** Then he it carries forth from the sanctuary to a small chapel at a nearby convent. Most of the congregation will follow, singing the sacred hymn, **Pange Lingua:**

Hail our Savior's glorious body,
Which His virgin mother bore.
Hail the blood, which shed for sinners,
Did a broken world restore.
Hail the sacrament most holy,
Flesh and Blood of Christ adore.

Text: *Pange Lingua,* Thomas Aquinas, 1227-1274; TR. By James Quinn, SJ, b. 1969;used by permission of Selah Publishing, Inc., NY Tune: Mode III; acc. By Eugene Lapierre, © 1694, GIA Publications, Inc.

The voices slowly die away in the darkness of the evening as the church is emptied. But some of us remain, as the men of the church oversee the solemn stripping of the altar and its surroundings. We sit in stony silence as tables, chairs, candles, flowers, lace cloths are taken up and silently carried away. The altar itself, though still in front of the rest of the sanctuary is moved into a corner, so that all that remains is the large crucifix, hanging on the wall. Anything else that cannot be removed will be draped.

As with people from other cultures, Catholics will often drape images and statuary as both a symbol of mourning and an illustration that the hosts are no longer there. The doors of the brass tabernacle are left open. The lights dim, and we are left with our thoughts and prayers. No other songs will be sung tonight. Holy Thursday ends in an eerie quiet, leaving the devout to keep watch. However, the sanctuary will remain open that believers may watch and pray as the Disciples tried to do so long ago.

My God, my God, why hast thou forsaken me?
Why art thou so far from helping me,
and from the words of my roaring?
Oh my God, I cry in the daytime, but thou hearest not;
And in the night season, and am not silent.
But thou art holy, O thou that inhabitest the praises of Israel.
Our fathers trusted in thee: they trusted, and thou didst deliver them.
They cried unto thee, and were delivered:
They trusted in thee and were not confounded.
But I am a worm, and no man; a reproach of men,
And despised of the people.
All they that see me laugh me to scorn:
They shoot out the lip; they shake the head saying,
"He trusted on the Lord that he would deliver him:
Let him deliver him, Seeing he delighted in him."
But thou art he that took me out of the womb:
Thou didst make me hope when I was upon my mother's breasts.
I was cast upon thee from the womb:
Thou art my God from my mother's belly.
Be not far from me; for trouble is near; for there is none to help.
Many bulls have compassed me:
Strong bulls of Bashan have beset me round.
They gaped upon me with their mouths,
As a ravenous and a roaring lion.
I am poured out like water, and all my bones are out of joint:
My heart is like wax, it is melted in the midst of my bowels.
My strength is dried up like a potsherd;
And my tongue cleaveth to my jaws;
Thou hast brought me unto the dust of death.
For dogs have compassed me:
The assembly of the wicked have enclosed me:
They pierced my hands and feet.
I may tell all my bones, they look and stare upon me.
They part my garments among them.
And cast lots upon my vesture.

Good Friday

The previous passage is from Psalm 22 (1-18, KJV), written at least 600 years before the birth of Christ. Yet, it seems to foretell the suffering that Christ would undergo on our behalf. Notice that the individual is beset by bulls and dogs. The bull was a favorite sacrificial animal of the Jewish priests, and the dog has always been hated in the Holy Land by both Jews and Arabs. Dogs are synonymous with non-Semitic infidels. Jesus was handed over by the Jewish Sanhedrin (the ruling religious body) to the Romans because they had no right to order an execution. We also need to bear in mind that deliberately piercing the body was forbidden in the Mosaic code, and crucifixion was relatively unknown in that region at the time the Psalm was written. But the writer records some of the pain and anguish of being crucified.

The problem with Good Friday is that modern Christians have sanitized the crucifixion, even to the point of holding no services on that day. Becoming fixated on the Resurrection, they tend to gloss over the suffering our Savior did for us. Furthermore, many Protestants have gone as far as to criticize Catholics for the use of crucifixes, asking why we have a "dead Christ" still suffering on the cross instead of the "triumphant risen Savior." Of course, they forget the words of Paul who wrote, *"But we preach Christ crucified, unto the Jews a stumbling block, and unto the Greeks foolishness." (1 Corinthians 1:23, KJV)*

Catholics hold Good Friday in great reverence. We must relive the pain and anguish of Jesus in order to more fully appreciate the glory and magnitude of Easter. The first thing that I want to do is to make the crucifixion a reality for my readers. So, let us begin with what history records about crucifying.

Though not credited with its invention, the first people to practice this type of execution on a large scale were the Persians. In the Behistum Inscription, Darius speaks of punishing rebels with crucifixion. Alexander the Great introduced it to the Mediterranean world, and it is believed that the Romans adopted the practice from the Carthaginians.

Rome reserved this form of execution for the lowest members of society, that of slaves and non-citizens. A citizen of Rome could not be put to death in this fashion. Crucifixion was one of the nastiest deaths ever devised by man. Crucified individuals earned sympathy even from Romans themselves, and Flavius Josephus, a Jewish historian in the time of Christ, refers to crucifixions as "the most wretched deaths."

First of all, the individual was stripped naked. Forget about the little loin cloth that Jesus wears in paintings and statuary. No Renaissance artist would have had the nerve to paint or sculpt an adult Christ in the nude, but that was the reality. Stripping an individual naked was part of the package, rendering the individual psychologically helpless and exposed. It was also a simple way to embarrass and degrade.

The condemned would then be tied between two pillars, spread-eagled, and whipped. Only the groin and the face were off limits, the rest of the body was open to attack. Jewish law forbade more than forty lashes. It was believed that a man could die if struck more than forty times, so the Jewish custom was thirty-nine lashes, in the case of miscounting and accidentally killing someone. But, Romans carried out the crucifixion and followed no such rule. Instead, the victim was beaten until it was determined that the person was near death. No clean whip marks here. The back, which bore the brunt of the beating, was reduced to the consistency of strawberry jam mixed with raw hamburger. The whip, also known as a *flagrum*, was a mass of leather thongs that were imbedded with bone and lead. These jagged pieces would tear and rip the flesh with each crack of the whip. The skin would be hanging off the back in strips.

Then, the victim is mocked as was Christ when the soldiers dressed our Savior in a purple robe and placed a crown of thorns upon His head declaring, **"Hail, the King of the Jews."** Historians are not certain which type of plant was used in the crown of thorns, but there are two probable candidates. Syrian Christ Thorn, which grows about a foot high and has two sharp curved thorns at the base of each leaf, was common in Palestine and plentiful at Golgotha where Christ died. Christ Thorn is also a possibility as its branches are easily braided and formed into a crown. The thorns of Christ Thorn also resemble spikes or nails.

After spitting on Jesus and beating him even more so with a rod, the soldiers lead him away to be crucified. Crucifixion begins with being strapped with a beam, called a **patibulum**, weighing around 110 lb. Imagine having something that heavy tied to raw, bleeding muscles. Then the person was forced to carry the patibulum through the streets to the place of death.

For a while, most scientists considered the practice of nailing to have been an unrealistic portrayal of crucifixion as the soft flesh of the hands and feet would not support a person's weight without pulling out and through. But in 1968, archeologist V. Tzaferis found a set of burial caves at Giv'at ha-Mivtar (Ras el-Masaref) which is located to the north of Jerusalem near Mount Scopus. The yield of the excavation was a set of remains that furnished proof of nailing. The victim had had a large spike driven through the heel bones. In light of using bone instead of soft tissue, the wrists would have been used rather than the palm. It is entirely possible that the spikes were driven through the bone and the medial nerve, which would have been agony. To provide further pain and misery, the body was twisted in order for the spike to be driven through the side of the ankles, rather than lying flat as depicted which increases the difficulty in raising oneself up to breathe. A seat, known as a **saedecula,** was attached to the cross to give the victim some support.

Roman torturers were masters at their craft. While the physical cruelty of the cross was clearly seen, there was also a silent problem that almost always killed in and of itself. The person had to push his/her own body up just to breathe. Listen to what a physician, Dr. Truman Davis, wrote concerning how Christ's body reacts to crucifixion:

> *As the arms fatigue, great waves of cramps sweep over the muscles, knotting them in deep, relentless throbbing pain. With these cramps comes the inability to push Himself upward. Hanging by His arms, the pectoral muscles are paralyzed and the intercostal muscles are unable to act. Air can be drawn into the lungs, but cannot be exhaled. Jesus fights to raise Himself in order to get even one short breath. Finally, carbon dioxide builds up in the lungs and in the bloodstream, and the cramps partially subside. Spasmodically, He is able to push Himself upward to exhale and bring in life-giving oxygen.*

Because being in this position was so torturous, the Romans would break the legs of the condemned in order to hasten death, so that taking in oxygen would be impossible. This was called **"crucifracture."** Another indication of crucifixion found with the remains in the burial caves was the fact that both shins had been intentionally fractured. Scripture says that the two thieves who died with Christ had their legs broken. Jesus' legs remained intact as he was already dead.

Of course, Christ's sacrifice ends with the thrust of the spear into His side issuing forth blood and water, which is evidence of rupturing the pericardial sac surrounding the heart as well as the heart itself. Normally, the sac contains 20 to 30 cc's of fluid, however, post mortems of individuals dead of ruptured hearts have had as much as 500 cc's of fluid and blood in the pericardial cavity. Given the reference John makes of blood and water issuing forth, Jesus more than likely succumbed from heart failure rather than suffocation.

This is probably more than most people want to know about the sacrifice of Good Friday, but it is important to resensitize ourselves to the harshness of the cross. Now, that we have explored what crucifixion actually is, we must trace Jesus' final journey to Golgotha. This is done through the **Stations of the Cross.**

The Stations of the Cross

The Stations of the Cross are usually a set of placards on the walls of Catholic churches, which follow the Via Dolorosa or the Way of Suffering. In early times, Christian pilgrims would often make at least one journey to Palestine to experience the Holy Land through Christ's eyes. These were a lucky few. Most could not afford to go and it was often a very dangerous trip. In light of this, Catholic theologians created a way to experience the Via Dolorosa in a safer, cost efficient way. Even the poorest Christian could "make a pilgrimage to the Holy Land" without the usual problems of making a long journey.

The pilgrimage is often done in the format of a service during the day or late in the evening, each Friday during the season of Lent. Because of other services on Good Friday, the Stations of the Cross are usually held on Good Friday afternoon. The service is a set of scriptures in a story format that is accompanied by prayers and even music in certain instances. Due to the lengthy use of scripture, I will dispense with the prayers and keep to the actual stations with their respective readings.

Beginning the journey…

Now before the feast of the Passover, when Jesus knew that His hour had come to depart out of this world to the Father, having loved His own who were in the world, he loved them to the end. When he had washed their feet and taken His garments and resumed His place, he said to them,

"This is my commandment, that you love one another as I have loved you. Greater love has no man than this, that a man lay down his life for his friends. You are my friends if you do what I command you. No longer do I call you servants, for the servant does not know what his master is doing, but I have called you friends, for all that I have heard from my Father I have made known to you. You did not choose me, but I chose you and appointed you that you should go and bear fruit and that your fruit should abide; so that whatever you ask the Father in my name, he may give it to you. This I command you, to love one another."

When Jesus had spoken these words, he went forth with His Disciples across the Kidron Valley, where there was a garden, which he and Disciples entered. Now Judas, who betrayed him, also knew the place; for Jesus often met there with His Disciples. So Judas, procuring a band of soldiers and some officers from the chief priest and Pharisees, went there with lanterns and torches and weapons.

So the band of soldiers and their captain and the officers of the Jews seized Jesus and bound him. First they led him to Annas… Annas then sent him bound to Caiaphas the high priest… Then they led Jesus from the house of Caiaphas to the praetorium. (John 13:1-5, 12-17; 15:12-17; 17:1, 11, 15-21; 18:1-3, 12-13, 24, 28)

The First Station- Jesus is condemned to death.

He (Pilate) entered the praetorium again and said to Jesus,
   "Where are you from?" But Jesus gave no answer.
   Pilate therefore said to him, "You will not speak to me? Do you not know that I have the power to release you, and the power to crucify you?"
   Jesus answered him, "You would have no power over me unless it had been given you from above; therefore he who delivered me to you has the greater sin."
   Upon this Pilate sought to release him, but the Jews cried out,
   "If you release this man, you are not Caesar's friend; every one who makes himself a king sets himself against Caesar." (John 19:9-16)

The Second Station- Jesus is scourged and crowned with thorns.

And the soldiers led him away inside the palace (that is, the praetorium); and they called together the whole battalion. And they clothed him in a purple cloak, and plaiting a crown of thorns they put it on him. And they began to salute him, "Hail, King of the Jews!"
   And they struck His head with a reed, and spat upon him, and they knelt down in homage to him. And when they had mocked him, they stripped him of the purple cloak, and put His own clothes on him. And they led him out to crucify him. (Mark 15:16-20)

The Third Station- Jesus falls for the first time. (We remember His frailty in the garden.)

(And falling on His knees he prayed) "Father, if you are willing, remove this cup from me; nevertheless not my will, but thine, be done."
   And there appeared to him an angel from heaven, strengthening him. And being in an agony he prayed more earnestly; and His sweat became like great drops of blood falling down upon the ground. And when he rose from prayer, he came to the Disciples and found them sleeping for sorrow. (Luke 22:42-45)

The Fourth Station- Jesus meets His mother. (We reflect upon the scorn of those who knew His family.)

And the crowd said: "Is not this the carpenter's son? Is not His mother called Mary? And are not His brethren James and John and Joseph and Simon and Judas? And are not all His sisters with us?"
   And they took offense at him. But Jesus said to them, "A prophet is not without honor except in his own country and in his own house." (Matthew 13:55-57)

The Fifth Station- Simon of Cyrene helps carry Jesus' cross.

As they were marching out they came upon a man of Cyrene, Simon by name; this man they compelled to carry His cross. And they came to a place called Golgotha, which means the place of a skull... (Matthew 27: 32-33)

The Sixth Station- A woman wipes the face of Jesus. We hear the words of the prophet Isaiah:

He had no form or comeliness that we should look at him, and no beauty that we should desire him. He was despised and rejected by men; a man of sorrows, and acquainted with grief; and as one from whom men hide their faces he was despised, and we esteemed him not.

Surely he has borne our griefs and carried our sorrows; yet we esteemed him stricken, smitten by God, and afflicted.

But he was wounded for our transgressions, he was bruised for our iniquities; upon him was the chastisement that made us whole, and with His stripes we are healed. (Isaiah 53:2-5)

The Seventh Station- Jesus falls for the second time (Christ once again shows us His humanity as he begs for release from Father in the garden.)

And going a little farther he fell on His face and prayed, "My Father, if it be possible let this cup pass from me; nevertheless, not as I will, but as thou wilt."

Again, for the second time, he went away and prayed, "My Father, if this cannot pass unless I drink it, thy will be done." (Matthew 26:39, 42)

The Eighth Station- Jesus addresses the women of Jerusalem.

And there followed him a great multitude of the people, and of the women who bewailed and lamented him. But Jesus turning to them said, "Daughters of Jerusalem, do not weep for me, but weep for yourselves and for your children. For behold, the days are coming when they will say, 'Blessed are the barren, and the wombs that never bore, and the breasts that never gave suck!' Then they will begin to say to the mountains, 'Fall on us'; and to the hill, 'Cover us.' For if they do this when the wood is green, what will happen when it is dry?"

Two others also, who were criminals, were led away to be put to death with him. (Luke 23:27-32)

The Ninth Station- Jesus Falls for the third time (We acknowledge that we must suffer as well in order to serve Christ. But God is our defender when we suffer.)

I cry with my voice to the Lord, with my voice I make supplication to the Lord, I pour out my complaint before him, I tell my trouble before him. When my spirit is faint, you know my way!

In the path where I walk they have hidden a trap for me. I look to the right and watch, but there is none who takes notice of me; no refuge remains to me, no man cares for me.

I cry to thee, O Lord; I say, thou art my refuge, my portion in the land of the living. Give heed to my cry; for I am brought very low! Deliver me from my persecutors; for they are too strong for me! (Psalm 142:1-6)

The Tenth Station- Jesus is stripped of His garments.

So they took Jesus, and he went out, his own cross to the place called the place of a skull, which is called in Hebrew, Golgotha.
When the soldiers had crucified Jesus, they took His garments and made four parts, one for each soldier; also His tunic. But the tunic was without seam, woven from top to bottom; so they said to one another, "Let us not tear it, but cast lots for it to see whose it shall be."
This was to fulfill the scripture. "They parted my garments among them, and for my clothing they cast lots." (John 19:17-18; 23-24)

The Eleventh Station- Jesus is nailed to the Cross.

And when they came to the place which is called the Skull, there they crucified Him, and the criminals, one on the right hand and one on the left. And Jesus said, "Father, forgive them; for they know not what they do."
And the people stood by, watching; but the rulers scoffed at him, saying, "He saved others; let Him save Himself, if He is the Christ of God, His Chosen One!" The soldiers also mocked Him, coming up and offering Him vinegar, and saying, "If you are the King of the Jews, save yourself!" There was also an inscription over him, "This is the King of the Jews." (Luke 23:33-34; 35-38)

The Twelfth Station- Jesus dies on the Cross.

It was now about the sixth hour, and there was darkness over the whole land until the ninth hour, while the sun's light failed; and the curtain of the Temple was torn in two. Then Jesus, crying with a loud voice, said, "Father, into Thy hands I commit my spirit!" And having said this He breathed His last.
Now when the centurion saw what had taken place, he praised God, and said, "Certainly this man was innocent!" And all the multitudes who assembled to see the sight, when they saw what had taken place, returned home beating their breasts. (Luke 23:44-48)

The Thirteenth Station- Jesus is taken down from the Cross.

So the soldiers did this. But standing by the cross of Jesus were His mother, and His mother's sister, Mary the wife of Clopas, and Mary Magdalene.
So the soldiers came and broke the legs of the first and of the other who had been crucified with Him; but when they came to Jesus and saw that He was already dead, they did not break His legs. But one of the soldiers pierced His side with a spear, and at once there came out blood and water.
After this Joseph of Arimathea, who was a Disciple of Jesus, but secretly, for fear of the Jews, asked Pilate that he might take away the body of Jesus, and Pilate gave him leave. So, he came and took away His body. (John 19:25; 32-34; 38)

The Fourteenth Station- Jesus is laid in the Tomb.

Nicodemus also, who had at first come to Him by night, came bringing a mixture of myrrh and aloes, about a hundred pounds' weight.
They took the body of Jesus, and bound it with linen cloths with the spices, as is the burial custom of the Jews. Now in the place where He was crucified there was a garden, and in the garden a new tomb where no one had ever been laid. So because of the Jewish day of Preparation, as the tomb was close at hand, they laid Jesus there. (John 19:40-42)

The Fifteenth Station- The Risen Christ appears to His Disciples and ascends into heaven.

That very day two of them were going to a village named Emmaus, about seven miles from Jerusalem, and talking with each other about all these things that had happened. While they were talking and discussing together, Jesus Himself drew near and went with them. But their eyes were kept from recognizing Him. And He said to them, "What is this conversation which you are holding with each other as you walk?" And they stood still, looking sad.
Then one of them, named Cleopas, answered Him, "Are you the only visitor to Jerusalem who does not know the things that have happened there in these days?"
And He said to them, "What things?"
And they said to Him, "Concerning Jesus of Nazareth..."
And He said to them, "O foolish men, and slow of heart to believe all that the prophets have spoken! Was it not necessary that the Christ should suffer these things and enter into His glory?" And beginning with Moses and all the prophets, He interpreted to them in all the scriptures the things concerning Himself.
So they drew near to the village to which they were going. He appeared to be going further, but they constrained Him, saying, "Stay with us, for it is toward evening and the day is now far spent." So He went in to stay with them.
When He was at table with them, He took the bread and blessed and broke it, and gave it to them. And their eyes were opened and they recognized Him; and He vanished out of their sight. They said to each other, "Did our hearts not burn within us, while He talked to us on the road, while He opened to us the scriptures?"
And they rose that same hour and returned to Jerusalem; and they found the eleven gathered together and those who were with them, who said, "The Lord has risen indeed, and has appeared to Simon!" Then they told what had happened on the road, and how He was known to them in the breaking of the bread.
As they were saying this, Jesus Himself stood among them, and said to them, "Peace to you."
Then He opened their minds to understand the scriptures, and said to them, "Thus it is written. That the Christ should suffer and on the third day rise from the dead, and that repentance and forgiveness of sins should be preached in His name to all nations, beginning from Jerusalem. You are witnesses of these things. And behold, I send the promise of my Father upon you; but stay in the city, until you are clothed with power from on high."
Then He led them out as far as Bethany, and lifting up His hands He blessed them. While He blessed them, He parted from them and was carried up into

heaven. And they worshipped Him, and returned to Jerusalem with great joy, and were continually in the temple blessing God. (Luke 24:13-19; 25-36; 45-53)

The Fifteenth Station is not part of the original tradition, but is a recent addition. Also, in 1991, Pope John Paul II recommended a change in the order of the Stations.

Special Note: All the previous readings were taken from a small booklet written by Father Julian Fuzer, O.F.M.

As I have stated earlier, the above service usually takes place in the afternoon. Some Churches have their Good Friday service as early as 3pm. The Easter Triduum Mass begins on Holy Thursday and ends with the Easter Vigil, Saturday evening. The only sacrament given on Holy Saturday is Eucharist, and then only as viaticum for the dying. At sundown Saturday, the Easter Vigil begins a new day.

Traditionally, I serve seafood on Friday evening. In a freshly cleaned home, I set my table and invite those I hold dear to a love feast. The main course is usually grain-fed catfish, baked and encrusted with Parmesan cheese and spices, accompanied with rice and dry white wine. Side dishes include white shoe peg corn in butter sauce and a green salad with snowflake yeast rolls on the side. The dessert could be something like homemade cheesecake with a pound of glazed strawberries or possibly lemon dessert bars. After the meal, we all journey back to the church.

It's always smart to come early in our parish. Good Friday draws people like a magnet. But now, the sanctuary is quiet, and we see only the figure of Christ in low lights. In Catholic churches, it is always customary at this time not to pass the crucifix without bowing. Yes, we know that Christ is not actually the figure on the cross above. It is merely a representation. This action is a lot like the respects shown the empty chair in the English Parliament. It is symbolic of the ever presence of the monarch. We know that Jesus is here with us. When we genuflect or bow, we are acknowledging His presence and showing respect. In addition to the occupied cross, there is a simple wooden cross standing in front of the pews. It is covered in three red cloths and has a kind of kneeling bench on either of its sides. This cross will play a major role in the service, as you will soon discover.

At the beginning, non-Catholics might be surprised to see the attending priests and deacons prostrate themselves before the cross. They lie, face down, and arms outstretched. This illustrates their absolute devotion to Christ and their willingness to die for and like Him.

Reading the passion from the Gospel, we (the congregation) are no longer onlookers as in the case of the Stations of the Cross. The congregation becomes the Jewish mob. This is a poignant reminder of human frailty and of our own sinful nature. It is also bears witness that in a real way, we have called for Christ's death. Our sins demand the blood of someone who is spotless and above reproach. But the hearts of the devout break with sorrow as we say, *"We have no king, but Caesar!" and "Crucify Him!"*

Next, we hear a litany of prayers. We pray for our Pope, the clergy, and our laity. We hold up to God baptismal candidates, our hope for the unity of Christians, and the Jewish people. We remember our public officials, those with special needs, non-Christians, and even those who do not believe in God.

There has been a great change in the intercessions regarding the Jews. According to the "Old Rite", we called them "Perfidious Jews," or "Treacherous Jews." Today our understanding has made us realize that we are all brothers.

O humble tree,
Gnarled and splintered from the woodsman's ax,
Today, your outstretched arms
Receive the Son of Man,
And are christened with His Blood
- The Author

The Veneration of the Cross

What does it mean to venerate something? When we venerate, we show respect and devotion. Society, in general, has many ways of venerating. We often hold people and objects in great esteem. For example, countries view their heroes and flags with great respect because of what they have come to symbolize. We see how angry Americans get when their flag is burned. It's not the material that is held dear, but the sacred memory of those who died for it.

The Bible reminds us of many things made of wood: the tree of life, Noah's ark, the wood used when Abraham almost sacrificed his son, Isaac, Jacob's angelic ladder, Aaron's walking stick, and even the branch used by Moses to make the bitter water sweet. How much more precious is the shape and wood of the cross on which the Son of God gave His life? This rough-hewn emblem helped to bring about the redemption of the world. (Celebremos, 158)

So, Catholics give honor to the cross on Good Friday. It is customary to come down in small groups of families and friends and kneel and pray to God at the foot of the cross. Monastic tradition dictates approaching it the way Moses did with the burning bush. This is holy ground, so we take off our shoes and come with bare feet. After praying, many will give the Old World salute as they leave, a light kiss as a mark of reverence. Once, I saw someone hug the cross, which made me cry. Others will bow or genuflect. In certain cultures, people have been known to dance as David danced before the Ark of the Covenant. (Celebremos, Lent & Holy Week, 156)

This deeply spiritual event begins with the slow showing of the cross. When each of three red cloths is removed, the priest, deacon, or cantor will sing:

"This is the wood of the cross, on which hung the Savior of the world."
The congregation sings back, *"Come let us worship."*

With each declaration, the cantor's voice will grow more and more urgent, as if to illustrate the gravity of such a sacrifice. Sometimes I have actually heard his voice break with raw emotion.

We approach the foot of the cross and are spiritually and mentally transported back in time to the dark glory of that day, two millennia ago. We see the blood and hear the ring and thunder of the hammers nailing hands and feet. There is also the haunting sound of rattling dice and the twisted joy of dividing up a condemned man's clothing. We might even feel Christ's thorny crown and the thrust of the lance. The angels are weeping, and the sun has left the sky.

And yet, in the midst of it all, there is unbelievable serenity. The air is heavy and a few windows have been opened for the night breeze. And the music, such music- hours of hymns reverberate the sanctuary as each small group comes forward to pay homage in such an intimate way. It's common to lose oneself to prayer and poignant reverie. Time seems to slow, and there is only the night and the company of Jesus.

Good Friday service ends with Holy Communion, and so the Blessed Sacrament is brought to the altar. Our Lord is present and we are infused with He who sacrificed so much for the world. The lights will once again dim as we quietly leave the sanctuary, washed clean with sorrow and tears. Our mourning is almost over.

Holy Saturday

Easter is also known as the Feast of Flowers, and that title lives up to its name in the region where I'm from. Besides the usual crocuses, buttercups, tulips and other spring plants, our pink and white dogwoods garnish many lawns as well as dot the forests like patches of lace. Ornamental trees such as cottonwoods and Bartlett pears also wax heavy with pink and white blossoms. There are clumps of purple wisteria and tons of vivid pink, white, purple, and red azaleas. All of these blooms are striking against the new green of the grass, the dark bark of the trees, and the blue of the sky. This setting is the backdrop of the grandest celebration of the Catholic year.

It is late Friday evening after the service when I begin my preparation for the following day. Unlike most Christians, I prefer to roast lamb as the primary meat of Easter. Christ ate lamb; therefore I eat lamb as a remembrance. For those of you who grimace at this, lamb is quite good if fixed properly. My first taste of it was at a Greek restaurant, run by a friend of the Gunn family in Tallahassee. I've been hooked ever since.

Lamb demands an alcohol or vinaigrette base in order to remove the gaminess of the meat and render the muscle fiber tender. We often roast it in Irish ale or in red wine and Dijon mustard. Add fresh rosemary, sage, thyme, onions, garlic, salt and pepper and you have a very tempting main course. I usually place all of this in a crock-pot, slowly cooking it overnight.

On Saturday morning, we awaken to the rich smell of the meat permeating the house. The lamb will usually be served with wild rice and almonds, glazed carrots, and a green salad with Parmesan/Romano cheese dressing. This meal is garnished with King's Hawaiian bread served steaming hot with honey and butter. While it is traditional to drink red wine with lamb, I prefer homemade sangria, cutting the alcohol with white grape juice and garnishing each glass with an orange slice. This softens the harshness often associated with red wine and cuts the alcohol content.

Of course, my Easter feast will end with my famous banana trifle, which I like to call "banana pudding on steroids." Forget the normal notion of banana pudding and think "rich." The filling itself is made with such ingredients as sweetened condensed milk, French vanilla pudding, and whipped cream. It slices like a cake and can last (but usually doesn't) up to five days in the refrigerator without weeping. This trifle is crowned in cookies and a layer of whipped cream and served in a crystal trophy bowl.

It's wise to avoid eating too much at lunchtime, as this supper will occur earlier than usual. Around 4:00, godchildren and family friends began arriving to help us polish off this repast. The table is set with flowers and greenery from nearby ornamental trees and lit with a large carved candle in its center.

By 5:45, it's almost time for Mass. Easter begins at sundown on Holy Saturday. Why? The Jewish culture has the custom of beginning the day at sunset, the previous evening. Remember that Jews begin their Sabbath on Friday evening. So, Catholics follow the same custom, especially for the Vigil Mass of Holy Saturday.

The smell of crackling pine greets the nose as we walk to the back of the building. The flames flare up and dance in the evening sky in the large bonfire. We see a number of parishioners milling about in their nicest clothes. The confirmation candidates are there with their families and friends, and we take time to say hello and welcome. As the sunlight wanes, the crowd grows in volume, expectantly waiting for the priests, acolytes, and our resident deacons.

Why do we have a bonfire? Well, Catholics, Lutherans, Episcopalians and Anglicans have a red glass cylinder that holds a flame near the altar. It always burns there through much of the year, signifying the presence of the Holy Spirit. The flame is removed on Holy Thursday during the stripping of the altar. It will be reborn in the freshly cut wood of the Easter bonfire, reminding us of the renewing quality of Easter, new fire and new life in Christ. Listen to the words of the priest:

Father, we share in the light of your glory
Through your Son, the light of the world,
Make this new fire holy,
And inflame us with new hope.
Purify our minds, by this Easter celebration
And bring us one day to the feast of eternal light.
We ask this through Christ our Lord. Amen.

Then, the large Paschal (Easter) Candle is marked with a cross and the number of the year. The priest prays:

Christ yesterday and today,
The beginning and the end,
Alpha, and Omega;
All time belongs to him
And all the ages:
To him be glory and power
Through him every age forever. Amen.

And inserting five grains of incense into the wax, held by wax nails, the prayer continues:

By His holy and glorious wounds,
May Christ our Lord guard us and keep us.
Amen.

The candle is lit with the new fire, and the priest proclaims:

May the light of Christ, rising in glory,
Dispel the darkness of our hearts and minds.
Amen.

With the candle blessed and prepared, the deacon will lift it up to heaven, and sing:

Christ our light,

Thanks be to God

The flame is then carried around to the front of the church, followed by the clergymen, and the candidates with their smaller candles, attending families and friends, and finally the congregation. At the door, our deacon will stop, hold the fire aloft and sing again:

Christ our light,

Thanks be to God

Upon entering the sanctuary, we find it dark and dimly lit. The windows and altar have been adorned with masses of trumpet lilies and azaleas. The church smells fresh and green. The candle is brought before the altar and the refrain is sung for a final time:

Christ our light,

Thanks be to God

Then, the Easter candle is used in lighting the candles of the confirmandi, who then light the tinier tapers of the congregation. Looking down from the rafters, one can see the light start from a single point, then go down the center of the church and spread to the outer walls, one flame that will become a sea of light. There is no music, just reverent silence.

We have a wonderful tenor who often serves as cantor in the Mass. Cantors get their history from the Jewish cantors and sound very much like them when they perform their duties. Cantors are singers, enshrining both scripture (the Psalms) and accompanying prayers in song. Tonight, his rich, melodic voice will fall over the people in a wave, as he sings:

Rejoice, heavenly powers! Sing, choirs of angels!
Exult, all creation around God's throne!
Jesus Christ, our King, is risen!
Sound the trumpet of salvation!

Rejoice, O earth, in shining splendor,
Radiant in the brightness of your King!
Christ has conquered! Glory fills you!

Darkness vanishes forever!
Rejoice, O Mother Church! Exult in glory!
The risen Saviour shines upon you!
Let this place resound with joy,
Echoing the song of all God's people!
Lift up your hearts!

We lift them up to the Lord

It is truly right
That with full hearts and minds and voices
We should praise the unseen God,
The all-powerful Father,
And His only Son, Our Lord Jesus Christ.

For Christ has ransomed us with His blood,

And paid for us the price of Adams's sin
To our eternal Father!

This is our Passover feast,
When Christ, the true lamb is slain,
Whose blood consecrates the homes of all believers.

This is the night
When first you saved our fathers:
You freed the people of Israel from slavery
And led them dry-shod through the sea

This is the night
When Christians everywhere,
Washed clean of sin and freed from all defilement,
Are restored to grace and grow together in holiness.

This is the night when Jesus Christ
Broke the chains of death
And rose triumphant from the grave
That good would life have been to us?
Had Christ not come as our Redeemer?

Father, how wonderful your care for us!
How boundless your merciful love!
To ransom a slave, you gave away your Son.

O happy fault, O necessary sin of Adam,
Which gained for us so great a Redeemer!

Most blest of all nights, chosen by God
To see Christ rising from the dead!

Of this night scripture says:
"The night will be as clear as day:
It will become my light, my joy."

The power of this holy night
Dispels all evil, washes guilt away,
Restores lost innocence,
Brings mourners joy;
It casts out hatred, brings us peace,
And humbles earthly pride

Night truly blest when heaven is wedded to earth
And man is reconciled with God!
Therefore, heavenly Father, in the joy of this night,
Receive our evening sacrifice of praise,
Your Church's solemn offering.

Accept this Easter candle,
A flame divided but undimmed,
A pillar of fire that glows to the honor of God

Let it mingle with the light of heaven
And continue burning to
Dispel the darkness of this night.

May the Morning Star which never sets
Find this flame still burning:
Christ, the Morning Star,
Who came back from the dead.
And shed His peaceful light on all mankind,
Your Son who lives and reigns forever and ever.
Amen.

    I know that some of you might have skipped over the preceding passage, but let me implore you to read back over it carefully, so you might grasp the beauty and eloquence of the Easter Proclamation. I cannot do it justice. Words are one aspect, but combine them with a good voice, and they transform into something extraordinary. One voice can make two millennia fall away, and the listener is transported to Jerusalem and the marvel that must have taken place in the tomb, unseen by human eyes. When you hear the Easter proclamation, you touch something very old and mysterious.
    We remember our sins and ask for God's mercy in the Mass Penitential Rite. Then we lift our voices and sing the Greater Gloria:

> *Glory to God in the highest,*
> *And on earth peace to people of good will.*
> *We praise you, we bless you, we adore you,*
> *We glorify you, we give thanks for your great glory,*
> *Lord God, heavenly king,*
> *O God, Almighty Father.*
> *Lord Jesus Christ,*
> *Only begotten son,*
> *Lord God, Lamb of God, Son of the Father,*
> *You take away the sins of the world,*
> *Have mercy on us;*
> *You take away the sins of the world,*
> *Receive our prayer;*
> *You are seated at the right hand of the Father,*
> *Have mercy on us.*
> *For you alone are the holy one,*
> *You alone are the Lord,*
> *You alone are the most high, Jesus Christ,*
> *With the Holy Spirit,*
> *In the glory of God the Father. Amen. (Cristo 12)*

As mentioned before Easter, we bring back two prayers that have been silent throughout the season of Lent: the Greater Gloria (which is sung before the scripture readings) and the Alleluia (which heralds the Gospel reading.) They are not used during Lent because Lent is a time of purification and mourning. But at Easter, our mourning becomes joy.

Holy Saturday can offer the congregation as many as seven Old Testament readings, interspersed with various Psalms:

*First Reading-*The creation of the world- Genesis 1:1-2:2

Second Reading- God puts Abraham to the test by asking for Isaac as a sacrifice. Genesis 22:1-18

Third Reading- God delivers the Israelites from the Egyptians, and the Egyptian army is drown in the sea.-Exodus 14:15-15:1

*The Fourth Reading-*Isaiah speaks of the mercy of God as the Redeemer and His loving call to the Israelites.-Isaiah 54:5-14

The Fifth Reading- God calls His people to renew their covenant with Him. Isaiah 55:1-11

The Sixth reading- From the Deuterocanonical books (Protestant Apocrypha), Baruch reproaches the Israelites for their lack of wisdom in refusing to follow God's commandments and extols the value of spiritual prudence in life. -Baruch 3:9-15, 32-4:4

*The Seventh Reading-*Ezekiel speaks of God's disappointment with the Israelites because they have disgraced His name among the nations. God has determined that His name will be restored as holy among the nations. -Ezekiel 36:16-28

Because of limited time, our church will usually choose the passages regarding the creation and the deliverance of the Israelites from the Egyptians, and then we hear the words of Paul:

Are you not aware that we who were baptized into Christ Jesus were baptized into His death? Through baptism into His death we were buried with Him, so that, just as Christ was raised from the dead by the glory of the Father, we too might live a new life.

If we have been united with Him through likeness to His death, so shall we be through a like resurrection. This we know: our old self was crucified with Him so that the sinful body might be destroyed and we might be slaves to sin no longer.

A man who is dead has been freed from sin. If we have died with Christ, we believe that we are also to live with Him. We know that Christ, once raised from the dead, will never die again; death has no more power over Him. His death was death to sin, once for all; His life is life for God. In the same way, you too must consider yourselves dead to sin but alive for God in Christ Jesus. (Romans 6:3-11)

After the three-fold Alleluia, we listen to the Easter story itself.

After the Sabbath, as the first day of the week was dawning, Mary Magdalene came with the other Mary to inspect the tomb. Suddenly, there was a mighty earthquake, as the angel of the Lord descended from heaven. He came to the stone, rolled it back, and sat on it. In appearance he resembled a flash of lightening while His garments were as dazzling as snow. The guards grew paralyzed with fear of him and fell down like dead men. Then the angel spoke, addressing the women: "Do not be frightened. I know you are looking for Jesus the crucified, but He is not here. He has been raised, exactly as He promised. Come and see the spot where He was laid. Then go quickly and tell His Disciples: ' He has been raised from the dead and now goes ahead of you to Galilee, where you will see Him.' That is the message I have for you."

They hurried away from the tomb half-overjoyed, half-fearful, and ran to carry the good news to His Disciples. Suddenly, without warning, Jesus stood before them and said, "Peace!"

The women came up and embraced His feet and did Him homage. At this Jesus said to them, "Do not be afraid! Go and carry the news to my brothers that are to go to Galilee, where they will see me." (Matthew 28:1-10)

If we examine the biblical passages used at the Vigil Mass of Holy Saturday, we see the continued story of God's love and witness the history of salvation, first with the deliverance of the Israelites from their Egyptian oppressors and finally with ultimate act of salvation, the defeat of death, sin, and the devil.

Following the homily or message, the priest will call the confirmandi and those to be baptized forward. They come, dressed in white robes, and kneel before the altar. Sponsors will lay hands on them as the Litany of the Saints is sung. The faithful invoke the prayers of heaven upon those joining the Church.

Our cantor sings and we answer him:
Lord have mercy
    Lord have mercy
Christ have mercy
    Christ have mercy
Lord have mercy
    Lord have mercy

Holy Mary, Mother of God, *pray for us*.
Saint Michael**, *pray for us.***
Holy angels of God, ***pray for us.***
Saint John, the Baptist, ***pray for us***.
Saint Joseph, ***pray for us.***
Saint Peter and Saint Paul, ***pray for u****s*.
Saint Andrew, ***pray for us.***
Saint John, ***pray for us.***
Saint Mary Magdalene, ***pray for us***.
Saint Stephen, ***pray for us***.
Saint Ignatius, ***pray for us***.
Saint Lawrence, ***pray for us.***

Saint Perpetua and Saint Felicity, *pray for us*.
Saint Agnes, *pray for us.*
Saint Gregory, *pray for us*.
Saint Augustine, *pray for us*.
Saint Athanasius, *pray for us*.
Saint Basil, *pray for us*.
Saint Martin, *pray for us*.
Saint Benedict, *pray for us.*
Saint Francis and Saint Dominic, *pray for us.*
Saint Francis Xavier, *pray for us.*
Saint John Vianey, *pray for us.*
Saint Catherine, *pray for us.*
Saint Teresa, *pray for us.*
All you holy men and women, *pray for us*.

Lord, be merciful,
> **Lord, save your people.**

From all evil,
> **Lord, save your people**.

From ev'ry sin,
> **Lord, save your people**.

From everlasting death,
> **Lord, save your people.**

By your coming as man,
> **Lord, save your people.**

By your death and rising to new life,
> **Lord, save your people.**

By your gift of the Holy Spirit,
> **Lord, save your people.**

Be merciful to us sinners,
> **Lord, hear our prayer.**

(if some confirmation candidates need to be baptized)
Give new life to these chosen ones by the grace of baptism,
> **Lord, hear our prayer.**

(otherwise)
By your grace, bless this font where your children will be reborn.
> **Lord, hear our prayer.**

Jesus, Son of the Living God,
> **Lord, hear our prayer.**

Christ, hear us.
> **Christ, hear us.**

Lord Jesus, hear our prayer.
> **Lord, Jesus, hear our prayer.**

Those confirmandi, who have not been previously baptized, will now be asked to renounce sin and profess the faith of the Catholic Church as defined by the Nicene Creed. Then, the congregation reaffirms its own baptismal vows.

Candidates are asked, *"Is it your will that you should be baptized in the faith of the Church which we have all professed with you?"*

The proper response is *"It is."*

To which the priest will say, *"_____, I baptize you in the name of the Father, and of the Son, and of the Holy Spirit."*

The congregation praises God as each person is baptized into the Church and will also be sprinkled with blessed water. This recalls our own baptismal vows.

The Mass continues with the sacrament of Confirmation. Each candidate is lifted up in silent prayer as the priest or bishop lay hands upon him or her and calls down the presence of the Holy Spirit. And taking chrism oil, the celebrant will address each individual using the name of that person's patron saint, saying, *"_____, be sealed with the gift of the Holy Spirit."*

The neophyte will then answer, "*Amen*"

Behold the Lamb of God,
Behold him who takes away the sins of the world.
Blessed are those who are called to the Supper of the Lamb.

Lord, I am not worthy that you should enter under my roof,
But only say the word, and my soul shall be healed.

The Priest consecrates the bread and wine; heaven comes down. Now, that the candidates have been confirmed into the Catholic faith, all the faithful are called to the Sacrament of Holy Eucharist. Everything in the Mass has led to this moment of great joy as the newest Catholics take their place around our sacred table. Jesus is there to welcome His lambs, and our neophytes *"taste and see the goodness of the Lord."*

Mass ends in song.

I have fixed my eyes on your hills,
Jerusalem, my destiny!
Thought I cannot see the end for me,
I cannot turn away.
We have set our hearts for the way;
This journey is our destiny,
Let no one walk alone.
The journey makes us one.
(Gather 390)

Text: Rory Cooney, b.1952 Tune: Roy Cooney, b.1952© 1990, GIA Publications, Inc.

Our hearts and souls turn towards the birthplace of the Christian faith, and we remember the promise of the "New Jerusalem." As we continue our journey, we are enriched by our new brothers and sisters who now call the Church, "Mother."

The Old Mother

A lion prowled the heavens when I was born.
And watched as I was, unknowingly, called, "Warrior Maid,"

For that is the meaning of my name.
A prophetic name- for I am summoned to a dreadful heritage.
I will not march on battlefields, but traverse the human mind.
I will not carry my sword in my hand, but in my heart.
For I behold an old woman against a barren sky.
She stands on stony earth and at her back is a dark and restless sea.

I can tell that she was once a great beauty.
But her skin is thin and yellow like old parchment.
And how she suffers- with raiment torn and shabby,
Her gaping wounds silently weep and streak the ancient fabric.

Afflicted by two thousand years of pain and misery.
Once upon a time, her children died for Roman pleasure.
Later her progeny fell to disgrace brought about by vices.
Others ran away and wanted no part of this family.
Now, those who still call her mother hide amid her robes,
Peeking out at the hideous spectacle.

Distant relations are gathering 'round, ready to stone and destroy.
They decree death upon her and her house.
She stares at me, eyes still bright with the radiance of Christ.
And through parched lips whispers a just challenge, "Defend me!"
Now, I, an adopted child of grace,
Must do the impossible and FIGHT!

So, arise my soul from your slumber,
Too long have you tarried in dreams.
Truth and knowledge be my armor,
And let me sharpen my pen as a soldier would his blade
May God anoint me with Holy Fire.
May Christ cover me with Precious Blood.
And Holy Spirit, fill my eyes.
So that I may complete my commission
And drink from the bitter cup.
This warrior's voice resounds the cry:
"Let this be my battlefield!"
-The Author

Part IV
Defending Mother Church

The Flipside of the Petrine Doctrine

When I decided to write this book, I never realized how much pain and confusion that it might cause. That is- until I reached this particular section which draws a sharp line between Catholics and Protestants, a line that cannot be erased no matter how much I might wish it. I continue to grieve, mourn, and weep inside, understanding that I must finish this commission and what that entails. I must beg you, the reader, to carefully reflect upon that which I am about to reveal, and understand that it gives me no pleasure to write these words. But I do what I must for the Glory of God, His Heavenly Kingdom, and for the edification of the Body of Christ. I wrote this book to bring Catholics and Protestants together in a productive dialogue, not a shouting match.

There is no Christian that I have ever met who did not believe that his/her church was the "True Church," and I have met Christians from every walk of life and every denomination. Most denominations acknowledge that Christians exist beyond their borders, but dispute the validity of other churches and denominations as being the "One True Church."

Catholics also believe that the Catholic Church is the "One True Church" founded by Christ upon Peter two thousand years ago. They believe that the "fullest flower of Christianity" grows in the heart of Rome. And while other churches and denominations illustrate aspects of Christianity, they do not contain within them "complete Christianity", as does the Catholic Church. The Pope can never truly acknowledge a Protestant leader as his equal. Why?

To answer this question, we must go back to the scriptures. Our answer lies in this particular passage: *"And I say that thou art Peter, and upon this rock, I will build my church; and the gates of Hell shall not prevail against it." (Matthew 16:18, KJV)*

All Protestant denominations are founded upon the premise that the original church from which they were formed was either wrong or spiritually dead, whether directly split from the Catholic Church or from another Protestant church. If we are to believe that the Catholic Church was wrong or spiritually dead, then logically, we must also conclude that "the gates of hell" did in fact prevail against the original church. This would make what Christ said to be a false statement. If this were a correct assumption, then Christianity is a false religion built upon a figure that either lied or was wrong. This simply cannot be.

Our Lord Jesus Christ was the Son of the Living God. He could never be wrong nor would He ever deliberately mislead us. If all Christians believe this statement, then the Protestant churches have a serious problem. If the gates of hell did not prevail against the Church, then the premise of the original Church being wrong or spiritually dead cannot stand. And finally, if the Church was still alive, then why go off and start another one? This is why the Pope cannot acknowledge a Protestant leader as an equal. By doing so, he would be refuting the Gospel itself and declaring by action that the Church was wrong or spiritually dead at one time. He would be saying that, in effect, the devil had won and the gates of hell had overwhelmed the church.

Now, some Protestant revisionists would have us believe that the Catholic Church was not founded at the time of Christ and by that, not the original church. This argument is false because of the proliferation of historical documents detailing the existence and efforts of various popes, bishops, priests, saints and lay people who were and still are affirmed as Catholic. Any classical history scholar should know this. In fact, there is more historical documentation concerning Catholicism than any other Christian faith- first as "catholic" which describes the universal body of Christ, then as "Catholic" which describes the faithful who did not reject Rome or the Russian and Greek Patriarchs. (Russian and Greek Churches did suffer a schism with Rome, but still have agreements with her due to their adherence to specific rites and practices, which are central to Catholicism.) There is absolutely no mention of non-Catholic denominations until 1500. And why would we have the term "Protestant?" A Protestant is a person who protests. If there wasn't a Catholic Church, then what exactly were they protesting?

Some scholars point to the spiritual failures of Catholics as reason for The Reformation. While there is no doubt that the Catholic leadership needed reform, the spirit of the Church has always remained inviolate. Protestants have trouble separating the spirit of Catholicism from her historical leaders. It is true that the Devil has done his absolute best to destroy her, (witness the sexual debacle of 2002), but he has always failed. That will never change. Although Mother Church has suffered from scandals too numerous to name and the influence of heretics who call themselves "Catholic," beneath it all lies a heart and spirit fashioned by Christ Himself, something that man can never ruin. Other churches have crumbled to dust, and disappeared with no mark of ever existing, but she hasn't. After twenty centuries, she still stands before you.

Should we judge Protestants as a whole by their own corrupt leadership as well? I often see a lot of "tunnel vision" when I talk to other Christians. Many would rather forget that Protestants are guilty of the same or similar offenses often associated with Catholicism. One of the hardest lessons that Nana taught me was the universality of sin and the spiritual frailty of mankind. For every evil deed done by a Catholic, there is a kindred wrong done by a Protestant. We have only to examine history to recognize that inevitable truth.

As an American, I can appreciate the dichotomy between religious ideals and reality. America has produced corrupt, even evil leaders. Yet, it would be grossly unfair to judge all Americans by the deeds of a few men. America's spirit still shines in spite of the political quagmires and ugly deeds that have stained her past. And it would also be a terrible injustice to judge all good and decent Catholics who embrace Christ on a daily basis by those who are unfit to be called Catholic or even Christian.

So, Catholics believe their church to be the True Church that Christ founded. But are there special marks, which distinguish Catholicism from the Protestant faiths? As a matter of fact, there are special attributes which only the Catholic Church has when compared with other churches. These marks are unity, holiness, universality (catholicity), and apostolicity.

1) The Catholic Church is **one** body. Protestant churches can vary greatly in doctrine, liturgical practices, and ways of government, even within their own denominations. Ever notice how some Protestant denominations continue to fracture and split amongst themselves. They do not generally recognize any authority in spiritual matters, except by their own judgment which is less than error-free. The Catholic Church is unified with one creed and the seven sacraments. It has but one shepherd, the Pope. There is true unity in doctrine, worship, and government, as Christ commanded us. Listen to His words: *And if a kingdom be divided against itself, that kingdom cannot stand. And if a house be divided against itself, that house cannot stand. (Mark 3:24-25, KJV)*

While the Catholic Church IS one body, it has multiple Rites, just as our bodies have multiple parts. The Maronite and Melkite Rites from Lebanon are Catholic Rites; Eastern Catholic. While their Rites, Rituals, and Rubrics are different, they are in union with Rome and are subject to the authority of the Pope. Here is another passage that stresses unity: *And other sheep I have, which are not of this fold: them I must also bring, and they shall hear my voice; and there shall be one fold and one shepherd. (John 10:16, KJV)*

Even just before the Ascension, Christ still stressed the importance of unity: *And now I am no more in the world, but these are in the world, and I come to thee. Holy Father, keep through Thine own name those whom Thou hast given Me, that they may be one, as we are. (John 17:11, KJV)*

2) The Catholic Church is **holy**. The Catholic Church was built by Christ Himself upon the person we know as Cephas or Simon Peter. Other denominations began with ordinary human beings such as Martin Luther, King Henry VIII, John Calvin and Charles Wesley. It's just not the same. All denominations are not created equally. Jesus chose each Disciple and anointed them in prayer, saying: *Sanctify them through Thy truth: Thy word is truth. As thou hast sent me into the world, even so have I also sent them into the world. And for their sakes I sanctify myself, that they also might be sanctified through the truth." (John 17:17-19, KJV)*

Our Savior also promised His Church that it would continue to work miracles as a sign of this holiness: *Verily, Verily, I say unto you, he that believeth in me, the works that I shall do he do also; and greater works than these shall he do; because I go unto my Father. (John 14:12, KJV)*

It is interesting to note that in this age of skepticism, the Catholic Church remains the seat of unexplained marvels and miraculous events. Many churches cannot accept the existence of miracles in the modern age.

3) The Catholic Church is **universal**. It is not limited to one particular nationality, race, ethnicity, class or sex. Catholicism respects people from all over the earth, not a particular segment of the populace. I remember hearing a Dominican monk speak of a Mass that was held in New York City in which prominent politicians and socialites sat in the same pews as the poor and disenfranchised. Everyone was given the same respect in God's house, as it should be. Christ told His Disciples: *Go ye therefore, and teach all nations, baptizing them in the name of the Father, and of the Son, and of the Holy Ghost: teaching them to observe all things whatsoever I have commanded you: and lo, I am with you alway, even unto the end of the world. Amen. (Matthew 28:19-20, KJV)*

We must also remember that the Catholic Church has uniformity that is binding throughout the world. Whereas we might have non-Catholic denominations everywhere, they are different everywhere as well and rarely completely agree with one another. Even if I go to a foreign country and cannot understand the language, I can still go to a Catholic Church and worship. My missal or prayer book allows me to follow the Mass and even has commentary in place of the priest's homily or sermon. Regional or national churches fail to truly teach all nations because their very names imply restrictions to certain geographic locals.

4) The Catholic Church is apostolic. Because Protestant denominations were born after the year 1500, they cannot historically and legally document their origin back to the Apostles. The Catholic Church's current leadership can lawfully and historically trace its spiritual lineage to the Apostles themselves. Apostolic Succession was instituted when Matthias was chosen to assume the authority of Judas Iscariot's Apostleship after the Crucifixion and Ascension of our Lord. Protestants reject the doctrine of Apostolic Succession, which is against Holy Scripture. (Refer to the chapter on Apostolic Succession.)

Common wisdom is that all Christian faiths are really the same. But when we compare the criteria of what the "True Church" needs to be, we are left with the inescapable conclusion that only Catholicism offers Christianity in its fullest flower. While many Protestant groups have some, even most of these characteristics, Catholicism has them ALL. There are genuine Christians and sincere, devout Christian priests and ministers outside of Catholicism; however, they do not enjoy the richness and depth of faith that Mother Church offers her children.

The Bishop's Slap

There is a very old custom in Catholicism that dates back to the earliest days of Christianity. When a candidate was finally confirmed as a full member in the Church, the Bishop would end the rite by slapping the individual. This was a grim reminder of what the person would face by becoming a Christian. As the denominations of Christianity formed, that slap informed the recipient that it would be painful to be a Catholic. Though the custom is no longer followed, I have felt the bishop's slap on many occasions.

To better understand why there is such pain, we must travel back in history. In America, Catholics, Lutherans, Anglicans, and Episcopalians generally have a good relationship with one another. This is from the idea of separation of church and state. The framers of the Constitution understood the importance of being free to honor God according to a person's convictions, not by royal edict. Unfortunately, since the English founded the original thirteen colonies, much of their legacy remains. This is particularly true in the southern states that were mostly settled by English Protestants. The North would later act as a receiving port to thousands of immigrants, and eventually be a haven for Catholics with the influx of Irish, French, Italian, Hispanic, Russian, and Greek peoples.

Being Catholic in Europe is not only a religious identity, but a political one as well, particularly in the United Kingdom. Much of the cruel treatment of Catholics finds its roots with the English monarch, King Henry VIII. Henry placed himself as Head of the Church of England and demanded his subjects acknowledge him as king in all things both temporal and spiritual. If a Catholic swore this oath of fealty, that person would be joining another church. In effect, this was self-excommunication from Rome.

For most Catholics, that was unthinkable. In their eyes, the English church was a sham and an effort to secure political power in the form of an heir to the throne. Many Englishmen refused, and paid the ultimate price for their dissension. The prisons swelled, and the executioner's block ran red with Catholic blood. While Henry's sister, Bloody Mary, did do some damage to Protestants in her short years, the Spanish Inquisition's death toll pales in comparison to the blood bath England endured during the reigns of both Henry VIII and Elizabeth I. We want to picture Queen Elizabeth as the "Virgin Queen" who encouraged Shakespeare and defeated the Spanish Armada, but we fail to grasp how ruthless she could be. Anyone perceived to be even sympathetic to Rome was executed. Scholars, noblemen, even close relatives such as Mary, Queen of Scots, were not spared her wrath.

If the bloodletting had stopped at these two monarchs, then most Catholics could let the whole affair go. But the mistreatment of Scotland and Ireland continues to haunt the English to this day. In his book, ***Highlanders: A History of the Scottish Clans,*** Fitzroy MacLean gives a detailed description of the wrath of the English throne against the decimated Jacobite clans after their crush at the Battle of Culloden. He writes:

> *Hundreds of Highland wounded were shot, bayoneted or, where it was more convenient, burned alive. Such prisoners as were taken, were treated in such a way that they died by hundreds and detachments of Government troops were sent out into the territory of the clans who had been loyal to Prince Charles to hunt down the fugitives, loot and burn the houses, drive away the cattle and devastate the country.* (225)

Many Scottish families fled, escaping to America for a new life. Among them was my husband's family, and (I believe) some of my own people. Though I was reared a

Protestant, my Scottish roots are more than likely Catholic because my family name was notoriously Catholic in Scotland. In many ways, I view becoming Catholic as coming "home."

Ever wonder why the IRA is so harsh against the loyalist government in Northern Ireland? It comes from centuries of imposed rule as well as social and economic measures against Catholics. The Irish were not allowed to have Catholic schools or openly teach their faith. Catholic lords could not hunt on their own land nor own an expensive horse. Distant relations who wanted a Catholic lord's land and prestige had only to join the Church of England, and they could take everything, completely bypassing accepted rules of inheritance. Irish culture was frowned upon. The Irish weren't even allowed to speak their own language. England had many colonies all over the world. Devotees from other religions had more freedom to worship than Catholic Christians. Had the Irish been afforded some of the freedoms that other English subjects were given, much of the violence in Ireland would have seriously been reduced. After all, civil unrest and domestic terrorism go hand in hand. (Wickwire 208-209)

Even loyal subjects of the Crown were sympathetic to the Irish cause. General Cornwallis, known for leading the fight against the American Revolution became a political advocate, pushing for clemency for Irish rebels as well as education and food for the populace. (Wickwire 228-231) Many noble families hid and befriended priests from the authorities at their own risk of imprisonment and death. This is why many English castles and mansions are riddled with secret passages and "priest holes," which were small rooms that kept someone tucked safely away from prying eyes.

Jonathan Swift wrote a sharp-witted rebuff of English policies in his ***A Modest Proposal,*** where he compared the English mindset toward the Irish in the vein of a farmer viewing livestock. He offered breeding suggestions and the use of "poppish" (Catholic) infants and children as tempting dishes for their English masters' tables. His point was that the English treated the Irish like cattle, so why not finish the job and use them as a source of food. Swift goes so far as to suggest cooking tips for these meals. (Abrams 2174-2180)

During the centuries between the birth of the Church of England and the present, it became popular to portray Catholics as evil degenerates. I took a class in early English literature and found myself upset at the malignment of Rome and her children. To add insult to injury, the teacher seemed unwilling to balance the text with opposing views. Want to feel outnumbered? Be a Catholic and participate in a class dominated by Protestants, taught by a Protestant, with a Pro-Protestant subject. But I think my classmates had a fondness for me. They'd often lament when I wasn't in class and say they missed my input. That particular type of heavy writing makes a great sleeping aid. I kept things interesting. Even so, the teacher would often dismiss us a few minutes early, when she saw vacant eyes about the classroom.

Now, please do not think me anti-British. I love the British people and have spent many hours enjoying their quirky, off-beat humor as well as exploring such literary masterworks as ***Jane Eyre, Pride And Prejudice, Wuthering Heights,*** *and* ***Horatio Hornblower.*** But my love of England is tempered with the knowledge that much of the harsh treatment of Catholics emanates directly or indirectly from how they wrote and what they did. Europeans had the Thirty Years War in which Protestants and Catholics rose up against one another, employing whole armies that laid waste to anything in their path. Yet, in the aftermath, much of the heat of that conflict has dissipated. Isn't it odd that Protestants and Catholics are still killing each other in the United Kingdom?

The English legacy of Catholic persecution is well represented in what is known as the "Bible Belt." Never mind the antics of the Ku Klux Klan, those "good and honorable" jackasses who use Christ to further their own agenda; there are more insidious and acceptable avenues to pursue when persecuting Catholics. The most effective of these is the tremendous social pressure to be a part of some other church- any other church but a Catholic one, often on the part of well-meaning, God fearing people. It's even worse if you have previously been in another denomination and were not raised as a "cradle Catholic." While it's generally ok to switch Protestant churches, it becomes an insult should you decide to become a citizen of Rome.

A few years ago I bumped into an old friend of the family, Henry Carvel, who was a minister. After catching up with the latest news on how everyone was, he casually asked me where I went to church. I mentioned the name of the only Catholic Church in town, and he looked at me as though I had physically struck him. I just smiled and wished him a pleasant evening.

But his reaction is rather mild compared to other experiences that have left harsh memories. One of my most vivid recollections happened on the Saturday following the 9/11 disaster, when I found myself walking with a group of Christians in a Pro-Life demonstration. After it became clear who I was and what church I belonged to, a former Catholic took it upon herself to explain to me how wrong and evil the Catholic Church was. When I began to mention Protestant atrocities and mistreatments to counter her accusations, she refused to listen. What was supposed to be a unifying experience in the body of Christ became an ugly diatribe. At a time when Americans were bonded by grief and the solace that comes with mutual suffering, all I came away with was a deep sorrow and the realization of how cruel Christians can be to their own kind.

Another poignant memory is the time I sat discussing my faith with a good friend from college at a favorite Mexican restaurant. A stranger heard me and ran up to our table to offer me a tract. I politely refused and sent him on his way. Marla seemed dumbfounded, but I wasn't, telling her that his behavior was typical. I do not hide my faith, but openly profess it; and of course, this gets more than its share of persecution. I find it odd that other Christians don't have to hide their church affiliations, while Catholics have a tendency of avoiding any mention of their faith.

If it were only me, then I could dismiss this treatment as a few aberrations, but my husband's life is littered with ignorant and prejudicial incidents. During an ecumenical activity for Christian youth in his hometown, one church dropped out because "those Catholics" had gotten involved. But Michael's worst memory of religious bigotry happened when his church was burglarized. In addition to taking sacred Eucharistic vessels, and writing profanity on the walls, the intruder desecrated the altar. And when the deputy sheriff arrived, he refused to go in and investigate the crime scene, saying that he had been taught that Catholics worship demons, and that if he went in, one would follow him home. So, this brave officer of the law sent a frightened teenage girl (the daughter of the church lady who cleaned the sanctuary) to see if the intruder was still there. He didn't care that she could have been harmed. Though this caused a great outcry among parishioners in the community, the officer was never punished for his dereliction of duty.

Admittedly, this is an extreme example. Most of the time, it is mild curiosity where teachers and classmates single Catholics out for cross-examination in grade school and college. Even the work place is often the scene of grand debates on Catholic theology once workers stumble across a Catholic who is open about the faith. But some cross-examinations turn nasty.

Recently, I read that another Catholic family, the Holmeses, in an adjacent town felt this same lack of religious tolerance when their son, Ben, attended a local Protestant school, which claimed that it accepted all Christian faiths. After a prayer in a Bible study, the young man made the sign of the cross. The attending teacher was deeply shocked saying, **"You've got to be kidding me."**

Cynthia Holmes, Ben's mother, was summoned to the principal's office where she was told that her son would have to attend the affiliated church of the school in order to stay enrolled. The principal called Catholics "idol worshippers," saying that they didn't have the same view of salvation as the denomination of the school. Cynthia refused to sacrifice her Catholic faith for her son's education, and the situation at school grew grim. This Christian school which had once been an enjoyable place became an offensive environment.

Although Ben was an "exemplary" student by even the principal's standards, he and his family were informed that he would not be allowed to return the following school year. This occurred after being summoned to a school board meeting in which the attending officials cross-examined the Holmeses on Catholic beliefs and views on salvation, never bothering with such relevant topics as grades and behavior. When questioned by the Catholic News and Herald, the principal refused to comment on the situation. (The Holmeses' names have not been changed; they are as they appear in the issue of the Catholic News and Herald.)

When I consider this story of religious intolerance, I become angry because I know that the prejudice will not die, but continue on. This happened in a school where young minds are taught and molded by well-meaning adults. I worry about how my own family views Michael and me, especially my nephews whom I love very much. My sisters and I are not very close. (This is largely due to age differences and personality conflicts.) Sometimes, I feel as though a wall separates their children from me. Do they truly know me at all? Or have their minds been colored against me? This is not to cast blame on my sisters. But I cannot be there to balance the occasional accusation that others make against my faith, and that, more than anything, troubles me. I would rather my nephews ask questions than say nothing at all. The more they ask the more foolishness I can dispel.

My teenage world was much different than that of most religious teens. I got the chance to learn and grow with a variety of different Christians from other churches including Catholics, Lutherans, and Episcopalians. This was largely due to the YMCA, a kind of friendly melting pot where I could meet a variety of people from different cultures and walks of life. I knew that there were differences in denominations, but considered them to be just as worthy as anyone else to be part of God's family. They were the individuals that I spent hours playing and learning with summer after summer. So, having been exposed to Catholicism, it was easy to connect and form a relationship with Michael.

However, over the past fifteen years, I have noticed a rising tide of anti-Catholicism grip my hometown. Much of this comes from independent Christian churches. While my husband and I are happy to invite a dialogue on the Bible and the scriptures, we are sad to hear the occasional remarks, labels, and declarations that have little to do reality and more to do with hearsay and common ignorance.

Now, I find the usual mistrust of Catholics blending with a kind of "knee-jerk" reaction to an influx of so many Northerners and Latinos, many of which are Catholic. A few native Southerners are afraid of losing their identity among a larger populace with a different culture. But to be fair, how much of Southern culture (and by large, western civilization) can be traced back to Catholic roots? The answer is that traces of my faith proliferate and thread themselves through Western culture in ways that many people seldom realize.

Let's begin with something as simple as the calendar. The calendar that the world follows is called the "Gregorian Calendar" named after Pope Gregory 13th who invented it. Western society would have to revert back to the Julian calendar or possibly the Judaic calendar. Can you imagine the kind of aggravation that would cause?

If the religious community wishes to rid itself of Catholicism, it will have to completely change when and how both Christmas and Easter are celebrated. Most historians agree that Christ was not born in the winter, but more than likely mid-summer. Shepherds do not "watch their flocks by night" in December, because it's too cold. Instead the sheep are herded and corralled to protect them from the harsh elements. Though Easter gets its name from the Teutonic goddess of spring, it was originally tied to Passover which, in turn, was (and still is) connected to the lunar cycle. That often meant that Easter would be celebrated on a weekday. Pope Gregory 13th found this arrangement to be unacceptable, and decreed that only Sunday was the proper day for Easter.

It was Catholicism that slowly replaced paganistic practices with devotion to the one true God. Both St. Valentine's and St. Patrick's Day are named for Catholic saints. Most of us know about St. Patrick, but few non-Catholics understand that St. Valentine was martyred for practicing Christianity, particularly marrying couples in Christian ceremonies. (American Catholic.org, 4/10/03, 1)

Catholics penned much of the greatest classical music ever written. So long, Mozart. Bye, bye, Beethoven. Many pieces such as Beethoven's *"Ode to Joy"* are still used in Protestant churches today. It is better known as *"Joyful, Joyful, We Adore Thee."* Do you like Vivaldi's *"Four Seasons*?" What about Giuseppe Verdi's works? Even Handel, famous for the work, *"Messiah"* was born and raised a Catholic. What about ballet and opera, which are companions to classical music? Both of these artistic disciplines were also born in predominantly Catholic countries.

The finest religious art ever created was at the hands of artisans under the patronage of the Catholic Church. It may be interesting to note that even Protestant bibles, especially the large family editions, feature glossy, full color prints of Renaissance art. If Catholicism is such a creeping evil, they'll need to tear those pages out.

How many of us like to eat ethnic foods such as Italian, Greek, French, or Spanish/Mexican dishes? Well, since Catholicism is deeply embedded into these various cultures, it would probably be best to refrain from all these wonderful dishes and save them for us. I suppose you could have German, English, Asian, and Eastern Indian cuisine, but anything from a Catholic country, particularly Mediterranean food, is out.

Christian symbols and church architecture have roots in Catholicism. Stained glass, gothic and Romanesque arches, steeples and spires, and even the way we position pews and place the altar originate from early Christianity- Catholic Christianity.

The professional world also bears curious signs of Catholic roots, particularly in the arenas of law, medicine, and science that still use Latin and Greek in their terminology. Latin and Greek were the primary languages of the Roman Empire and would later become the primary languages of the Christian faith. And in the early days, if one wanted to learn those languages, that person would attend a monastery, an abbey or a convent. These institutions were the first European "colleges." It wasn't until after Vatican II that the Mass was said in the vernacular language of each country.

What about the privacy that individuals enjoy with their doctors, lawyers, and clergymen (even non-Christian spiritual advisers)? This idea comes from the secrecy of the confessional. How many of us are willing to give the privilege of confidentiality up? That question got a stern answer in the 1990s when someone in the government wanted to force clergymen to divulge confidences. There was open defiance from every sector of American society, and the American people said, *"Absolutely not!"*

Did you know that the American pledge of allegiance was changed due to Catholicism? Lately, there has been great debate for or against removing the words *"under God"* from the pledge. Many Catholic bashers are up in arms at the prospect of removing those words, but do not realize that it was the Knights of Columbus, a Catholic organization, that began the campaign to put them there in the first place. On April 22, 1951, its Board of Directors started a grass roots movement that ended at the White House when President Eisenhower signed and made it official that we as a nation would put God in our national pledge. As of June 14,1954 (Flag Day), America became "one nation, under God"- all due to the efforts of loyal, devout, and patriotic Catholics. (Baer 2)

I hope that my readers understand what I am trying to say. It is nothing but the height of arrogant hypocrisy to use the Catholic calendar, adopt Catholic traditions, enjoy Catholic music, artwork, and even the food born out of Catholic cultures worldwide, then call us everything but holy. It is an absurd injustice to employ Catholic symbolism, architecture, languages, and standards of confidentiality and idealism, and then turn and brand us infidels. Much of the beauty associated with western culture is a direct or indirect result of the influence of Catholicism.

What many Protestant radicals fail to understand is that the Catholic Church is mother, grandmother, and even great grandmother of every other Christian denomination on this planet, no matter how independent they may claim to be. While people may disagree with her on a number of issues, Holy Mother Church must be accorded the respect she deserves. Anything less is ignoring the historical and spiritual ancestry of modern Christianity and in a very real way, disrespecting our own spiritual origin for she is inextricably linked with it.

I was there when the darkness came creeping,
When it covered the earth as a voluminous cloak,
And prophecy's daughter stole beside me,
And whispered ,"Christiani non sint."
-The Author

Endgame

Early in the Roman Empire, there was a set of military conflicts known as the Punic Wars in which Rome fought a city-state called Carthage. During the final conflict, the edict **Carthago non sit** was issued against the Carthaginians. When the Romans finally took Carthage, carnage and fire ensued. The Greek writer Appian (AD 200) spoke of Roman *"army servants using hooks to drag both dead and living to be flung pell-mell, with the debris of the houses, into the pits from which still moving heads and limbs could sometimes be seen emerging, only to be crushed by the galloping horses." (Lancel 426*)

Carthage, the jewel of Africa, one of the most beautiful cities of the ancient world, glowed as one massive funeral pyre. Was it all embellishment after 350 years of stories and whispered events? Hardly. Appian remains the key source on Carthage. Archeologists continue to document and prove his words as they unearth the charred remains of both the city and its inhabitants (Lancel 425-426). Yes, the Romans erected another city and called it Carthage, but the real Carthage was obliterated. The words **Carthago non sit** meant that Carthage, and the Carthaginians, could not be allowed to exist. Therefore, the term "Carthaginian Peace" means absolute destruction – in modern terms, genocide. Now, let's move forward in Roman history when the edict, **Christiani non sint** was issued. If we look at the fate of Carthage, the gravity of that sentence becomes very clear. Christians, in Nero's day, were facing certain death, and many were sacrificed for their belief in Jesus.

Today, some believers feel that the world is facing a new age of barbarism likened to that dark time when Christians met in secret to escape a grisly death. If this is true, then why do Christians set about destroying each other from within the Christian faith? If these people are right, it will take both Protestants and Catholics working together to battle the coming darkness. It is doubtful that the enemy will stop and consider which denomination we come from. There will only be interest in eradicating Christianity as a whole. While both sides of Christendom may never agree on everything, we should all be able to agree on the life and divinity of Christ, the forgiveness of sins, discipleship, and eternal life. These concepts lie at the heart of what it means to be a Christian.

When I see Christianity as a whole, I see a complete body of believers, not just one denomination. Yet many Christians think it's perfectly ok to carve up the body of Christ, to separate the bone and sinew and divide the flesh- an arm here, a leg there. Why not open the chest and take out the heart? Then, there are those in their zeal for perfection who pick at the whole carcass like obscene vultures. When witnessing this kind of cruelty inflicted by two millennia of politics, divisions and splits, we have to ask ourselves if we are furthering the cause of Christ or serving a darker purpose.

Popular wisdom dictates that evil is chaotic, but that is a wrong assumption. True evil is deliberate and methodical, not unplanned. This becomes very clear when we study the great villains in history. They had organized "methods of madness." Adolph Hitler is a prime example. He indoctrinated the German nation using a set pattern of propaganda and nationalism. But Hitler pales besides the efforts, schemes, and calculations of Lucifer who is the Prince of Darkness and the Father of Lies.

Any great military tactician will tell you that one of the best ways to defeat a large enemy is to cause division and infighting between groups and factions within the camp. And while they're busy tearing each other apart, the opposing forces can bring in the troops and mop up. Rumors, innuendo, misinformation (ignorance) and disinformation (deliberate lies) are the earmarks of this tactic. If we look closely, we see the same kind of problems within the Protestant/Catholic conflict. ***Someone wrote that… I didn't know… I didn't mean… I was taught that… My preacher said…***

The reality is that many people do not wish to think and consider for themselves. They want all the hard decisions and policies made for them and no responsibility when it all backfires. Society gives villains their power, and like it or not, Christians further a diabolical cause when they seek to divide the Body of Christ.

In writing this book, I had no illusions of "converting the world" to Catholicism. I know that many of my readers will continue to differ with my faith on a number of issues, and that is to be expected. Conversion will always remain a matter of the heart and nothing to be forced into. My job was to share what I have learned; God will do the rest in His own time. But I hope that the evidence that I have provided will prove that we are, once and for all, biblical in our teachings and deeply Christian. Few things hurt more than having my faith branded "the whore of Babylon" and hearing my beloved Pope called "the Antichrist."

Unfortunately, this seems to be a common refrain that has echoed through the centuries. It was simply not enough to disagree with us. Many Protestants have reduced Catholics to the status of pagans or heretics and still do today. There will always be Protestants who will seek to wipe Catholicism out by any means necessary, but I wonder if they will be able to justify their actions when they stand before Christ and witness the immeasurable harm they have done.

Christianity is like a shattered mirror, once created to reflect back the glory of God. Over time, it lost its pristine beauty, and man, not God, smashed this masterpiece instead of working to bring it back to its former glory. We are all pieces of broken light with sharp edges. But Jesus is not content to let us glisten in the dirt. He continues to sift and retrieve each piece no matter how small or sharp. One day, we shall all be cast into the fire and emerge one complete body of believers. Will Christ then turn to us and reveal his bloody hands? These wounds won't be from the Crucifixion, but newly torn flesh inflicted by well-meaning Christians.

God wants to help us to recreate ourselves in the New Millennium. We were once one priestly people. We can be so again, though not under our own power. Only the Holy Spirit can break our hearts and open our minds, so that we may tear down the wall that separates Protestants and Catholics. Many say that this is an impossible dream, but nothing is impossible with God.

Editors

Principle Editor/Writer
  Kelly Dawn Stuard-Will
Assistant Editor
  Timothy Michael Will
Doctrinal Editor
  Father John Putnam, Jr., B.S., S.T.B., M. Div., J.C.L.
Historical Editor
  Father Stephan Heimann, M. Div.

Works Cited

About the RCIA. Pamphlet 17830D-6-90, 1991 ed. South Deerfield, MA : Channing L. Bete Co., 1984.

About the Sacrament of Anointing the Sick. Pamphlet 1770B-9-83, 1986 ed. South Deerfield, MA: Channing L. Bete Co., 1983.

About the Sacrament of Confirmation. Pamphlet 17624E-8-90, 2000 ed. South Deerfield, MA: Channing L. Bete Co., 1982.

About the Sacrament of Holy Orders. Pamphlet 1774A-5-83, 1983 ed. South Deerfield, MA: Channing L. Bete Co., 1986.

About the Sacrament of Marriage. Pamphlet 17616D-10-90, 1999 ed. South Deerfield, MA: Channing L. Bete Co., 1982.

About the Sacrament of Reconciliation. Pamphlet 17392E-6-90, 2000 ed. South Deerfield, MA: Channing L. Bete Co., 1979.

Abrams, M. H., Ed. The Norton Anthology of English Literature. 5th Ed. New York: W. W. Norton & Co., 1986.

Akin, James, The Practical Problems of *Sola Scriptura*,
  <http://www.cin.org/users/james/files/practicl.htm>

Allee, John Gage, ed. Webster's Encyclopedia of Dictionaries. 1978 ed. Ottenheimer Publishers, Inc., 1958.

"All Catholic Church Ecumenical Councils – All the Decrees
  <http://www.piar.hu/councils/~index.htm>

Anatolios, Khaled, and Stephen F. Brown. World Religions: Catholicism and Orthodox Christianity. New York: Facts on File, Inc., 2002.

A

Baer, Dr. John W., <u>The Pledge of Allegiance, A Short History</u>. <http://history.vineyard.net/pledge.htm>

Batastini, Robert J., and Michael A. Cymbala, Eds. <u>Gather Comprehensive Hymnal</u>. Chicago, IL. G.I.A. Publications, Inc., 1994

Batastini, Robert J., Robert H. Oldershaw, Richard Proulx, and Daniel G. Reuning, Eds. <u>Worship II Hymnal and Missal</u>. Chicago, IL. G.I.A. Publications, Inc., 1975

Beliefnet, "Prayer for the Dead"
<http://www.beliefnet.com/boards/message_list.asp?pageID=2&discussionID=219859>

Buetner, Fr. Matthew, Dr. Alice van Hilledrand. <u>Understanding the Mystery of the Mass</u>.Goleta, GA, Queenship Publishing, 2006

Catholic Answers, "Christ in the Eucharist"
<http://www.catholic.com/library/Christ_in_the_Eucharist.asp>

<u>Catholic News & Herald</u>, West, Msgr. Mauricio W. Pub. Charlotte, NC

Choy, Chi Kang, <u>Hanukka</u>,
<http://mbhs.bergtraum.k12.ny.us/user/c6677/hanuk.html>

Clarke-Copeland, Judi, <u>Origin of Holidays: History of Ash Wednesday</u>
<http://www.information-entertainment.com/Holidays/ashwed.html>

Clarke-Copeland, Judi, <u>Origin of Holidays: History of Easter</u>
<http://www.information-entertainment.com/Holidays/easter.html>

Clarke-Copeland, Judi, <u>Origin of Holidays: History of All Saints' Day</u>
<http://www.information-entertainment.com/Holidays/allsaints.html>

Clough, Shepard B., Ed. <u>A History of the Western World: Ancient Times to 1715</u>. Boston, MA: D. C. Heath and Co., 1964

CNN/AP. <u>Education: Study Details School Sexual Misconduct</u>.
<http://robots.cnn.com/2004/EDUCATION/07/01/school.sexual.misconduct.ap>

Coffman, Chaim, <u>History of Chanuka</u>, 3/19/03.
<http://www.chanuka.com/history.shtml>

Davis, C. Truman. <u>A Physician Testifies About the Crucifixion</u>.
<http://www.konnections.com/Kcundick/crucifix.html>

Diamant, Anita, <u>Shiva: Seven Days of Mourning</u>,
<Http://www.jhom.com.topics/seven/shiva.html>

Dodds, Bill. "Making Saints." Columbia November 2000: 16-19.

Enya, Nicky Ryan, and Roma Ryan, arr. Enya: Shepherd Moons. New York: Wise Publications, 1991.

Ferretto, Joseph Cardinal, "Indulgenced Works: The Enchiridion of Indulgences." 1968 Orig. pub. Liberia Editrice Vatican, Vatican City, 1968.

Fisher, C.H., Once Saved, Always Saved, <http://www.truthkeepers.net/osas.htm>

Fuzer, Julian. Stations of the Cross. Cincinnati, OH: World Library of Sacred Music, Inc., 1966.

Gallegos, Joseph A., Perpetual Virginity of the Blessed Virgin Mary. <http://www.cin.org/users/jgallegos/virgin.htm>

Grant, Michael. The History of Ancient Israel. New York: Charles Scribner's Sons, 1984.

Gross, David. Hippocrene Practical English-Hebrew/Hebrew-English Dictionary. New York: Hippocrene Books, 1991

Hamilton, Edith. Mythology. Boston, MA: Little, Brown, and Co., 1942

Hardy, James, narr. Castle Ghosts of Ireland. Prod. Eben Foggit and Edward Windsor. Dir. Gary Birch., TLC Prod. Peter Koper. The Learning Channel. 1997.

Horn, Geoffrey M. Barron's Book Notes: Old Testament. Woodbury, NY: Barron's Educational Series, Inc. 1986.

Inglis, Rewey Belle, and Josephine Spear, Eds. Adventures in English Literature. New York: Harcourt, Brace, & World, Inc., 1952.

Jones, Alexander, ed. Jerusalem Bible. New York: Doubleday and Co., Inc., 1966, 1967, &1968

Knights of Columbus, The Pledge of Allegiance. <http://exit.i-55.com/~minkusmj/Pledge.html>

Lancel, Serge. Carthage: A History. Trans. Antonia Nevill. Cambridge, MA: Blackwell Publishers, 1995

Latourette, Kenneth Scott. A History of Christianity. San Francisco, CA: Harper Collins, 1975.

Laux, John., and Carl J. Ryan. Introduction to the Bible. New York: Benziger Brothers, 1932.

Limb, John J., ed. Unidos en Cristo. Portland OR. Oregon Catholic Press, June 18-Nov. 26, 2000.

Living Bible Encyclopedia in Story and Pictures. New York, NY: H.S. Stuttman Co, Inc., 1968.

Maclean, Fitzroy. Highlanders: a History of the Scottish Clans. New York: Viking Studio Books, 1995.

Madhury, Ray, Michael Crassweller, & Andrew Boyce-Lewis, Assyro-Babylonian Pantheon. <http://library.thinkquest.org/12865/mray/pbab.htm>

Maier, Paul L., First Easter: The True and Unfamiliar Story. New York: Harper & Row, Publishers, 1973

Martin, Michael. "Rosarium de Beata Virgine Maria" Jan. 1, 2003 <http://home.earthlink.net/~thesaurus>

Martin, Ralph. F.I.R.E.: "Faith". Rally, Belmont Abbey, NC, Sept. 18, 1999.

Morrow, Louis LaRavoire. My Catholic Faith. Kenosha, WI: Pan-American Copyright Convention, 1966.

Opisso, Br. Anthony, MD, The Perpetual Virginity of Mary. <http://www.cin.org/users/james/files/talmud.htm>

Origins of St. Valentine. <http://www.americancatholic.org/Features/Valentines Day>

Paluch, Margaret A., and Mary L. Rafferty, pubs Celebremos Apr. 7 - Aug. 10, 2002. Schiller Park, IL: World Library Publications, 2002

Perry, Dr. Leonard, Plants of the Winter Solstice. <http://pss.uvm.edu/ppp/articles/solstice.htm>

Pohle, J. "The Real Presence of Christ in the Eucharist." Transc. Charles Sweeney, SJ <http://www.newadvent.org/cathen/00573a.htm>

Pope Paul VI, Humanae Vitae: A Challenge to Love. Trans Janet E. Smith. New Hope, KY: New Hope Publications, 1991

"Purgatory and Praying for the Dead" <http://www.lumenverum.com/apologetics/prgatory.htm>

Ratzinger, Joseph Cardinal. Catechism of the Catholic Church, 2nd ed. United States Catholic Conference, Inc., Washington, District of Columbia, US-Libreria Editrice Vaticana, Rome, Italy. 1994.`

Rudge, Bill J., The Resurrection: Myth or Fact?, <http://www.billrudge.org/Specialarticles/mythfact.htm>

Simkoff, Archpriest Nicholas, "Prayers for the Dead."
<http://www.stnicholas-oca.org/prayer4dead.htm>

Soule, Becket W., <u>The Catholic Teaching on Annulment: Preserving the Sanctity of Marriage</u>. Pamphlet 301 4/00. New Haven: Knights of Columbus Supreme Council, 1997.

Spaeth, Frank, ed. <u>Phantom Army of the Civil War, and other Southern Ghost Stories</u>. Castle Books, div. Of Book Sales, Inc. Edison, NJ, 2000

Stockhart, Hal. "Origin of 'The Twelve Days of Christmas'." Sacred Heart Newsletter. Bulletin. Salisbury: Sacred Heart Catholic Church, 2000.

<u>Uncle John's Great Big Bathroom Reader</u>. Ashland, OR: Bathroom Readers' Press. 1998.

USCCB, United States Council of Catholic Bishops. <www.usccb.org>

Valentim, Antoine. <u>The Bible Defends the Catholic Church: Baptism</u>. <http://web.globalserv.net/~bumblebee/ecclesia/baptism2.htm>

Valentim, Antoine. <u>The Bible Defends the Catholic Church: Infant Baptism</u>. <http://web.globalserv.net/~bumblebee/ecclesia/baptism.htm>

Valentim, Antoine. <u>The Bible Defends the Catholic Church: The "Brothers" of Jesus</u>. <http://web.globalserv.net/~bumblebee/ecclesia/brothers.htm>

Valentim, Antoine. <u>The Bible Defends the Catholic Church: Eucharist</u>. <http://web.globalserv.net/~bumblebee/ecclesia/eucharist.htm>

Valentim, Antoine. <u>The Bible Defends the Catholic Church: Purgatory</u>. <http://web.globalserv.net/~bumblebee/ecclesia/purgator.htm>

Valentim, Antoine. <u>The Bible Defends the Catholic Church: Salvation (Once and for All?)</u> <http://web.globalserv.net/~bumblebee/ecclesia/salvatio.htm>

Valentim, Antoine. <u>The Bible Defends the Catholic Church: Sola Fide</u>. <http://web.globalserv.net/~bumblebee/ecclesia/solafide.htm>

Valentim, Antoine. <u>The Bible Defends the Catholic Church: Sola Scriptura</u>. <http://web.globalserv.net/~bumblebee/ecclesia/solascri.htm>

Valentim, Antoine. <u>The Bible Defends the Catholic Church: Statues, images, and relics</u>. <http://web.globalserv.net/~bumblebee/ecclesia/statues.htm>

Valentim, Antoine. <u>A Biblical Defense of Mary.</u> <http://web.globalserv.net/~bumblebee/ecclesia/mary.htm>

White, James. "A Brief Definition of the Trinity."
<http://www.aomin.org/trinitydef.html>

Wickwire, Franklin & Mary, Cornwallis: The Imperial Years. Chapel Hill, NC: University of North Carolina Press, 1980.

Wilhelm, J. Catholic Encyclopedia: General Councils.
<http://www.newadvent.org/cathen/04423f.htm>

Wilson, Alastair. Teach Yourself: Latin Dictionary. Chicago, IL: NTC Publishing Group, 1992

Witherington, Ben, III, & Hershel Shanks. In the Name of the Brother.
<http://www.usaweekend.com/03_issues/030413/030413jesus.html>

www.ingramcontent.com/pod-product-compliance
Lightning Source LLC
Chambersburg PA
CBHW032041150426
43194CB00006B/381